WEAR SOME ARMOR IN YOUR HAIR

WEAR SOME ARMOR IN YOUR HAIR

Urban Renewal and the 1968 Democratic
National Convention in Lincoln Park

Brian Mullgardt

SOUTHERN ILLINOIS UNIVERSITY PRESS | CARBONDALE

Southern Illinois University Press
www.siupress.com

Copyright © 2024 by the Board of Trustees,
Southern Illinois University

27 26 25 24   4 3 2 1

Cover illustration: Photo of protestors by Art Shay, Gallery VICTOR and the
Art Shay Archive

Library of Congress Cataloging-in-Publication Data

Names: Mullgardt, Brian, — author.
Title: Wear some armor in your hair : urban renewal and the 1968
    Democratic National Convention in Lincoln Park / Brian Mullgardt.
Other titles: Urban renewal and the 1968 Democratic National Convention
    in Lincoln Park
Identifiers: LCCN 2023033035 (print) | LCCN 2023033036 (ebook) |
    ISBN 9780809339358 (paperback) | ISBN 9780809339365 (ebook)
Subjects: LCSH: Lincoln Park (Chicago, Ill. : City section)—History—
    20th century. | Democratic National Convention (1968 : Chicago, Ill.) |
    Lincoln Park (Chicago, Ill. : City section)—Politics and government—
    20th century. | Urban renewal—Illinois—Chicago—History—20th
    century. | Gentrification—Illinois—Chicago—History—20th century. |
    Counterculture—Illinois—Chicago—History—20th century. |
    Vietnam War, 1961-1975—Protest movements—Illinois—Chicago, |
    Youth International Party—Illinois—Chicago. | Riots—Illinois—
    Chicago—History—20th century. | Chicago (Ill.)—Race relations—
    History—20th century. | BISAC: HISTORY / United States / 20th
    Century | POLITICAL SCIENCE / Public Policy / City Planning &
    Urban Development
Classification: LCC F548.68.L5 M855 2024 (print) |
    LCC F548.68.L5 (ebook) | DDC 977.3/110904—dc23/eng/20240213
LC record available at https://lccn.loc.gov/2023033035
LC ebook record available at https://lccn.loc.gov/2023033036

Printed on recycled paper ♻

SIU
Southern Illinois University System

CONTENTS

Gallery of illustrations begins on page 89

ACKNOWLEDGMENTS

As a social and cultural historian intent on writing a social history of the 1968 Democratic National Convention, I discovered a much larger story during my research and instead ended up with a book that is a social history but also an urban history, religious history, countercultural history, history of liberalism . . . a mix of new territories for me, some daunting, all engaging. In navigating them, I owe thanks to the following: Peter C. Baldwin read multiple drafts of this manuscript in various forms, provided sources and advice, and remained incredibly supportive of this project from the beginning. Kathryn DeGraff at DePaul University's Special Collections and Archives was generous with her time and resources during the earliest stages of my research. Damon Bach provided his keen insight on the counterculture. Robbie Lieberman read chapters and offered sagacious comments. Ed Schmitt shared resources and his insight on the publishing process. Devin Hunter's input, especially on Chicago and urban history, was instrumental. My colleague and friend Dan Monroe offered thoughts on various chapters and was an asset in my obtaining two sabbaticals and financial support, for which I also thank Millikin University.

Library staff at the University of Wisconsin-Parkside tracked down hard-to-find sources and digitized them for me. Millikin librarians, notably Rachel Bicicchi, helped me obtain precious microfilm and images. Sylvia Frank Rodrigue and Jen Egan at Southern Illinois University Press provided encouragement and patience. The anonymous reviewers at SIU Press gave me invaluable guidance and suggestions.

Victor Armendariz, owner of Gallery VICTOR, provided the cover photo and permission. Some content from chapter 4 appeared in the Fall 2014 issue of *Chicago History*, and parts of chapters 3 and 4 appeared in the *Journal of Illinois History*, Winter 2008.

Lastly, the Bartosz, Mullgardt, Temple, and Webster families, and especially my wife, Kim Bartosz, provided support in innumerable ways.

CCC	Conservation Community Council
CCLP	Concerned Citizens of Lincoln Park
CCSF	Concerned Citizens Survival Front
CPD	Chicago Police Department
DUR	Department of Urban Renewal
GNRP	General Neighborhood Renewal Plan
LPCA	Lincoln Park Conservation Association
LPTM	Lincoln Park Town Meeting
NSCM	North Side Cooperative Ministry
OTTA	Old Town Triangle Association
YIP	Youth International Party
YLO	Young Lords Organization

WEAR SOME ARMOR IN YOUR HAIR

Introduction

On Wednesday night, August 28, 1968, some ninety million television viewers watched Chicago Police Department officers attack demonstrators in a moment now infamous in the history of the 1960s.[1] It began when approximately seven thousand people protesting both the Vietnam War and the Democratic Party marched to Chicago's downtown at Michigan Avenue and Balbo Street. These demonstrators, some chanting "Fuck LBJ," "Hell no, we won't go," and "Pigs eat shit," stood outside of the Hilton Hotel opposite helmet clad policemen gripping menacing batons. Some demonstrators threw bottles and rocks at officers who were then ordered to clear the crowd. Chaos followed.[2] While some policemen acted calmly and responsibly, others, some chanting "Kill, kill, kill," beat people.[3] Others sprayed mace.[4] Policemen dragged protesters into paddy wagons, sometimes clubbing their captives as they slammed them into the vans.[5] Some protesters fought back, and others chanted, "the whole world is watching." The broadcast melee lasted only about twenty minutes, but violence continued for hours.[6]

The scene inside the Democratic National Convention, also televised, is just as notorious. While barbed wire covered army jeeps patrolled nearby streets as part of an absurd defense strategy, Mayor Richard J. Daley shouted at Senator Abraham Ribicoff inside the hall. Democrats bickered and screamed at each other, one angrily addressing police brutality outside. The same violence transpiring on the street found its way inside the convention and nearby Hilton Hotel as officers attacked anyone they saw fit to pummel.

What started out as a week-long protest in Chicago's Lincoln Park, several miles north of the convention, had turned into days of skirmishes, sometimes violent, between protester and police officer. Now, the nation watched what the National Commission on the Causes and Prevention of Violence, the group charged with investigating the bloodshed, labeled a "police riot."[7] In its wake, presidential candidate Richard Nixon called for "law and order" in the streets. For those active in "the Movement," that spectrum of civil rights, antiwar, countercultural, and leftist activism, Chicago was proof positive that Americans lived in a repressive police state where anyone advocating change had to be even more concerned for their personal safety and suspicious of authorities.

The incident at Michigan and Balbo, the drama inside the convention hall, and the antics of the Youth International Party (aka Yippie) in the months and days before have, thanks in part to vivid television coverage, been packaged together as a pivotal moment in 1960s history, one complete with colorful characters both fiery and whimsical, rising tension, and a violent climax. In the traditional telling, Yippie leaders and Richard Daley took center stage, while those beaten on the streets played supporting roles. However, focusing on the twenty-minute televised "riot" fails to place all the key historical actors in frame and offers a limited view of events. There was another important drama in Chicago that week that better informs us about not only the city, but the nation, in the 1960s. Within the broad spectacle of convention week, a very local protest transpired, largely off camera, one that mirrored national disagreements about the power of the state versus the rights of its citizens that brought to a head long-simmering problems on the North Side of Chicago. Pulling the camera back and examining more than just Wednesday night provides the full picture.

On Tuesday, August 27, at approximately 11 P.M., ministers carrying an eight-foot cross entered Lincoln Park. This was in response to increasing police violence over the previous two days and about enforcement of the rarely imposed 11 P.M. curfew in the park. About two thousand people watched as the ministers began a religious service. Local clergymen spoke, others made public statements and sang hymns, but many present were mainly waiting for the Chicago police to again clear the park. While officers prepared to advance and special mace-spraying trucks moved into position, some demonstrators argued loudly for violence in the streets. Others were adamant that they peacefully stand their ground. Protesters scrambled to build a barricade of picnic tables and trash cans between the ministers and approaching officers. Clergymen advised those who would listen to "sit or split": either leave now or sit down, lock arms, and remain calm.[8] Then, demonstrators sat and tied handkerchiefs across their faces to combat the whitish chemical fog now bursting out of shells and spewing from trucks.[9] As the gas rolled in shortly after 12:30, one minister vowed, "This is our Park. We will not be moved."[10]

Gas mask–clad officers then entered the park swinging clubs, knocking one minister unconscious. Stinging mace drifted in the air. Nightsticks crashed down on muscle and bone. Scared and confused demonstrators scrambled to find safety. Protesters fired back with rocks and bottles as the gas curled its way into the surrounding neighborhood. The police repeated that the area was to be cleared, but brick and rock missiles pelted their cars as they chased down demonstrators.[11] That night alone, Chicago police officers arrested some 160 persons, while seven policemen and more than sixty demonstrators experienced injury.[12] Abe Peck, hippie activist and editor of the Chicago underground paper *Seed*, referred to the Tuesday night conflict as "the elemental struggle" for local countercultural members.[13] The whole world may have watched on Wednesday, but few Americans saw this pivotal moment for Lincoln Park residents on Tuesday, an instant with many layers that encapsulated late-1960s America.

This local protest involved more than Yippies, Daley, and violence. In a decade when the American clergy debated its relevance, ministers led the protest in Lincoln Park. In an era when the counterculture grew, hips helped plan Chicago's demonstration alongside "average" area residents making this a grassroots protest in a time when "average" people joined together in the south and north to combat entrenched powers. In an era when cities underwent urban renewal programs that displaced many in the name of progress, Lincoln Park was home to residents advancing an urban renewal plan.

This study examines how, on Chicago's North Side, urban renewal and gentrification, liberalism, the counterculture, police violence, the 1968 Democratic National Convention, and grassroots activism molded the development of a neighborhood and the city in the postwar years. Early top-down works on the history of the 1960s chronicle civil rights, antiwar, and New Left leaders.[14] Scholars later shifted the focus from national to local leadership on college campuses and in student organizations.[15] This study answers the call by historians to analyze the 1960s at the grassroots by examining how ordinary citizens molded urban renewal, gentrification, and the events of August of 1968.[16] *Wear Some Armor in Your Hair* also contributes to Chicago history by placing Lincoln Park within the history of postwar development of the city.

The story of the Democratic National Convention of 1968 sits within the larger story of the development of the Lincoln Park neighborhood from 1948 to 1974, an area that hosted the North Side's first large-scale urban renewal project.[17] After World War II, ideas about the neighborhood's identity were as varied as its architecture. Two visions of community emerged before August 1968. White liberals belonging to the area's neighborhood organizations united under the umbrella group the Lincoln Park Conservation Association (LPCA) and began to advance their dream for the area in the 1950s. From day one they fused their group to Chicago's power structure, working with city officials to have the area declared eligible for urban renewal aid and obtaining funds from the federal government, the state of Illinois, and the city to further their vision, one that claimed to embrace diversity. By the 1960s, some white Americans avoided directly addressing race as an issue then they discussed neighborhood change. Instead, they offered up "individual rights" and other coded language in their objections to governmental oversight of development. As in other parts of the nation, white liberals in Lincoln Park did not openly discriminate in their plans, but instead objected to high-rise and public housing—edifices rather than people. Lincoln "Parkers" of the Democratic 43rd ward did not overtly seek to exclude nonwhite and poor residents from the area but wanted to cushion themselves in a secure zone, pursuing a kind of domestic containment.[18]

Scholars have examined and treated urban renewal and gentrification as separate subjects. For example, one anthropologist defines gentrification as:

> an economic and social process whereby private capital (real estate firms, developers) and individual homeowners and renters reinvest in fiscally neglected neighborhoods through housing rehabilitation, loft conversions, and the construction of new housing stock. *Unlike urban renewal* (italics mine), gentrification is a gradual process, occurring one building or block at a time, slowly reconfiguring the neighborhood landscape of consumption and residence by displacing poor and working-class residents unable to afford to live in 'revitalized' neighborhoods with rising rents, property taxes, and new businesses catering to an upscale clientele.[19]

One historian noted that gentrifiers he chronicled were "veterans in the fight against urban renewal."[20]

And yet, dividing and easily defining the two can be challenging. Two scholars offer, "When historians refer to 'urban renewal,' they are not describing one singular policy. Rather, they are describing a host of programs and policies that wrought a series of radical interventions on the urban built environment."[21] Another refers to both "gentrifier" and "gentrification" as "chaotic conceptions."[22]

In urban renewal histories, generally, government and residents native to an area work together to affect change, while in gentrification studies citizens from outside a neighborhood descend on and alter it. Both stories of renewal and gentrification, however, often end up at the same conclusion: the displacement of poorer residents and/or persons of color.

However, the end of the story is not the only similarity between the two areas of study. For example, scholars of both gentrification and urban renewal concern themselves with the intent and nature of those advocating neighborhood change. The history of gentrification has received increasing attention by historians, and offers alternative and sophisticated views of the process that go beyond pitting gentrifiers on one side and their victims on the other. Studies of gentrification seek to reframe its meaning and impact, arguing that those promoting it were more than two-dimensional forces of exclusion.[23] Some argue that, especially for leftists and those in the counterculture, cities were "emancipatory" havens away from suburban conformity.[24] Others argue that a "New Middle Class" of urban residents created culturally sophisticated lifestyles in neighborhoods.[25] In the "revanchist city," however, gentrification was revenge directed at the poor and persons of color.[26] Japonica Brown-Saracino offers up three kinds of gentrifiers: traditional "pioneers" who displace native residents, "social preservationists" not out for financial gain who seek to resist gentrification while inadvertently carrying it out, and the middle ground "social homesteaders" who value buildings and the environment over the native population, despite not wanting them removed.[27]

Similarly, scholars have recently argued that urban renewal was an idea with multiple origins, both modernist and profit-driven, that evolved out of the conflicts of World War II and the Cold War.[28] One urban historian argues that renewal was "spatial apartheid," another calls it "both visionary and pragmatic."[29] Andrew J. Diamond refers to 1950s and 1960s urban renewal as "a form of warfare."[30] Samuel Zipp and Michael Carrier challenge us to see that early proponents of urban renewal were, in fact, "idealists."[31] Others note, "In retrospect, we can think of urban renewal as a distinct moment in American history, replete with triumphs and disasters."[32] Blacks themselves could, and did, embrace urban renewal, and were agents of gen-trification.[33] In Philadelphia, residents and the city worked together to pro-duce a renewal program that didn't displace Blacks.[34]

Additional overlap is found in studies examining how concerns over the local environment and ecology grounded each. Brown-Saracino's social homesteaders cared about the local environment, and other renewers saw cities as renewable resources.[35] In Atlanta, arguments centered on renewal as being about buildings, or people.[36] The role of art and artists is another key focus of renewal and gentrification scholars.[37] Periodization is also in question in both fields. While British sociologist Ruth Glass first used the term "gentrification" in 1964, Carolyn Whitzman traces it back to the late nineteenth century in Toronto.[38] In his study of Lincoln Park, Daniel Kay Hertz argues that the gentrification of the neighborhood dates back to the early twentieth century.[39] Urban historians also convincingly push the timeline of urban renewal back prior to the post–World War II years.[40]

The roles of liberals and liberalism is also important in both. New Deal liberals in Brooklyn liked central planning and government cooperation, while brownstoners wanted a more independent, decentralized approach.[41] Liberals in Philadelphia's West Mount Airy successfully integrated that neighborhood.[42] Arnold Hirsch notes how liberals, during and immedi-ately after World War II, embraced "liberal environmentalism."[43]

The story of Lincoln Park contains much overlap between renewal and gentrification. It went from a phase of gentrification (although the term had not yet been coined), to urban renewal, to gentrification, speaking to the elastic and adaptable nature of development and displacement. In the late 1940s, largely white, liberal residents in the Old Town section began rehab-bing buildings and established an art fair. By the early 1960s, after residents worked with city officials to research and draft a plan, urban renewal was up and running. And, after both the erosion and transformation of the local movement to make renewal more inclusive and President Richard Nixon's termination of urban renewal nationwide in 1973, local residents in Old Town and other areas continued to gentrify the area.

As in Brooklyn, Lincoln Park gentrifiers initiated urban renewal at the grassroots level and fought for what they thought was a "real" and "diverse" neighborhood.[44] Like New York's SoHo, Lincoln Park was also a neighbor-hood where artists and those outside the mainstream took part in urban renewal. And, as in Harlem where Black Power influenced gentrification,

1960s forces such as the counterculture, antiwar movement, and religious activism molded it.[45]

White Lincoln Parkers who spearheaded renewal efforts in the 1950s fall under what gentrification scholars term consumption, or demand-side, interpretations of the process. As opposed to production, or supply-side, interpretations that emphasize economic opportunities and political policies, in consumption interpretations gentrifiers interested in and concerned by social diversity, historic preservation, and job proximity are the prime movers; people, rather than structures, implement and guide gentrification efforts.[46] In Lincoln Park, already established residents, not outsiders, proudly emphasized the necessity of "diversity," as early as the 1950s and engaged, by the 1970s, in historic preservation. These first-phase activists were establishment liberals, concerned with neighborhood authenticity, as they defined it, and *less* with residents. As such, they were more internal homesteaders promoting change from within than ruthless pioneers who cared about residents not at all. Theirs was a more complicated and contradictory vision of renewal. They wanted to preserve what I term the cosmetic diversity of 1950s Lincoln Park, a place where pockets of nonwhite residents lived among a group of people with varied European backgrounds. They sought to change the physical, not the ethnic or racial, landscape through urban renewal. To those liberals promoting this vision, urban renewal meant securing their enclave, not necessarily excluding others from it.

The white, liberal clergymen who stood their ground for their right to the park in the face of gas and clubs that Tuesday night in 1968 belonged to the North Side Cooperative Ministry (NSCM), a coalition of more than twenty churches on Chicago's North Side that offered the second vision of Lincoln Park. NSCM ministers and other neighborhood inhabitants countered LPCA's vision with a more broadly inclusive definition of community open to more minorities and low-income families. During the 1960s, members of the clergy nationwide assumed more active roles as churches questioned their relevancy in the postwar world. As early as the 1940s and 1950s, what Mark Wild refers to as a "renewalist vanguard" of ministers embraced secularism and worked to make churches more relevant.[47] In Chicago, ministers following in this vein clashed openly but nonviolently with LPCA in the 1960s. They formed committees, studied the neighborhood, publicly criticized the conservation association, sought influential positions on LPCA, and even picketed the organization to further their cause.

In showing how white liberal proponents of ethnic European diversity, as they defined "diversity," carried out their vision of Lincoln Park, this book adds to the analysis of the postwar gentrifier. Clergymen of the North Side Cooperative Ministry were also members of the Lincoln Park Conservation Agency, and LPCA members did warm to demands for low- and moderate-income housing in urban renewal planning. Both groups embraced grassroots organization, but while LPCA worked with the city's leadership, the ministers and their expanding band of allies held tightly to the power of the people. They, like the Woodlawn Organization south of Lincoln Park that fought for Black rights, were also ahead of their time.[48] Their vision and activism in the 1950s and 1960s, like those of other neighborhood-first-focused groups in Chicago, predated the nationwide rise of neighborhood movements of the 1970s in cities like New York, Boston, and Washington, DC, in what Suleiman Osman calls "The Decade of the Neighborhood."[49]

Both groups consisted of liberal white Chicagoans, and by examining the clash of ideas, this study further contributes to the history of postwar liberalism among white Americans by examining, at the local level, their beliefs and actions. Some authors have asserted that 1960s liberalism faced a backlash in the latter years of the decade when American voters leaned right.[50] Other works argue that the events of the late 1960s were the culmination of longstanding beliefs.[51] This study argues that white liberals on Chicago's North Side had conflicting views regarding class, ethnicity, and race rather than one coherent vision, and in carrying out their plan did not strike back but doubled down to meet their challengers while finding common ground with them.

A third community, with a less defined vision, emerged in Lincoln Park in the mid-1960s: the counterculture. The intersection of the counterculture and urban development at the local level has been examined only rarely.[52] The Old Town area of Lincoln Park hosted both hips and commerce, its Wells Street home to head shops and Crate&Barrel, a place where ministers worked with freaks (as those most committed to the hip life preferred to be called). Publicized by the mainstream media and the underground paper *Seed*, Chicago's hip scene thrived by 1967. This study opens a new chapter in Chicago history by tracing the rise of Chicago's counterculture, and more generally contributes to the subject of the 1960s counterculture itself.[53] In analyzing its resemblance to the national cultural movement, while detailing its unique traits, it addresses to what extent activism in Chicago was driven by national leaders or was locally autonomous. In Old Town, local hips initially took direction from the Diggers of Haight-Ashbury in San Francisco in developing a hip enclave. However, while the Haight was a designated hip zone, Old Town interwove commercial development, the counterculture, political action, and, most uniquely, the clergy. Damon Bach argues that different strains of American hips existed in the 1960s, from "Hybrid Counterculturalists," "Cultural Activists," to "Cultural Revolutionaries."[54] Likewise, in the G.I. coffeehouse movement one found a mixed bag of persons.[55] Chicago's distinctive hip area housed ministers and businessmen and as such was not characterized by a false binary of hip versus square. This blend of worlds forces us to reexamine how we think of the 1960s counterculture, alternately portrayed as a cultural sideshow, an easily co-opted marketing tool, or a drain on serious political activism. In Chicago it was actually a more complicated and committed social and political movement. It also played a role, albeit unknowingly, in gentrification as the influx of artists, writers, and musicians in the 1960s paved the way for renewal and gentrification, as it did later in San Francisco's Haight and New York's East Village.

When Yippie leaders announced that they intended to hold a national protest, a "Festival of Life" in Chicago during the 1968 Democratic National Convention, the group inadvertently shifted the focus in Lincoln Park from urban renewal and community identity to protest planning and survival. Yippie leaders Abbie Hoffman and Jerry Rubin traveled the nation in the summer of 1968, making outlandish threats about their convention plans. Rubin spouted, "I support everything which puts people into motion, which creates disruption and controversy, which creates chaos and rebirth" and that the government was "reachable only through the language of power and violence."[56]

Meanwhile, Lincoln Park residents planned the nuts-and-bolts of convention week protests and, especially in Old Town, bore the brunt of police harassment ordered by Mayor Daley, who was intent on blocking the demonstration. Abbie Hoffman later wrote of the organizing for Chicago as if residents were marginal, but they were actually an independent, guiding force before and during convention week, ultimately adding new meaning to this national event.[57] Expecting violence—*Seed*'s Abe Peck warned those coming to the city to "wear some armor in your hair" rather than flowers—and experienced in organizing over urban renewal, residents worked independently of Yippie in the months prior to August 1968.[58] Some collaborated with the police to prevent a hippie invasion. Others, such as the Free City Survival Committee composed of local hips and ministers, acted at the forefront of demonstration planning, working day-to-day to make it possible for protesters to sleep, eat, and travel in the city. Neighborhood activists who worked to promote inclusion in urban renewal now sought park space along with food, shelter, and legal and medical aid for the festival coming to their neighborhood. Free City went to great lengths to work with the city to secure a permit for the Festival of Life. Holding meetings and filing paperwork seems completely at odds with the hip life, and Chicago hips again force us to rethink both the makeup of the counterculture and its actions. Rather than impede mass politics as depicted in histories of the New Left, the Chicago counterculture moved them forward in a reasoned and sensible manner. Chicago hips were not fair-weather activists at best, stoned fools siphoning energy from the Movement at worst, but instead were community leaders and ground forces in the preparation for a national demonstration.

Numerous scholars have assessed the national meanings of the violence in Chicago during convention week.[59] Additionally, participants have interpreted the conflicts surrounding it.[60] Only two full-length historical works focus on this legendary event.[61] This work is a companion piece to those two important studies. This conflict was both a flashpoint in 1960s activism on the national scale, and on the local, a watershed in a longstanding feud over urban renewal and community identity in Lincoln Park at a time when Americans across the nation debated national identity and neighborhood demography.

When the festival began, Yippie leaders finally realized the potential for police violence that protesters faced and encouraged them to leave the park. Chicagoans, now unwittingly transforming a national event into a local one, refused. Reverend Larry Dutenhaver later called the church service of Tuesday night "a community event," noting the local dimension Chicago residents added to the national demonstration.[62] Mike Royko offered that the meaning of the violence in Lincoln Park was "as simple as a child's game of king-of-the-hill."[63] Abbie Hoffman proclaimed, "We've won the battle of Chicago, and just because they wouldn't let us sleep in the park. That's what it's all about—the right to sleep in the park and do our own thing."[64]

A demonstration originally designed to protest a war and the political party that expanded it also became part of a local fight over space underway for years. Years later, Rubin told Peck, "We manipulated you in the sense that our goal was national, not local."[65] In reality, Lincoln Park residents manipulated the festival, making it a local protest in addition to a national one. Those embracing a Lincoln Park open to demonstration dealt with those police officers ordered to close it.[66] Many in the area knew things would be bad, but they didn't expect police officers to remove their badges and chant "Kill, kill" while beating unarmed protesters. Rather than hiding, these residents, in increased numbers, stood up to police, negotiated with them, protected others, and, with increased support from the area, aided the wounded.

Without the Yippies, the demonstration would not have been born. And yet without Chicagoans, the protest would have floundered, or been far bloodier. National leaders and local leaders created an event with multiple meanings. The key roles played by Chicago residents indicate that the nature of the demonstration was neither national nor local, but *both*. The scene at Michigan and Balbo was just one televised event; the true significance of that incident can only be understood when we pull back the camera to include the supporting players and look at the weeks, and years, before and after that famous 1960s snapshot. In doing so, we see a richer postwar United States defined by conflict between entrenched interests, even those that voted democrat, and the grassroots.

The police violence of convention week arguably changed the nation, and definitely affected the neighborhood, in 1969. *Wear Some Armor in Your Hair* also adds to the growing dialogue about the impact of violence on postwar urban development.[67] In places like Newark, Baltimore, and New Haven, violence had a profound impact on urban change.[68] In Chicago, the police violence of August of 1968 ushered in a more confrontational atmosphere on the North Side as activists now feared police more than ever, some arguing for "revolution."

In this way, Chicago followed the national trajectory of the 1960s. First-wave historians of that era have argued that idealism, dedication, and nonviolent protest characterized the early years of the decade, only to give way to chaos, violence, and anger after 1968.[69] Chicago's story provides some support to this narrative. Newcomers to Lincoln Park activism after 1968 brought with them the strategy of confrontation. Those promoting a more inclusive neighborhood became fearful of the police, and some began to accept confrontation as a means for change. They then took roles as monitors of police behavior, joining with those previously uninvolved in community activism. This confederacy included members of NSCM, the Concerned Citizens of Lincoln Park (soon to be the Concerned Citizens Survival Front), and the Puerto Rican gang the Young Lords, politicized in part by the police violence of convention week. The Lords were the most visible, and to some frightening, group in 1969 Lincoln Park. They disrupted community meetings and seized property to make their voice heard. Additionally, the murder of a Young Lord, a local minister and his wife, Black Panthers Mark Clark and Fred Hampton, and the bombing of two alderman's offices, intensified fears in the area. Gentrification met militarization in the wake of the festival as an area once simmering now boiled.

Both 1965 and 1968 have been labeled as key years of the decade.[70] For Lincoln Park, 1969 was crucial. The police violence during the Democratic National Convention set a new tone in the area as suspicion, aggression, and combativeness replaced the peaceful petition signing and picketing of the early decade.[71] LPCA white liberals, now actually more accepting of low-income residents, recoiled at the new, confrontational approach by gang members and their allies, one that stepped outside the acceptable parameters of disagreement. The very white liberals who claimed that they supported a more diverse plan for urban renewal and in fact approved more moderate- and low-income housing in renewal plans, now claimed to merely object to the tactics of those advocating for it. They also continued to work with authorities to secure their vision for the area in the face of the tension that lingered after August of 1968. Scared by Lords outbursts, local violence, and a belief that NSCM and its allies funded militant, extremist groups, they sidestepped the issues of economic, racial, and ethnic diversity in the neighborhood and focused on community violence as those working for a more open Lincoln Park were now demonized. Some neighborhood organizations worked closely with the police, and two LPCA leaders testified to Congress that ministry leaders promoted communism, aided the Lords, and had ties to the antiwar group Students for a Democratic Society. At the same time, members of Chicago's Red Squad, a police unit formed to infiltrate leftist groups, harassed activists.

The original movement for inclusion held on for a time, then faded, but new actors made their voices heard in the 1970s. As Rhonda Y. Williams cautions us "about offering a tidy conclusion to the era of expansive Black Power politics," a simple implosion of activism, nor a backlash against it, did not occur in Lincoln Park.[72] And as when the Black Panthers refused to recognize the police, which Nikhil Pal Singh argues was not only a success, but "something far more dangerous than is generally acknowledged," when other groups in Lincoln Park rose up after the police violence of 1968, they too denied the legitimacy of the state and succeeded in making their voices heard.[73] Key leaders in the inclusion movement became disillusioned and left the area, yet other activists emerged after their departure. Meanwhile, members of the Old Town Triangle Association, housed on the wealthy east side of the neighborhood, obtained government protection of structures as historic landmarks. While the area gentrified, other Chicagoans acted in new and different ways, and as such declension did not happen in full, but a transition occurred as new actors emerged.

Where Lincoln Park's story diverges from other parts of Chicago in the postwar years is that the conflict there resulted not in a shift from a white to a Black neighborhood, but that it remained a white-dominated zone. Historians Arnold Hirsch and Amanda I. Seligman detail how white Chicagoans sought to affect the development of the city.[74] Hirsch's path-breaking work on the South Side traced the creation of a "second ghetto" through the "fierce application of a containment policy" by white residents in concert with Chicago city government.[75] Some Lincoln Park residents, working with city officials, contained *themselves* in a predominately white, affluent enclave, forcing low- and moderate-income residents into other parts of the city, thus altering Chicago's demographic makeup. Lincoln Park mirrors Hirsch's examination of urban renewal in the Hyde Park neighborhood, where he reveals a lip-service to diversity in a renewal plan that ultimately ended in a predominately white area. Seligman's West Side white activists, like those in Lincoln Park, were concerned with the possibility of "blight." However, they failed in their attempts to keep their neighborhood from changing because they lacked access to political levers of power, whereas middle- and upper-middle-class Lincoln Park residents connected with city officials right away and worked with them to carry out their plans. While the West Side went "from white to black," the North Side's Lincoln Park went from predominately white to somewhat less predominately white, establishing itself as a bedroom community housing people who worked in the downtown, the focus of Mayor Daley's urban development plans.[76]

Lincoln Park was at the nexus of defining issues of the 1960s, including urban renewal, liberalism, the rise, fall, and transformation of the counter-culture, religious revival, police–community relations, and the antiwar movement, and as such provides a valuable local lens through which to re-examine national trends. This book merges 1960s history, Chicago history, social and urban history to explore how Chicago both followed and devi-ated from the national narrative in the postwar era. The story of Lincoln Park, Chicago, is in many ways the story of 1960s activism writ small, and in other ways challenges us to view national trends differently.

CHAPTER ONE

Diversity and Renewal

"Its meaning depends on who is saying it. Diversity for upper class
people means cobblestone streets and a tennis club on Armitage and
Halsted. Do you think a man coming home from a factory after working
ten hours will go play tennis? Come on!"[1]
—Lincoln Park businessman

Postwar Chicago

Years before the arrival of hips and before the batons and chanting in the
streets in August of 1968, the direction of urban renewal divided Lincoln
Park. In 1948, residents of the Old Town section on Lincoln Park's southeast side formed the Old Town Triangle Association (OTTA) to revitalize
their area.[2] Other neighborhoods soon followed and by the early 1950s,
seven North Side neighborhoods possessed their own organizations. These
groups merged with local business interests into the Lincoln Park Conservation Association in 1954, and sought city and federal aid to promote their
vision of postwar Lincoln Park: a "diverse," family-centered neighborhood,
an idea that dovetailed nicely with Mayor Daley's vision of a ring of white,
middle-class neighborhoods surrounding the downtown Loop business
district.

Their concern came after years of nationwide debate about the future of
America's cities. In the early twentieth century, politicians and social re-
formers began a dialogue over the nature of cities and the role of the federal
government in their development.[3] After World War II, the debate over
American cities revived with "blight," and the flight to the suburbs as key
concerns.[4] Blight "meant the process of physical deterioration that destroyed property values and undermined the quality of urban life. More-
over, blight was often referred to as a kind of cancer, an insidious, spreading
phenomenon that could kill a city if not removed or forced into remission."[5]
It also, supposedly, fueled white flight to the suburbs.[6]

Nationally, urban planners, commentators, and others offered solutions to the perceived plight of the modern city.[7] In New York, Kansas City, and Los Angeles, those embracing slum clearance as the way of the future debated modernists envisioning urban renovation as a means to better citizens.[8] Some believed the government should play a larger role in aiding cities, and in 1949 the federal government agreed to pay two-thirds of the cost of demolition, land, and construction in renewal projects under the Taft-Ellender-Wagner bill that became the Housing Act of 1949.[9] The 1954 Housing Act expanded this in a combination of urban renewal and urban redevelopment programs to curb slums and blight.[10] In Chicago, use of the word "blight" dated back to at least 1932. In postwar Chicago, the idea of designating spaces "conservation areas" became popular while labeling an area "blighted" became controversial as it meant bulldozing and running residents out, however, Illinois lawmakers in the 1950s did not develop a standard definition for either.[11] The language white Chicagoans used, in Lincoln Park and elsewhere, mirrored how some whites expressed their views on race in the postwar United States. These views had been subtly changing across the nation as white Americans, whether consciously or not, began to alter their conceptions of and concerns about race, blending them with newfound worries over the real estate market and neighborhood property, views that allowed them to claim to embrace diversity, however they defined it, while walling out persons of color, or at least minimizing their presence.[12] In suburbs across the nation, white Americans embraced a "new racial thinking" in which they abandoned older, overt beliefs in racial hierarchy and talked instead of "property instead of people."[13] In Brownsville, Brooklyn, white residents who embraced public housing and protested against segregation but still were, as one remembered, "liberal on race . . . but were not liberal on interpersonal relations" fled their neighborhood.[14] Such contradictory views reveal racism's "ever shifting yet present structure" and fueled concerns over city development in Chicago and elsewhere after World War II.[15] Additionally, white Chicagoans placed great value on what they considered ethnic identity, so much so that one 1932 study noted that realtors ranked ethnic groups from most to least desirable.[16]

Chicago's city government pursued urban renewal by working with local neighborhood groups. The Chicago Land Clearance Commission, created by the 1947 Illinois Blighted Areas Redevelopment Act, cleared areas and sold them to developers. In 1955, the city established the Community

Conservation Board that designated areas "Conservation."[17] Mayor Richard J. Daley, elected in 1955, went further. He envisioned a revitalized downtown as key to developing the city in the postwar years. In his first four years in office he poured money into developing the Loop.[18] In doing so he allied with Chicago's business community and promoted urban renewal in the area lest it become, as one developer predicted, "The Central Business District Slum."[19] City government and business then worked together as the Chicago Central Area Committee to develop the downtown and adjacent residential areas.[20] Daley and the committee wanted this district restored and protected, surrounded by a periphery of neighborhoods full of middle-class homes.

If done well, urban renewal (first called "redevelopment") revitalized areas. However, Chicago renewal plans in the 1950s bulldozed buildings and ejected the poor and nonwhite more than beautified neighborhoods. For example, the Illinois Institute of Technology, Michael Reese Hospital, and the New York Life Insurance Company had already worked with the city to tear down homes and build high-rises and offices.

The largest development prior to Lincoln Park was the Hyde Park-Kenwood renewal program, one that in some ways created the template for Lincoln Park's efforts. It began in 1952 when the University of Chicago sponsored the South East Chicago Commission to develop and implement its renewal program, in place in 1958. The Hyde Park-Kenwood Community Conference helped gain acceptance of the plan from residents on the South Side. While critics lambasted the program for driving out Black and low-income families, the city completed the plan in part due to local residents. That same year, Daley introduced his program to build a University of Illinois campus in Chicago, one that could buffer the business district. Residents of the predominately Italian first ward who faced removal protested.[21] Following this was the clearing of land for the Carl Sandburg Village south of Lincoln Park. This was a high-income complex housing thousands of well-to-do white professionals, begun in 1962 and finalized in 1966.[22] The village consisted of six, twenty-nine-story towers and a dozen artist studios, among other buildings.[23] Only in the case of the Woodlawn neighborhood, on the city's South Side, did the city listen to the demands of low-income residents.[24]

One of Daley's chief concerns was the growth of the Black population adjacent to the city's business district, a worry that mirrored those of white

Chicagoans who had no place for Blacks in the postwar years. The city, post–World War II, was largely segregated, with Blacks living mainly on the south side. Chicago experienced numerous riots since 1944, and many of these were racial in nature, sparked over living space.[25] Historians studying African American history in postwar Chicago have identified a pattern of violence spanning the 1950s and 1960s.[26] Blacks and whites clashed throughout the 1950s, notably the South and West Sides, as "turf battles ensued over access to schools, parks, playgrounds, and beaches, in addition to housing."[27] White residents, anxious to segregate Black families after the war, used urban renewal and vigilante justice to combat integration. Between 1944 and 1946, forty-six residences occupied by Blacks in predominantly white neighborhoods experienced vandalism, arson, and bombings. In Cicero in 1951, a large housing riot erupted during which National Guardsmen and Cook County Sheriffs helped the local police.[28] Attempts to integrate Trumbull Park led to violence in 1955.[29] The Martin Kennelly and Richard J. Daley mayoral administrations remained mute as white Chicagoans lashed out against what they saw as encroachment by Blacks.[30]

Postwar Lincoln Park

While violence occurred elsewhere in the city, Lincoln Park was calm, its streets relatively safe. The Lincoln Park neighborhood sits on Chicago's North Side along Lake Michigan, enclosed within Diversey Avenue to the north, Lincoln Park itself to the east, North Avenue as its southern boundary, and Clybourn Avenue along its west. Development of the area first began in the nineteenth century.[31] After the incorporation of Chicago as a city in 1837, the federal government offered land grants for what would become Lincoln Park. A large influx of German immigrants in 1838 comprised the area's earliest population and remained as an influential presence for years.[32] Irish immigrants followed. It developed into a residential community between 1871 and 1895.[33] The city then developed the bulk of the neighborhood between 1880 and 1904, and over 60 percent of structures built then still stood in 1960.[34] In the 1910s, additional factories were built along the Chicago River and Poles, Slovaks, Serbians, Romanians, Hungarians, and Italians moved there for jobs. A Black enclave developed in the mid-1920s on Maud Avenue near Armitage and Diversey Avenues and "expanded to 1,358 persons by 1960."[35]

The area's identity was, however, in many ways undefined after the Second World War. On the one hand, it was a mishmash of ethnicities where residents spoke affectionately about the area's "diversity." On the other hand, however, distinct eastern and western sections existed within the predominately white neighborhood. The east side housed wealthier, educated residents living in brick and concrete homes. On the west side (starting around Halsted street), working-class and lower-income residents occupied wooden houses near both the Chicago River and industry near it. Most residents rented and worked a variety of jobs, some within walking distance, others in the nearby Loop. The neighborhood survived depression and war as homeowners converted residences into apartments. As the 1950s dawned, the area then entered into a period of de-conversion of apartments back into single-family homes.

Residents often remarked on their neighborhood's "diversity," and in terms of businesses, the area was quite varied, with eighteen institutions including eight hospitals, DePaul University, McCormick Theological Seminary, Francis Parker School, a public library, a retirement home, and a Salvation Army center in the area. It also had eleven elementary schools and one public high school.[36] Completion of the Chicago subway after World War II gave Lincoln Park a station at North Avenue and Clybourn, minutes from the Loop.[37] Between 1947and 1957, twenty manufacturers in Lincoln Park relocated to the suburbs. However, thirty-three other establishments moved *to* it.[38]

Jobs also varied. For men, blue-collar work dominated; only three census tracts reported that more than half of males worked white-collar jobs. In every tract, a larger number of women were in white-collar jobs than men. The larger pattern, especially among men, was that more white-collar workers lived in the eastern part.[39] For example, after World War II, radio and TV persons moved to Old Town because of its proximity to the Loop.[40]

When off the clock, residents had a variety of recreational options as well. The area had over twenty-two billiard halls. Eleven bowling alleys also existed along with eleven dance halls. In 1949, there were 284 retail liquor licenses registered in the area.[41]

The neighborhood offered residents diverse architectural styles as well, boasting row houses, mansions, flats, and Victorian homes in various conditions. The reason for this variety was, in part, due to the 1871 fire. After the disaster the city passed the Fire Ordinance of 1872, restricting the construction of wooden buildings. In Lincoln Park, buildings east of Wells Street and Lincoln Avenue close to the park would have to be built of stone and brick. On the west side of the neighborhood, however, less expensive wooden frame homes could be erected.[42]

However, between 1919 and 1950, virtually no new building occurred (with exception of along the park). University of Chicago sociology professors noted that from 1920 to 1940 "there was comparatively little residential construction in the community."[43] Residential building during the Depression and war had virtually ground to a halt as homes turned into rooming houses.[44] During World War II the government refrained from developing the area and encouraged dividing existing structures into apartments to house migrant workers from the southern United States who relocated to the city in pursuit of wartime jobs.[45] By the 1940s, approximately 10 percent of structures had fallen into "disrespectful disrepair," and 15 percent had been converted to apartments.[46] A local artist offered "two houses over, some people rented their second floor rooms to a couple of people. Fifteen to twenty people moved in—gypsies. There were cars parked in the middle of the street—Cadillacs—with people running in and out." One Lincoln Park resident commented, "After the war there was less pressure on housing . . . the people were poor, with problems."[47]

By the 1950s, the area was home to spacious homes on the wealthy East Side and to the emerging Cabrini Green housing project on the far southwestern border.[48] The most common structures were two- and three-story buildings. With factories located on the West Side, two-story, two-family wooden-frame (or brick) structures grew to house Irish, German, and Polish workers. On the east side of Halsted stood more rooming houses and high-rise buildings. Clark Street had the largest number of housing units.[49] East of Clark Street were pricey, single-family wood and brick homes, and some two- and three-story multifamily apartments.

By 1950, over 20 percent of all structures had been converted to multiple family units, and "not one entire street of single-family houses could be found in the community."[50] In that decade, more than three hundred rooming houses were de-converted back into apartments or homes. Two-family structures were 20 percent of housing, while 38.6 percent of housing units had ten or more structures. In 1960, 14 percent of housing units in the neighborhood were owner occupied.[51] The population in 1950 was 102,000, but in 1960 it was 89,000.[52]

The area was diverse in its buildings, vocations, businesses, and recreational spots. In terms of its people, however, Lincoln Park was both "diverse" and not. As opposed to other parts of postwar Chicago where racial makeup was changing, the 82,622 white residents of Lincoln Park were the majority. In 1950, only 205 African Americans lived in the neighborhood, and "other races" accounted for only 1,664 persons.[53] However, a small influx of other peoples to the 1,185-acre neighborhood did begin after the war.[54] One priest raised in Lincoln Park commented that, "There was a large segment of hillbillies."[55] The south and west boundary of North Avenue became a Black and Hispanic enclave, and a Japanese population grew. Add to this the increased presence of artists and bohemians in the southeast, and a seemingly diverse population emerged.[56]

In reality, though, the area was diverse in terms of its residents of European descent. In the 1950s, Germans and Italians were the largest ethnic groups at 19.6 percent and 13 percent of the population. Poles followed (7.2 percent), then Irish (5 percent), Austrians (4.6 percent), Hungarians (4.4 percent), and Russians (4.4 percent). Germans were spread out evenly throughout the neighborhood, while Italians and Poles clustered.[57]

Blacks and Latinos, however, were small, largely segregated presences. The 1960 Census showed 1,256 Blacks in Lincoln Park, "mostly concentrated along the River Branch and in the extreme southwest section, where the post-fire relief shanties are still most prominent."[58] From 1952 to 1962, there was a "significant increase in Latin American residents living along North Avenue."[59] By 1960, there were 1,800 Puerto Ricans in the area, mainly in the central to eastern parts of the neighborhood.[60]

As for economic variance, families that made less than $5,500 annually lived on the far northwestern corner of the neighborhood; residents who made $5,500–$6,600 lived in the center, and those who made $6,000–$8,500 lived on the far eastern border by the park. Additionally, the median value of owner-occupied homes, and the rent for nonowners, was highest on the east side along the park.[61] Homes along the lake and park sold for more than elsewhere. Clark Street and Diversey was home to the only "thriving" shopping center in the area.[62] Those on the east side, north of Armitage, made more than anyone in the neighborhood. One resident later noted that, "The people of the high-rise buildings live apart from the rest of the community . . . They belong to a higher economic group and have more cosmopolitan taste and other attitudes than most other citizens of the community."[63]

Educational patterns mirrored economic ones. The least educated residents tended to be in the western and southern portions of the area, with the eastern section being the most educated. Generally, the less educated tended to live on the west side, with some exceptions (tracts 12 and 108), while the most educated residents lived on the far eastern side across from the park.[64]

While wealthier, more educated, and white families tended to live on the east side near the lake while poorer nonwhites tended to live on the west side, with its peppering of Asians, Latinos, Appalachians, artists, and Blacks, the area was, in comparison to neighborhoods like Mayor Daley's Bridgeport, comparatively varied. However, the 1950 *Community Fact Book for Chicago* grimly predicted that, "the increase in conversions and the expansion of industry forecast the end of much of Lincoln Park as a residential community."[65]

The Lincoln Park Conservation Association

To combat the grim forecast, residents formed the Lincoln Park Conservation Association (LPCA) in 1954. Nationwide, residents of cities such as St. Louis, Baltimore, Detroit, and Pittsburgh formed grassroots associations to guide the growth of their neighborhoods.[66] Chicago residents initially, in 1949, formed the Association of Community Councils, on which Lincoln Park's Malcolm Shanower was a leader.[67] Prior to the formation of LPCA, residents of the Old Town and Mid-North sections formed the Old Town Triangle and Mid-North Associations, in 1948 and 1951, respectively, to combat what they saw as decline. These groups next helped form the LPCA.

LPCA's approach to renewal continued a pattern set by city officials, businessmen, and scholars combining urban study with cooperation between city government and private citizens. For years Chicago had been at the forefront of urban studies and city planning. The Chicago Plan Commission had, in 1943, released its *Master Plan of Residential Use of Chicago* that advocated clearing out "slums" and the "conservation" of neighborhoods spearheaded by homeowners' associations. In 1947, the newly created Chicago Land Clearance Commission allied itself with businessmen to pursue urban redevelopment, and in 1948 released its study *Ten Square Miles of Chicago*. The University of Chicago also took an active role in studying the city and promoting a citywide program of conservation and clearance. In 1952, Mayor Kennelly created an Interim Commission on Conservation that, a year later, published its *Preventing Tomorrow's Slums*. City officials and area businessmen were also instrumental in passing the 1953 Illinois Urban Community Conservation Act. The approach that developed involved the city clearing blighted areas, and local community groups spearheading conservation.[68]

LPCA proceeded in a similar manner, first studying the area then working with government to promote conservation. Informing its members about the Conservation Act, LPCA argued, "the legislative principle unique to this Act is that . . . planning should be more than a merely super-imposition of planning technique on a disinterested neighborhood."[69] Those interested in Lincoln Park would take initiative and work with the city to pursue their goals. The 1953 Urban Community Conservation Act allowed and encouraged participation by local groups in the urban renewal process, and established a Community Conservation Board (CCB) authorized to assign spaces of forty or more acres as "conservation areas." Unlike previous state legislation that promoted the clearing of slums, this allowed neighborhoods not yet designated slums, but facing that possibility, to be labeled conservation areas.[70]

To pursue their goals, Lincoln Park residents first turned to the Lincoln Park Conservation Association's predecessor, the Lincoln Park Community Council (LPCC), one subgroup of the Association of Community Councils.[71] From its inception, the LPCC was methodical, setting the tone for future action. From 1951 through 1953, members held meetings to discuss the possibility of starting a conservation plan for Lincoln Park.[72] The group also met with members of the Mid-North and Old Town Triangle Associations to engage in a joint study.[73]

Lincoln Park residents also met with city officials, forging an important alliance. In 1953, the city of Chicago established the Office of Housing and Redevelopment to select which neighborhoods it would renew and its coordinator addressed a meeting sponsored by the LPCC to discuss possibly starting a formal conservation program.[74] One councilman reported to the group that the area "would in time become slums unless something was done to arrest deterioration."[75] LPCC members then began the long path of urban renewal, the term that now replaced "conservation" after passage of the 1954 Housing Act.[76] To obtain funds and take action, they would have to conduct a study of the neighborhood and convince the city to declare it a conservation area. Then they needed to work with the city to determine what actions the they would take.

Why didn't they just flee? Gerald Suttles regards the motives behind urban residents' banding together "as a more or less self-conscious effort to withdraw into a 'defensible space' where residents could try to regulate the process of redevelopment." One theoretical model of neighborhood investment asserts that residents' desire for financial return on investment spurs improvement. Another argues that when residents meet a certain "threshold" (investing a certain amount of time and money into a neighborhood) others will essentially bow to community pressure and follow.[77] In each case, the resident expects some return on investment.[78]

Some Lincoln Parkers were interested in the buildings themselves, the area's "atmosphere," and others maintained that they wanted to live in a "diverse" area. Others wanted to maintain the existing demographic qualities of the neighborhood. While they spoke of diversity, Blacks, Puerto Ricans, Chinese, and poor whites faced "a somewhat arms-length attitude."[79] Albert Hunter notes that the LPCC was an attempt to reverse "what until a few years ago were natural processes of invasion, movement, and decay." The origin of such activity "is often the threat of real or anticipated invasion."[80]

The next step in renewal was forming a tighter organization over which residents could have more control in developing their plan.[81] Members of the OTTA and Mid-North Association joined together to forge this group, one that did not replace local organizations but brought them together to speak as one voice to the city. Meeting first in March,[82] they then chartered the Lincoln Park Conservation Association on April 20, 1954.[83] The organization's first executive director commented, "The purpose of our organization is to prevent slums and retain this area as one of the most desirable residential districts in the city."[84] LPCA intended to "protect the civic welfare, to improve the conditions of life, work, recreation, health, and safety; to foster and develop a neighborhood plan; and to aide [sic.], assist, and sponsor neighborhood activities."[85] A later executive director argued, "We want to conserve Lincoln Park as we know it."[86]

From its inception, the organization's establishment liberals had ties to city hall, a public–private relationship seen previously in other parts of the city.[87] LPCA president Paul Gerhardt, Jr., was a city building commissioner, and the city architect of Chicago.[88] He noted that LPCA would, "have direct access to a special branch of the mayor's office, and thru that branch, to the operating city departments—building, zoning, police, fire, board of education, traffic and sanitation."[89] They were also deeply involved with public service. Conservation Association Vice-President Pierre Blouke, also an architect, advised the federal government's Home Owners Loan Corporation and believed that the "most important single form of shelter" was the single-family, "relatively low value" home.[90] Group secretary John A. Cook, an attorney, helped found the OTTA before the Conservation Association.[91] The organization's first set of directors included Reverend William T. Gaughan of DePaul, Reverend Eldon Lindberg of the Fullerton Covenant Presbyterian Church, and G. E. Potts of McCormick Theological Seminary. Edgar Crilly, son of the designer of Crilly Court, was also on the board of the Jazz Institute of Chicago.[92] Gerhardt, writing about his profession, argued that architects "must . . . act in consonance with a changing world, but with firm convictions, steadfast ideals, and courageous leadership" and noted that the "present-day architect" possessed a "progressive attitude."[93] LPCA president Malcolm Shanower, in the years to come, would become a director of Job Opportunities Through Better Skills, a job training program.[94] These were not rapacious capitalists out to create a gated community, but more a blend of idealist, establishment liberals, and "social homesteaders," only they were not invaders from outside, but established residents.

The association consisted not only of community members worried about the future, but of fellow neighbors DePaul University, McCormick Theological Seminary, Aetna Bank, The Welfare Community Council, Alexian Brothers, and Children's Memorial, Augustana Lutheran, and Columbus Hospitals.[95] Learning a lesson from Hyde Park, the larger institutions did not want to become the center of controversy that the University of Chicago was during its participation in urban renewal. Each kept a low profile.[96] One resident believed that "Virtually every member of the LPCA lives in the community (and about 80% of them own their homes) or has a business or non-commercial investment in it."[97] A 1970 study of leadership speaks to the consistency of this makeup. It noted, "Most people, both those who are LPCA members and those who are not, characterized the membership as white, middle-class homeowners. Classification of the members of the Board of Directors shows that better than one-third are professional people...Approximately one-fourth are business executives...while about eighteen percent are small businessmen in the area. The remainder are housewives or retired."[98]

Membership rose to 650, with a board of directors of thirty-six. The group eventually reached one thousand members, and maintained this throughout the 1960s.[99] By August of 1954, the organization was large enough to require an office and an executive director.[100] It initially presented city and building zone complaints to the Building Department. By April of 1958 the group reported some 350 grievances, and by August 1960 thirty cases awaited court action. The group handled so many complaints that it hired an additional staff member. It also started a real estate service to assist the renting and selling of Lincoln Park residential property.[101] Additionally, park residents organized a Senior Citizen Center, an annual "Brotherhood Week Dinner," campaigns to clean up the area and to plant trees, and a community Christmas tree.[102]

In forging an alliance with the city residents largely avoided contact with one local politician, their alderman "Paddy" Bauler who was, by the 1960s, a relic of a corrupt age. He was "the best alderman money can buy" and the "Clown Prince of City Hall," known as much for his backroom dealings in his saloon/headquarters as his extroverted, beer-drinking persona.[103] Since taking his aldermanic seat in 1933 he made a name for himself by notoriously claiming that "Chicago ain't ready for reform" when Mayor Daley was elected in 1955.[104] While his speakeasy and, later, tavern was active (he held ward meetings in its basement), he was, according to one author, "virtually silent" on the City Council itself.[105] He did, however, hand out patronage jobs, and was proud that each of his seventy-six precinct captains held some kind of state, county, or city employment.[106] Beyond that, especially in the 1960s, he was not an active voice in politics.[107] Those interested in changing Lincoln Park were wise to avoid Bauler who was at best colorful, at worst a corrupt clown ineffective at battling city hall. For example, he opposed the development of the Carl Sandburg Village, but Mayor Daley simply ignored him.[108]

The city of Chicago, without Bauler's involvement, moved to further cement the alliance between government and the private sector in advancing renewal. In what it claimed was an attempt to form a group with wider representation than the association, in April of 1956 Chicago city officials appointed fifty-two members of the business sector, clergy, and military to form a new conservation committee. Of that group, the Community Conservation Board of nine to fifteen members would work closely with the Daley administration and make formal recommendations to the city.[109] The tie between city government and LPCA, forged during the early years of North Side renewal, was instrumental. In the years to come, prominent Lincoln Park residents could pick up the phone or send a telegram or letter to the Department of Urban Renewal (DUR), police commanders, and Daley himself and expect some response. In turn, as Daley moved his plan for Loop development further, he had allies in Lincoln Park to whom he could turn.

On June 20, 1956, LPCA held a public meeting to discuss designating Lincoln Park a conservation area. The association also appealed to the city's Community Conservation Board for a public program to supplement the private funds already used to improve the area. Some three hundred Lincoln Park residents urged the board to declare the neighborhood a conservation area. Using 1950 census data, the group asserted that in 201 blocks of Lincoln Park there existed 7,729 residential units in either poor condition or lacking private toilets or baths. Field inspections indicated that many residences were overcrowded, and that the 2.9 acres of recreation space failed to properly serve the 5,569 schoolchildren of the area. LPCA president George M. Proctor reviewed the area's lack of upkeep. The Reverend Comerford O'Malley, president of DePaul University, argued that the neighborhood's diversity made it truly representative of the city, and thus deserving of aid. Resident Robert Preble, president of Encyclopedia Britannica, urged support, commenting, "Preventative medicine is much easier and more pleasant to take than major surgery." Residents also complained of high traffic dangerous to children, and argued that the conservation program would result in loan benefits.[110]

The city listened. Just over a month later, on July 12, 1956, the CCB designated the neighborhood a conservation area, making it the third Chicago neighborhood officially declared one.[111] In December, further demonstrating the close ties between LPCA and city hall, the Community Conservation Board sponsored a tour of the conservation area. Approximately twenty-five city department officials, along with Lincoln Park community leaders, took the bus tour, which highlighted resident efforts and challenges.[112]

One benefit of conservation would be more widespread funds. Lincoln Park Savings and Loans had previously refused to cooperate with redevelopment and redlined the area. While some local banks provided loans, it was up to residents themselves to fund restoration projects.[113] The president of the Ranch Triangle Association informed the CCB commissioner that, "buildings have been maintained throughout the industry and skill of the owner himself." Echoing this, the Sheffield Neighborhood Association President indicated that his neighborhood really needed "help in urging banks to make loans to reliable persons in the area."[114] Lincoln Park residents committed to renewal applied to the federal government for $307, 353, for a conservation plan for the area so those already revamping homes would receive aid. LPCA executive director Malcolm Shanower commented, "This shows that private individuals and private capital can do it if there is certainty the rest of the community is going to be conserved and the investment won't be lost."[115]

Their efforts paid off. In August of 1960, the federal government promised the Community Conservation Board some $300,000 to survey the area and plan for renewal under the auspices of a General Neighborhood Renewal Program (GNRP) to be completed in ten years' time.[116] Under a GNRP, residents and officials would work together create a general plan establishing broad goals and objectives. As Lincoln Park was so large, urban planners felt that handling it all at once would be impossible, so they would carry out smaller projects over time.

The media later publicized the plan and city officials presented it throughout the community to stimulate discussion and gather opinions.[117] The CCB asked neighborhood associations to submit their suggestions for the renewal effort. The federal Housing and Home Finance Agency received a general plan, written by the city with resident input, for approval in August of 1961. More communication between the Department of Urban Renewal and Lincoln Park residents followed.

By 1961, members of LPCA and the Department of Urban Renewal now worked with the new Conservation Community Council (CCC), a mayor-appointed group of Lincoln Park residents. This body officially represented LPCA and Lincoln Park residents to city units such as the CCB and the DUR.[118] Next, LPCA members met with urban renewal officials to promote the idea of beginning renewal in the Old Town, Mid-North, and Lincoln Central areas. Members felt that the strong neighborhood organizations in these areas would carry urban renewal through and so should be the program's pioneers.[119] At the same time, groups like Mid-North also held meetings to discuss a renewal plan.[120]

Diversity?

Early in 1961, six neighborhood associations in Lincoln Park began to submit, via letters, their suggestions and vision for the GNRP to the Conservation Board. Each association provided a profile of its respective neighborhood and mentioned specific problems it wanted addressed. These organizations radiated pride, and expressed concern that their neighborhoods were in decline. They also emphasized the heterogeneous nature of their respective areas, while repeatedly using the words "community" and "family" to describe them. Taken together, they painted a portrait of a quaint, small-town area populated by "traditional" families interested in the kind of urban renewal that would preserve the current demographic makeup and restore buildings as they once were.

On the city's West Side, white Chicagoans feared that "Blighted buildings jeopardized the health and well being of residents, who suffered from the physical threat presented by the decay and the moral hazard of living in a degraded environment."[121] Similarly, Lincoln Park organizations expressed anxiety about deterioration. The Old Town Triangle Association referred to "the existing blight and near-slum conditions" in the neighborhood.[122] The Lincoln Central Association took pride in the fact its residents' "charm and character . . . has survived even the years of slow deterioration."[123] The Mid-North Association argued that the "housing problems of the Second World War, and the difficulties of enforcing building and maintenance laws, resulted in some illegal and unsafe overcrowding and deterioration of some of our buildings."[124] The Park West Community Association noted the "run-down character" of its shopping centers."[125]

However, the groups also felt that Lincoln Park was quaint and unique, that the plan had to maintain these aspects, and that the city re-create past conditions and architectural styles. They also highlighted locally owned businesses in the area, and emphasized a small-town feel. The Mid-North Association sought a way "to return some feeling of communal life to our neighborhood" and "to return as closely as possible to the pattern established when this community was built." Alluding to high-rise housing, members of the Sheffield group wrote that they "appreciate the old, stable looking character of our neighborhood, and would, therefore, hope that planners, architects and builders would not design and build new structures which are completely out of harmony and character with what remains." In addition, the Old Town Triangle Association felt buildings should be zoned "to preserve and enhance the residential character of this neighborhood." The Lincoln Central Association's first recommendation was "the conservation of as many existing buildings as is feasible."[126]

The depictions of a mixed Lincoln Park put forth by the neighborhood organizations might have stunned Black and Puerto Rican residents, segregated largely to its west side. The Lincoln Central Association wrote of the "heterogeneous nature of the local population." The Mid-North Association claimed its "residents seek the exchange and diversity of the city, and reject the distance and isolation of the suburbs" and that it possessed a "unique character." The Sheffield Neighborhood Association asserted that "The great span in ages, ethnic group backgrounds, interests, and vocations create an atmosphere in the neighborhood that we would like to maintain."[127] Sheffield residents offered, "Our members appreciate their neighbors with whom they are now living."[128] Perhaps Mid-North best summed up what Lincoln Park neighborhood groups meant by "diverse." Rather than noting racial, sexual, or ethnic variance, Mid-North offered:

> The cultural diversity of Mid-North is not the least of its advantages. As opposed to some of the other areas of the city, ours is not a one institution, one industry, or one income-level community. It contains elements of many economic, religious and occupational groups. None of its six major institutions exercises a dominant influence on the life of the community, nor do they provide disproportionate numbers of residents. We have many single people, as well as families; retired older people who prefer to live in an area which is not exclusively a family-oriented one, and young working people who wish to be close to work opportunities.[129]

However, an emphasis on the traditional nuclear family contradicted the value placed on "diversity." The organizations clearly wanted a residential area composed of home-owning families. The Lincoln Central Association stated that attracting new members "including young families with children" to be a primary goal of the group. The Park West Community Association indicated that the "area is predominantly a family residential area" and that in development "emphasis on family living consideration should be given." The Sheffield Neighborhood Association felt that "We are in an ideal location for family dwelling. Because of this we hope that future planning will keep industry in the area to a minimum, and that the predominantly residential character of the neighborhood will be maintained."[130]

Chicago's North Side, and Lincoln Park, did indeed have a reputation for diversity. A. J. Liebling wrote of Lincoln Park:

The Forty-Third Ward is one of the most diversified in the city . . . Toward the ward's southwest frontier there is a Negro slum . . . in its center is the residue of the original German colony, and within its boundaries are also blocs of Nisei, Finns, Hungarians, Italians, Irish, Syrians, Armenians, Swedes, and Poles . . . Parts of the ward look like a city, parts like a pleasant suburb, and large tracts like the less favored sections of a blighted mill town."[131]

Paddy Bauler noted "We got nice people in this ward . . . Nice Germans, nice Poles, nice Irish, nice Jews, nice colored people, and so on, and recently we been getting a lot of Japanese, which are moving north across Division Street, and they are a very nice high-class class of Japanese."[132] One Puerto Rican resident remembered that 1960s era Lincoln Park was integrated, and offered, "I can't tell you that I suffered from racism from our neighbors, because it was all liberals. They didn't have any problem living with all of us. It was very mixed."[133]

The reality, however, was that postwar Lincoln Park was more cosmetically diverse in that it seemed to be mixed, but was by no means a largely integrated, or racially diverse, neighborhood. One OTTA member offered,

There are very few Negroes actually within the bounds of the Triangle itself although adjacent neighborhoods to the south have a majority of Negroes. In general, I think it is fair to characterize the majority of the Triangle residents as integration minded, though the rent level, because of the success of [urban renewal], has probably been the principal reason for the lack of integration.[134]

Puerto Rican immigrant, and future community leader, Jose "Cha Cha" Jimenez, arrived in Lincoln Park in 1950, and recalled the heterogeneousness, and division, of the area:

Lincoln Park as a whole seemed mixed but it was internally divided along racial lines. You also had people from Appalachia and indigenous people there. Primarily there was a lot of Puerto Rican, hillbilly and indigenous people living nearby. But the saloon owners were still Irish and Italian.[135]

He also, around the age of ten when his family first moved to the area, routinely ran from the white gang who chased him on his way to school.[136]

The lack of uniform integration also extended to representation in LPCA. In 1956 the association offered a revealing sense of who it was, and who it was not, in a self-authored resume and history. The group noted that the neighborhood contained Italians, Japanese, Germans, Blacks, Mexicans, rural whites, Puerto Ricans, and others. However, it pointed out that "Except in the cases of the Italians and Nisei, there is little opportunity to contact their people as groups because of the lack of organization and leadership within their own ranks."[137]

To some in Lincoln Park, demographic changes most likely made it seem that the area was "diverse." For example, between 1950 and 1960, the overall population of the area dropped 13.2 percent.[138] The white population of Lincoln Park declined by 7.6 percent as some 15,939 whites left the area, while nonwhites increased by 2,379 (49.2 percent).[139] However, Blacks still only made up 1.5 percent of the Lincoln Park population in 1960.[140] Puerto Ricans were only 2.5 percent of the population. In terms of economic diversity, 32.5 percent of men worked in manufacturing, while 34.7 percent worked in white-collar occupations. Those with incomes of less than $3,000 were 15.4 percent, while 16.7 percent earned over $10,000. Compared to its southern neighbor the Near North Side, which contained 23,114 (30.6 percent) African American families, Lincoln Park was none too diverse.[141] Turnover and an influx of nonwhite residents may have brought some to their conclusion that Lincoln Park was "diverse."

In other Chicago neighborhoods, racism was obvious among white city residents. In Lincoln Park, middle- and upper-middle-class whites spearheading urban renewal did not openly attack or even refer to nonwhite, or poor, residents in recommendations to the city. Neighborhood groups viewed themselves as open-minded "liberals" and chose to sidestep the poor and/or nonwhite. Residents instead focused on public housing. The Ranch Triangle Association was the most direct, and asked that if any buildings were found to be "beyond conservation" that they be replaced with single-family homes, and indicated, "In no case would we welcome high-rise or public housing." The Mid-North Association said it "would resist strongly any attempts to bring high-rise architecture, mass demolition and modern apartment living to our community on a wholesale scale." The Sheffield Neighborhood Association coolly noted, "We believe that we have the maximum number of people that we can creatively and efficiently integrate into our community."[142] In response to an LPCA questionnaire about urban planning, the Old Town Triangle Association offered:

PUBLIC HOUSING (caps in original): The Old Town Planning Committee feels that because of Old Town's limited area, and because of nearby high-density public housing, with more under construction, the answer is a limited number of low-density public housing units scattered throughout the area. These could be newly built, or rehabs of existing structures. In no instance [should public housing] replace existing buildings or displace residents.[143]

A survey sent only to Old Town residents asked "How do you feel on this subject of high-rises and high density?" Four percent of respondents were in favor, 53 percent were against, and 43 percent had no response.[144] In that same survey, the Triangle Association voiced its belief that public housing "should be specifically for the elderly, must be low-rise, low-density and offer priority to people in the area who may be dislocated by Urban Renewal."[145]

The city again listened. In a letter to OTTA President David Landis, D. E. Mackelman wrote, "We would concur with your wish that the unique character of the neighborhood should be preserved and this would be insured through the provisions of maximum rehabilitation, and clearance only where necessary."[146]

Focusing on the threat posed by crooked realtors who plotted to build high-rise apartments, rather than the residents of said apartments, was another way for Lincoln Park groups to advance their cosmetically diverse vision of the neighborhood without looking openly exclusionary. In late 1963, the OTTA reported on plans for a twenty-eight-story, 228-unit condominium project bounded by Ogden, Lincoln Park West, and Armitage. In its newsletter, the association assured members that "A condominium is an apartment building in where each tenant buys his own apartment within the building."[147] However, by 1966, the same newsletter reported that residents had become leery of real estate developers asking for zoning changes, as those led to the construction of high-rises without community approval.[148] Elastic zoning laws, residents feared, allowed "the speculator who wants a profitable project" to move into the area and build things such as "His apartment buildings (many of them just high priced slums for transients), taverns, gas stations, and sprawling supermarkets located helter-skelter, without rhyme or reason, will make our community not just a planner's nightmare but also a sad place to live in. The people who make up this community—who *are* [emphasis in original] this community—whether tenants or property owners, will be replaced by transients."[149] In 1965, the OTTA warned "Beware of 'Sharp Operators'—just sell to the DUR!"[150]

That neighborhood groups avoided overtly addressing racial concerns regarding future residents of Lincoln Park parallels urban developments in other US cities where whites who wanted to keep Blacks out of their neighborhoods did not always resort to public name-calling or the use of epithets, nor did they openly say they wanted restricted zones. Instead, they used coded language and alternative reasons. For example, in Lawrence, Kansas, white residents spoke not of race, but of individualism, freedom, and the rights of private property owners when they addressed potential neighborhood changes.[151] In Southern California, whites linked civil rights not to race or racism, but to disorder, and argued that civil rights legislation unfairly overstepped states' rights.[152] In Detroit, one homeowners group focused on the rights of the homeowner in determining the future of neighborhoods.[153] In 1964, even Republican presidential candidate Barry Goldwater realized he "had to eschew racial extremism and couch his strong opposition to the civil rights bill in moderate terms."[154] As Hyde Park-Kenwood residents discussed their neighborhood conservation plans in the 1950s, some wanted to emphasize that their goal was a "safe, clean, well-serviced community" to avoid the mention of race, or class, at all.[155] By the 1950s in Hyde Park-Kenwood, race had become a hot-button topic, one to be avoided, if possible, in public discussion.[156] One study of the area revealed that residents either tended to avoid race as a problem, deny that racial problems existed, or define neighborhood problems along class, rather than racial, lines.[157] The Mid-North Association, in 1966, noted that

> Public reaction to a firm stand by Mid-North against public housing in the area might well lead to a critical situation from the standpoint of

human relations . . . although we do not want any more public housing in the area, we must be realistic in our approach to the problem and avoid an arbitrary stand which might precipitate a dangerous human relations crisis.[158]

White liberals in Lincoln Park, then, liked integration more in theory than practice. Politically, Lincoln Park was part of the 43rd ward of the City of Chicago, and residents traditionally voted democratic in mayoral elections, handing Daley the ward in 1955, 1959, 1963, and 1967.[159] The very same white, middle-, and upper-middle-class residents of Lincoln Park who voted democrat and spearheaded urban renewal efforts sidestepped the issue of race like other white liberals did in the 1950s and 1960s. The issue of race and "rights" had been key to liberalism since the 1940s, when Blacks in the Democratic party became more assertive in making it a concern, and as white liberals sought to distinguish their political beliefs from the authoritarian governments the US was at odds with during and after World War II.[160] And yet, "corporate liberals," as labeled by members of the Left, worked as "liberals in service to large business corporations" who "defended the existing distribution of wealth and power in America," rather than fighting for equal rights.[161] The paradox between belief and action was not confined to political orientation. Jewish Americans in the postwar years on the one hand favored and fought for Black civil rights, but at the same time moved out of their neighborhoods when Blacks moved in, largely due to fears over personal safety, decreased real estate values, and the condition of schools. Cheryl Greenberg notes, "It was neither politics nor simple racism that led these Jews to move. Had it been the former, they would never have supported civil rights activity at all. Had it been the latter, they would have left long before. Rather, the combination of racially based fears and class-based anxieties pushed these liberal urban residents at last into their own version of segregation."[162] Black Chicago activists were themselves limited in how they could focus on city development. In their fight, they felt they needed to abandon critiques of class to fight racial discrimination in housing.[163]

The white neighborhood organizations of Democratic-leaning Lincoln Park held similarly conflicted beliefs. They viewed themselves as living in a "diverse" area, and they wanted to preserve the enclaves in which they resided. The neighborhood organizations saw the 2 percent of the population that was nonwhite in the foreground of community makeup. In pursuing a renewal plan of preservation and conservation they were, in reality, favoring the white middle class and advancing an exclusionary plan for renewal. Some did so wittingly: in 1964, the Chair of the Human Relations Committee of the Mid-North Association felt that "serious consideration should be given to the matter of *whom* [emphasis in original] we propose to welcome into our neighborhood."[164] Others did so less consciously: in considering the future of the GNRP in 1966, the Mid-North Association noted that "the Board accordingly suggested taking a positive stance on human rights (with active implementation); and at the same time, resisting the introduction of low income housing in our area."[165] Perhaps one resident best summarized ideas regarding diversity in Lincoln Park this way: "There were certain contradictions in what we wanted. We wanted it to be an integrated neighborhood. And we wanted it to be clean, remodeled, and respectable."[166]

The General Neighborhood Renewal Plan

By January of 1962, the federal government approved the plan.[167] Lincoln Park residents who sat on the Conservation Council approved the GNRP in May. Approval from the Chicago City Council followed in June and in February of 1963 the Housing and Home Finance Agency followed suit. After the city council signed on, private money to finance rehabilitation flooded Lincoln Park. Wrecking balls swung, bulldozers leveled buildings, and some residents began to move out. The building commissioner reported that the city issued 356 permits for projects, totaling 3.5 million dollars.[168] In 1962, area residents and city agencies worked together to demolish twenty structures, and LPCA handled 350 cases.[169] In 1963, the Department of Urban Renewal began a survey of 2,289 buildings to determine their place in the plan.[170] The Chicago Urban Renewal commissioner reported that the Housing and Home Financing agency would add some $6,000,000 to the $3,500,000 already set aside. The Lincoln Park Program would span ten to twelve years, with the federal government providing $24,221,711 and the city $12,110, 856.[171] The federal government authorized "detailed planning" for Lincoln Park Project I in April 1963 while the city continued to work with community members to finalize plans. DUR officials met with various residents' groups 120 times before presenting the

Preliminary Proposals for the GNRP and its Lincoln Park Project I on February 18, 1964. Additionally, residents discussed the proposals at more than one hundred community meetings.[172] In 1963, the OTTA touted the plan thusly:

> We are for urban renewal. The many abuses and blunders of such programs, in Chicago and elsewhere, do not furnish sufficient reason for opposition to urban renewal as a whole; we are simply against the repetition of the abuses and blunders. We believe the Lincoln Park General Neighborhood Plan can be the most successful urban renewal project in the history of the United States . . . We do not want urban renewal failure— politically, economically, or in planning. We want a success, and we are prepared to fight for it.[173]

In the pamphlet released to detail the GNRP in 1965, the Department of Urban Renewal claimed that "from the beginning, planning for the Lincoln Park Community has been a joint effort involving city agencies and the community" and that it listened to additional input given it by communities. The city did heed its residential partners' wishes in designing the General Neighborhood Renewal Plan and Lincoln Park Project I, to the point where parts of the GNRP read as if ghostwritten by neighborhood groups. The introduction lists its ten "major goals and objectives." Goal two states that renewal projects "must all be designed to strengthen the residential base of the community by providing facilities which create and enhance a desirable environment for family living," and goal six indicates, "The distinctiveness of the community must be preserved and encouraged through the planning process." Goal four echoes the associations' claims of variety, indicating that the "preservation of diversity in housing accommodations, income, occupation, age, and environmental experiences is a major planning goal."[174]

The plan also contained charcoal sketches of proposed changes that further indicate the DUR agreed with the neighborhood organizations in terms of community makeup. The drawings promote a vision of a clean, tree-lined neighborhood populated by young middle-class whites, sometimes with children in tow. In some sketches the people appear as white and wear business attire. The illustrated Convenience Center, an outdoor mall of sorts, is spotless. White couples walk through, two with shopping bags. Other drawings show young white couples and parents with children roaming tree-lined, tidy streets, the men clad in V-necked sweaters and sport jackets, the women in dresses.

There was one way in which the plan differed from the requests of residents. While neighborhood associations testified to the mix of individuals in their respective areas, the plan specifically stated that "Various income levels" would be included in the allotment of residential dwelling units. These levels were to be present in both low density (maximum of thirty dwelling units per acre) and medium density (eighty units per acre) housing.[175] Only the Lincoln Central Association made any overtures to low-income groups when it offered its suggestions for the plan, stating "It is most important to us that all families now living in substandard units should have housing which is up to standard. If this necessitates providing public housing for some, in the form of low-rise buildings scattered throughout the neighborhood, we would have no objection."[176] The original plan for public housing in Project I called for two sites to be developed for low-income families. One site was to be at Webster and Clark Streets (with one hundred dwelling units per acre), and the other between Burling and Halsted Streets (eighty dwelling units per acre) for public housing for the elderly. An additional two sites, on North Avenue between Sedgwick and Hudson streets, and one on Sedgwick Street north of Wisconsin, were to be developed at a density of no more than thirty units per acre.[177] While it may seem that the DUR had the interests of the poor and elderly in mind, the sites designated in the Land Use Plan of Project I were located on the outskirts of the Project I area. One small development lay between Hudson and Sedgwick, and another off West Wisconsin Street, but most of the housing remained segregated to the low-income West Side, assuring that no new shift in the community dynamic would occur.

CHAPTER TWO

Inclusion and Renewal

"The church must act where others do not!"
—North Side Cooperative Ministry

Religious Activism in the Postwar United States

In the 1940s and 1950s, a new generation of liberal Protestant ministers across the nation, some viewing themselves as a vanguard and inspired by the World Council of Churches, became more interested in working with laypersons and secular institutions on social and political matters, and by the early 1960s Chicago was home to such clergymen, some of whom would be instrumental in 1968.[1] Rather than migrate to the suburbs like their predecessors, these ministers, mostly white and middle class, joined in the debates over urban renewal.[2] Calls for "a major reappraisal of the most assured grounds of the historic Judeo-Christian consensus" could be found in best-selling books that advocated a secular interpretation of the Bible.[3] James Hudnut-Beumler argued that the "culture-supporting" religion of the 1950s became the "confrontational, politically factious religious ethos" of the 1960s as numerous jeremiads appeared, all calling the role of the church into question.[4] Dietrich Bonhoeffer and Gabriel Vahanian found new audiences for their death-of-God theologies.[5] Bonhoeffer argued for a "religionless Christianity."[6] Vahanian insisted that modern culture did not need God, and that the religion of the 1950s was a "desperate character" of the Christian faith.[7] The September 1955 *Christian Century* piece "The Church in Suburban Captivity" attacked suburbs as havens of materialism and superficial relationships, arguing that attendance in church came only out of blind obligation and social pressure rather than faith. Suburbia had "imposed its mindset on the church" and in the end isolated it from members' daily lives.[8]

To wrest power away from out-of-touch church elites, specialized ministries became common in the 1960s. In light of the emphasis media placed on the "new morality" and ethical debate, "nearly every church body in America decided . . . that the time had come to appoint a commission for the re-examination, not only of sexual ethics, but also of the theological and philosophical grounds for its making any kind of moral pronounce-ment."[9] A wave of books attempted to define this "new morality," which stressed ethics and love, eschewing legalism and the authority of the church.[10] In 1962, clergy representing ten protestant denominations met to discuss whether or not the differences between the Episcopalian, Method-ist, Presbyterian, and Congregationalist churches could be overcome in or-der to form one single church.[11] Additionally, in 1963 the National Council of Churches voted to admit Jews and Roman Catholics into its policymak-ing groups.[12]

Calls for the reexamination and revitalization of religion are not surpris-ing considering how many Americans felt church influence had waned. Gallup, in 1957, asked, "At the present time, do you think religion as a whole is increasing its influence on American life or losing its influence?" Four-teen percent of respondents felt religion was in decline. In 1962, the re-sponse to that question was 32 percent in the affirmative. Gallup also found that 53 percent of America's youth felt similarly, as indicated by a 1962 sur-vey in which 53 percent of respondents were between the ages of eighteen and twenty-four. Many youths claimed this was because they felt church was irrelevant to their lives, that materialism had overtaken faith, that in-creased crime and immorality indicated organized religion was losing in-fluence, and that churches interfered in lives when they had no business, while failing to address relevant societal and political issues.[13]

"Renewal," to many of faith, referred to "the church's constant transfor-mation process as it seeks to self-reflect, repent from past short-sightedness, and become more whole."[14] Some found a link between revitalized debates over the purpose of the church and arguments over urban renewal. One professor of church history argued that the church had changed radically in the 1960s due to the rise of an "urban crisis and racial crisis" combined with lack of governmental concern for the escalation of the Vietnam war.[15] Urbanization meant that the local church was not just local anymore. New immigrants and expanding city limits altered neighborhoods where the local church had once been the center. Clergymen changed as well. They were "less authoritative" and assumed they would be working for societal change and be involved in conflict. New training for ministers included submersion into the city itself and sometimes enclaves such as "skid row, youth street organizations, hippies, the 'gay' world, the black ghetto, and the white Appalachian ghetto," where ministers would interact with the local population sans collar and title. Additionally, clergymen underwent training in social planning.[16]

The North Side Cooperative Ministry

Churchgoers in Lincoln Park were as aware of the questions the church asked itself as they were familiar with the phrase "the dying churches."[17] In the early 1960s, clergymen on Chicago's North Side began to feel as if their ministries had failed in many ways and formed the North Side Cooperative Ministry (NSCM) to revitalize them. NSCM pursued its concerns as it slowly created a vision of the community that reached out to white and nonwhite residents, rich and poor. Like LPCA, this was no band of rampaging radicals, but a cautious and optimistic group. Rev. David Doering, NSCM's first coordinator, wrote that its origin sprang from discussions among church and laymen as "churches faced the irrelevance of past ministries and the indifference of the people of the city."[18] Concerned with urban renewal, crime, and youth without guidance, they decided to band together.

Eight protestant churches birthed the ministry between 1961 and 1962, which members called "little more than a sharing of ideas and dreams that certain laymen and ministers have had for some time."[19] Founders wrote that "despite our past courageous discipleship, [we] acknowledge that we find ourselves, as churches, with signs of unfaithfulness in an unfaithful world. Many of us have declining memberships, unstable finances, deteriorating buildings, discouraged and apathetic memberships, indifferent and irrelevant parishes."[20] The group addressed the fact that many "unchurched" citizens lived on the North Side, and asserted that it was the responsibility of NSCM to reach out to these people.[21] Founders did not establish the group to force people into church pews. One laywoman commented, "If I thought this was just a stepping stone for bringing these people into the church, I'd quit." Another member offered, "You talk to a businessman about God; he rolls up his eyeballs." Another commented, "It's not that you're trying to change the world. But when you come to die, you like to feel you have kicked over a piece of sand."[22] Believing that they

had failed to unify or reach the North Side, NSCM vowed to promote cooperation among churches, more closely monitor the needs of the North Side,
and respond accordingly.

The clergymen who comprised NSCM were activists even before the
group's formal inception. On September 13, 1962, a constitution would
be drawn, as would "concrete plans" for a coffee shop for youth. Meanwhile,
five of its members served jail time in Albany, Georgia, for answering Martin Luther King's call for an end to segregation. On October 11, the ministry co-sponsored an open meeting with Chicago residents to address the
question, "How can and should the church stand on such social issues?" To
appeal to all members of the community, NSCM also established a Puerto
Rican and an Indian Ministry.[23]

On October 25, 1962, the North Side Cooperative Ministry passed a
constitution, and on Palm Sunday of 1963, founders formally named
NSCM as an "experiment," comprised of churches from Near North, Lincoln Park, and Lake View. The ministry intended to last only until Palm
Sunday of 1966. At that time, members would evaluate their efforts and decide whether to continue.[24] The budget for that first year was set at $13,000.[25]
By 1965, the ministry boasted some four hundred laymen and clergy and
united twenty-six churches of six denominations.[26] However, one pastor
reported that it still only involved an estimated 5 percent of the people in
area churches.[27]

Rev. Doering was thirty-three years old when he began as coordinator at
NSCM. He was a graduate of nearby McCormick Theological Seminary,
and a master's student in Philosophy of Culture and Aesthetics and Philosophy of Religions at Indiana University. Hired in June of 1962 for six
months under a Presbyterian grant to "see what could be done in mission
development with churches and agencies in the Near North, Lincoln Park,
[and] Lake View communities of the north side of Chicago," he organized
and worked for NSCM for the remainder of the 1960s and early 1970s.[28]

The early incarnation of NSCM was, if anything, methodical. In order to
more effectively minister to the elderly, youth, and ethnic groups, members
set out in either a direct, one-on-one manner or via task forces to tackle
issues such as housing, education, and juvenile delinquency. For any NSCM
project the group demanded that at least two churches of separate denominations participate, that the project possess built-in methods for evaluation
of effectiveness, and that the lay leadership take charge.[29] Like ministers in

the 1950s who were "characterized by an almost compulsive introspection," members initially studied and reported on social issues as they planned.[30] Doering wrote that in the group's early stages "ideas were checked with census reports, research and observations. The needs of the people of the area were studied and programs proposed to meet these needs." He noted that over a year of research and planning was undertaken prior to the ministry's formation and that committees "studied census tracts and statistics, and interviewed experts and men-on-the streets to see what the real needs of the people are and what kind of ministries could be developed to meet the needs of the community."[31] The group also wrote position papers.[32] Members formed study groups and subcommittees, and held seminars and retreats to examine cultural and ethnic issues. NSCM also solicited the advice of members via questionnaires.[33] Members also created a one-hundred-page "dream book" of plans and hopes for things like a coffee-house and ministries to Black and Latin American groups.[34]

From the onset, NSCM decided on a multiplatform approach. Doering claimed that early on in the group's history, studies it conducted revealed that the community needed specialized ministries for specialized groups.[35] He also asserted that the church could only meet "the complexity of needs through a complexity of ministries ministering to a multiplicity of people with diverse needs."[36] Eight months into the ministry's existence, he released his first annual report. In it, he lauded the group for its new ministries to the young and elderly and responded to criticism that NSCM had taken on too much, commenting that "maybe we should do more than less." He concluded by encouraging further cooperation between denominations, asking them to "plan ourselves to become involved with [the] race issue, urban renewal, middle-aged single adults, older couples, youth . . . in significant ways through specialized ministries and even specialized churches if need be."[37]

The Door

According to NSCM's reading of the 1960 census, its area of Chicago "contains one of the largest concentrations of young adults in the United States, and yet the lack of attractive and active programs in that area have been limited to the large youth group at the Fourth Presbyterian Church." The group then began developing a specialized ministry to reach out to the "over

20,000 young adults in the age range of 20–29."[38] NSCM organized many different youth-oriented ministries, including one aimed at dropouts and troubled teens, one exploring the arts and the church, and others addressing social issues. In November of 1962, its Committee on Young Adults began a discussion of the possibility of opening a coffeehouse to "spark the interest and capture the imagination of young adults who are not interested in a customary church program." It would also assist youth in finding direction, demonstrating their talents, and expressing their beliefs. The committee recommended that art exhibits, poetry readings, folk music performances, and an open book store be included, housed in Old Town, a perfect location given its annual art fair.[39] By fall of 1963, the coffeehouse was underway, and NSCM called for volunteers to wait tables or assist in the painting and rehabilitation of the shop.[40]

The Door, as the "coffee house-book store ministering to young adults" came to be called, opened on Tuesday, November 19, at 3124 North Broadway. It operated Tuesday through Saturday evenings, opening at 8 P.M. NSCM promised entertainment for Friday and Saturday nights.[41] By February of 1964, the ministry hired a reverend to manage the Door, and another to coordinate youth ministries. This Youth Project, as the group called it, was part of the Youth and Education Division of NSCM, which also included its Reading Room and Tutoring centers. A board of directors consisting of both laymen and ministers guided the Door, planned events, and evaluated its effectiveness.[42] Typical of the ministry's methodical style, the coordinator was to begin his work by taking an inventory of the youth programming of local area churches, and those laymen willing to assist in it. He was then to be the contact for any future summer programs directed at youth.[43]

In the summer of 1966, the Door extended its hours to every day of the week, noon to 11 P.M. weekdays, and noon to midnight Fridays and Saturdays. Rev. Jon Tuttle, also a graduate of McCormick Theological Seminary, began full time for the summer with the hope he could stay on at least as a part-time employee in the fall.[44] The Door began to stock books ranging in topics from theology to social problems and current literature in the hopes of improving its financial situation and attracting people to come in and share ideas. In 1966 it served between three hundred and five hundred young adults per week. By 1968, 45 percent of the NSCM's budget went to the Door. Doering also appealed for additional outside funding to allow the ministry to divert its monies to the issues of housing, education, race relations, and the war in Vietnam.[45] The encouraging progress of the Door led to the formation, in conjunction with St. James United Church of Christ, of a second coffeehouse: The Cellar, in the Old Town area, was open two nights a week in the basement of building next to St. James. It was to offer "a program of art, discussion, speeches and entertainment." The ministry also proposed studying the "attitudes and ideas of people who frequent The Door."[46]

Urban Renewal

NSCM also concerned itself with renewal. In September of 1962 organizers circulated a petition to Shell Oil and the World Real Estate Company requesting that the companies cease construction of a service station and apartment house, respectively, in Lincoln Park. The group admonished Shell Oil for "violating the Lincoln Park Urban Renewal Plan" by placing its service station on land designated for the expansion of Augustana Hospital. The World company planned to build on an area reserved for park space, and members found this unacceptable.[47] In November 1962 NSCM announced the upcoming viewing of *Good Night, Socrates*, a "film which treats the removal of a Greek ethnic group which resided in a Halsted area which was cleared by Urban Renewal." It also announced an upcoming Community Conservation Workshop sponsored by the Lincoln Park Conservation Association and encouraged members to attend, claiming this was a "Prerequisite to Operation Urban Renewal, NSCM exploration of demonstrative housing" for elderly and low-income groups.[48] By February of 1963, talk centered on low-cost housing for the elderly. Members expressed concern that the apartments housing the elderly were being cleared for urban renewal and claimed, "The church must act where others do not!"[49] In February 1964 NSCM announced a consultation to be held on February 24 at 10 A.M. with an official from the Department of City Planning, and that the GNRP's Project I would be presented on February 18 at 7:30 P.M. at nearby Waller High School.[50]

While LPCA's vision of Lincoln Park maintained cosmetic diversity, NSCM sought to include as many different peoples as possible as it studied, planned, and acted. In the spring of 1965, the group formed its Integrated Housing Task Force. Calling itself a "study-action group," it claimed that "special effort will be exerted to overcome the ghetto pattern imposed on the vast majority of Negroes in the ghetto."[51] The ministry began by preparing a brochure entitled "Let's Explore the Myths and Facts About Integrated Housing in the City of Chicago" and discussed the issue at meetings throughout the North Side. The group also formed a subcommittee to deal with the issue of 221D3 (low-income) housing. Its most hands-on, and ambitious, approach was the placement of Latino and Black families into predominantly white neighborhoods. White volunteers from the task force responded to newspaper ads for available dwellings, making telephone calls as if they were prospective renters to gauge whether or not landlords discriminated. The group placed approximately four or five families over six months, but due to the timidity of some applicants and the lack of real estate savvy on behalf of volunteers, discontinued the service.[52]

Keeping in tune with its flexible approach, NSCM also defined its membership flexibly and sought to be as inclusive as possible, even reaching out to LPCA. On September 10, 1962, David Doering sent LPCA executive director William Friedlander an invitation to join ministers to receive a study conducted by the Church Federation's Research Department and discuss church and city planning in Lincoln Park. Doering closed by informing Friedlander that one of the goals of the new organization was "to stimulate active interest in the area and to communicate facts concerning urban renewal in Lincoln Park, and for the bordering communities to begin to see the effects such renewal will have on them."[53] Friedlander replied that while he would be out of town, LPCA member William A. Hutchinson would attend in his stead.[54]

NSCM continued to seek LPCA's cooperation. Doering requested that Friedlander appear at NSCM's public hearing on October 16, 1965, at which the ministry would evaluate its effectiveness. As the ministers stepped forward to extend a hand, the Conservation Association stepped back. Friedlander, in a humbly written letter, declined the invitation on the grounds that he did "not understand, except perhaps in a very general, intuitive way, the goals of the organization, the philosophical problems and other related matters." Yet despite his ignorance, he offered some observations and suggestions for the ministry, including that NSCM "may be trying to do too many things," and that it should stick to the priorities of housing, race relations, improvement of education, and employment for minorities.[55]

In 1966, Friedlander informed NSCM, via letter to Doering, that he felt that it failed to recognize achievements made by *his* group. He expressed his disappointment that, in a recent bulletin distributed by NSCM, which reviewed civil rights activities in the area, the group failed to include

LPCA's Human Relations Committee. He also took NSCM to task for failing to recognize the association's "Human Relations Network" that performed some of the same things, he argued, as NSCM's Emergency Task Force. According to Friedlander, LPCA designed this network to provide assistance during the summer, its "time of high racial tension."[56] He also made the first motion to form the Human Relations Committee in 1962.[57]

The ministry pressed on even without the LPCA. In 1966, NSCM reassessed its effectiveness in dealing with the homeless. Members felt that the situation of the poor on the North Side was not improving, and that of the reasons for this, "the one that should be particularly disturbing to those of us who believe in the radical message of Jesus Christ, is that the Church should be one of those reasons." The group also referred to itself as the "Christian avant-garde" and some members envisioned a more aggressive approach for the next year, in which volunteers would be asked to "spend time in laundromats and other public 'wells'" to more directly connect with the community.[58]

In July 1968 NSCM clergy staff reflected on the three phases they saw the ministry go through. They saw it begin as a "pastoral kind of ministry in which the church . . . ministered to the world" via tutoring, visiting the elderly, or the Door. Its next phase was its task force phase, followed by "the more recent emphasis on co-opting action and movement going on in the world." The staff also claimed that the church failed to renew itself and create change in general, thus it would "suspend for the time being our confessions of failure" and instead ask itself, "What do we want to become?"[59]

Inclusive Activism

What the ministry wanted to become was an umbrella activist group successfully pursuing many goals at once. Throughout the mid-1960s, NSCM continued reaching out to neglected groups, including Black and gay populations, concerned itself with housing, and found allies in other organizations. As it acted, it created a local activist network that would remain in place through the demonstrations of convention week in 1968. NSCM increased its attention to civil rights seen earlier in the actions of those clergymen jailed in Albany and worked with other civil rights groups.[60] Ministers and a Near North Civil Rights Group containing Congress of Racial Equality members "evolved out of the highly successful civil rights rally of Dr. Martin

Luther King last summer" and met every Tuesday evening. The group also sought a library for the Cabrini-Green area. A Tenant Action Council wanted to fight slum conditions, and an End the Slums Group desired to create a "slum union of Public Housing and Slum tenants working in the Near North area." In September 1966, "Several NSCM pastors and laymen were involved intensively in the Old Town Gardens and rent strike and demonstrations and arrests," coordinated via NSCM's Ministry on Social and Racial Justice.[61]

The ministry's Housing Task Force also concerned itself with Blacks by "finding and placing Negro families in the Lincoln Park and Lake View areas." Members clipped residential advertisements from newspapers, and, as others had before, posed as potential tenants, calling landlords to find out if the dwellings were available "on a non-discriminatory basis." Additionally, Rev. Larry Dutenhaver led the 221D3 Housing Committee, which, in conjunction with members of LPCA, sought to develop low- and middle-income housing in Lincoln Park, indicating that while some in leadership positions in LPCA did not agree with the ministers, others did, at least enough to work with them.[62]

In 1967, NSCM proposed a real estate clinic be established, staffed by volunteers, to encourage cooperation between residents and realtors and ultimately promote integration. In proposing this, the group revealed findings from a study it conducted. It argued that 32.2 percent of the combined populations of Lake View, Lincoln Park, and the Near North Side were Black. Members also found that "community organizations object to 'importing' minority groups (economic and racial) into the area to achieve or maintain diversified community or integrated community." Given the difficulties persons of color faced in avoiding discrimination in housing, the organization sought to "stimulate the open rental and sale of privately owned housing in the area." It also suggested that free legal aid be provided at the real estate clinic, which would keep a list of real estate openings submitted by church members. The last alternative the group provided was establishment of a real estate agency to facilitate integration.[63]

What the ministry really excelled at was self-examination and criticism on a level that would make the original Martin Luther blush. As ever, the organization asked itself what more it could accomplish, and how it could improve. Critical of its own makeup, the group asked that more Blacks get involved, as "we are so middle class and white." NSCM members asserted that two of the largest issues facing it were, "Not whether to let our community remain white or integrate it, but whether we will work to integrate it so it will not become [a] negro ghetto," and "Not whether the Negroes can be helped by being allowed to live with the whites, but how deprived the whites will be if they are not allowed to live in a mixed integrated society."[64] NSCM also formed an Emergency Task Force. The group offered, "with summer approaching and the real possibility of Civil Rights disturbances in our area the Ministry for Social and Racial Justice (of NSCM) is concerned that an Emergency Task Force be formed of people who are willing to be on emergency call during the summer to help calm any disturbance or rioting." The ministry believed that a force such as this "served to avert rioting in other communities."[65]

NSCM's inclusive vision of community also included the gay population of Lincoln Park in proposing a special Ministry to the Homosexual by May of 1966 and then, typical of the organization, engaging in a nine-month study to see if there was really a need for such a ministry. Members hoped that it would "bridge the gaps which exist between the mass of the homosexual community and the residential community, the legal community, the religious community and the psychiatric community." They argued "that we are responsible for the large homosexual community in our area" and participated in what it called the "newly formed Council on Religion and the Homosexual."[66] By late May of 1967, NSCM solicited funding for a Ministry to the Homosexual that would emphasize "services of pastoral care and psychiatric help."[67] Doering asserted that the North Side faced a "concentration of homosexuals" and proposed this ministry to achieve "a better adjustment to accepted social behavior and hopefully an adjustment to heterosexuality." This ministry planned to work in the typical on-the-street style of NSCM. Staff would administer its "pastoral care" in bars, churches, and offices in the area. Pastors would make first contact with a gay resident, followed by an interview with the clergyman and a therapist to see if the person was the right fit for a therapy/discussion group. While the attempt to convert gays was certainly misguided, that the organization recognized them at all is notable when even Abbie Hoffman ridiculed a fellow activist about his homosexuality.[68]

By early 1968, NSCM grew strong enough that other groups sought sponsorship (via its nonprofit corporation) and financial support. In May and June, the group the Quiet Answer asked for such aid and revealed tensions in the area that only grew in time. The organization sought to form a serviceman-oriented program that would establish a coffee shop to allow returning veterans to share experiences from the war. In asking for sponsorship, the group stated, "We are well aware that we will be hassled eventually, legally and otherwise, by local 'authorities.' With this reality in mind, the need for sponsorship by a 'respectable' group . . . becomes a necessity if the project is to become successful."[69]

That the Quiet Answer appealed to NSCM for aid to its Vietnam-centered coffeehouse is not surprising as the war concerned the group, and the nation. Across the United States, "citizen activists" began a movement to challenge US involvement in Vietnam.[70] In November of 1966, NSCM established the exploration of Vietnam and its effects on the community as one of its "top priorities."[71] As per usual tactics, members first studied the war, writing to congressmen for clarification as needed. Additionally, they attended the December 1966 conference of the newly formed Clergy and Laymen Concerned About Vietnam. During the next Lent NSCM held a sacrificial meal of rice and tea every Wednesday to disseminate information gleaned from newspapers, while others continued writing letters to congressmen and newspaper editors to open communication on the issue. Members felt that many churchgoers remained passive when it came to Vietnam, and that was unacceptable. Therefore, the organization dedicated its next Holy Week to the subject of the war. It arranged for speakers, and coverage in newspapers and on radio and television. The Door also developed a study group, and asked churches to take special offerings for the "Napalm Children of Viet Nam" in Maundy Thursday and Good Friday services. Doering asserted that those involved in Holy Week activities were not radicals, but many of the same middle-of-the-road types the group sought to educate. The hope was that more people would join study groups, or even attend an upcoming Peace March that included Dr. Benjamin Spock and Martin Luther King, Jr. NSCM also developed a brochure titled "25 cents and 25 minutes" that listed the names and addresses of five political figures to which members could express their views in five minutes at five cents a letter. The ministry continued holding Wednesday meetings and arranging for guest speakers into 1967.[72]

The Clergy and Laymen Concerned About Vietnam planned to establish two new coffeehouses, named Amnesty One and Two, by the 1968 convention. The Door served as ground zero for church involvement in Old

Town.[73] By April of 1968, the Door was self-sufficient enough to open its own account with the Belmont National Bank.[74] Studies, meetings, and petitions were the tactics of a methodical, rational organization. However, as change failed to materialize, some citizens would embrace more direct means of promoting inclusion in Lincoln Park just as activists across the nation began rethinking passive resistance.

Concerned Citizens of Lincoln Park

The years of privately funded rehabilitation combined with increased demolition decreased the amount of affordable housing, causing rental rates to skyrocket. This further alienated residents who wanted a more inclusive area. Approximately 7,500 families who could not afford to live in a renewed Lincoln Park were forced to relocate throughout the 1960s, and this troubled some in LPCA and NSCM. While the ministry branched out, LPCA by the mid-1960s boasted some one thousand members, but only some seventy-five persons were actually active, and even less than twenty controlled the group.[75] This helps to explain why the association remained aloof to NSCM's concerns in the years before the Democratic National Convention. When Dr. Marvin Rosner, LPCA president, decided to renovate a rooming house, which once held fifteen people, for his own family, it epitomized the lack of regard LPCA leadership had for the poor, outraging those promoting inclusion.[76]

Debates over the next phase of renewal further heightened tensions. The initial planning for Phase II of the GNRP came to LPCA's board of directors on July 14, 1966. Of the seven recommendations in the plan, the one regarding low-income housing was important. Phase II recommended against high-rises, but offered that "adequate housing for all residents of Lincoln Park and maintenance of economic diversity should be the goals of urban renewal in the Lincoln Park Conservation area." Low-income housing would be included sporadically throughout the neighborhood in the form of low-density units.[77] Here was some acceptance of a more inclusive area and indicates the possibility that, with persistent effort and meaningful dialogue, North Side white liberals and their city allies could have been convinced to expand housing for lower-income residents.

However, that failed to materialize. In September of 1966, some members of LPCA advocated amending renewal planning to provide for more low-income housing. Their voices then went unheard in city government as their opponents moved stealthily to block them: they omitted mention of low-income housing from the official recommendations sent to the Department of Urban Renewal.[78]

Outraged, pro–low-income LPCA members wrote to the DUR and the Lincoln Park Conservation Association as the Concerned Citizens of Lincoln Park (CCLP) in October 1966. Concerned Citizens focused mainly on including lower-income groups in renewal, and sought to work *within* LPCA to force it to confront the issue. CCLP was voluntary, demanded no dues, and had no official membership or staff.[79] Members claimed they were

> deeply shocked at the failure of the Lincoln Park Conservation Association to include any provision of housing for low income residents of Lincoln Park, or to provide any adequate priority for housing of moderate income families, in the list of priorities sent to the Department of Urban Renewal in regard to Phase II planning.[80]

The group referred to the original General Neighborhood Renewal Plan's goal of "preservation of diversity in housing accommodations, income, occupation, age, and environmental experience" in its attack on LPCA. It also outlined the measures it wanted the Conservation Association to address in urban planning. CCLP demanded that urban renewal provide housing for low- and moderate-income families and asked that such housing be distributed "throughout the Lincoln Park community." No longer were these groups to be segregated to the West Side. Additionally, the Citizens specifically demanded "this housing is made available on a non-discriminatory basis."[81]

The shift to a more assertive position in 1966 aligned with trends across the nation. This was the year in which Stokely Carmichael coined the term "Black Power," Students for a Democratic Society and the Student Nonviolent Coordinating Committee denounced the war in Vietnam, and twenty-thousand people marched against the war in New York City. Locally, it was also the year in which students at the University of Chicago protested the draft, and when Martin Luther King relocated his family to the city, facing violent white resistance.[82] In Lincoln Park activists wanting a more inclusive area now blended fiery words with action. What was once a debate between two liberal organizations now began to transform into a divide between the centrist, establishment, homesteading liberals of LPCA and the more inclusive liberals in Concerned Citizens.

Petitions quickly gave way to protest as those advocating change now more forcefully entered the public arena to advance their vision. Members of LPCA's Human Relations Committee, led by Rev. James Reed of the Parish of the Holy Covenant, protested the omission of more low-income housing to the DUR, picketing the December1966 meeting of the LPCA board.[83] Concerned Citizens demanded that Phase II add a priority for more low-income housing.[84] In calling Lincoln Park residents to join them in the strike, the group explained it wanted "to prompt the Association to adopt clear priorities to the Department of Urban Renewal in Lincoln Park for 1.) an adequate amount of low and moderate-income housing, and 2.) a phased program of demolition and reconstruction which will allow residents whose housing must be replaced to remain in the community." It also charged that "LPCA purports to represent the entire community" and, by not doing so, the Citizens felt they must

> demonstrate to record our insistence that the LPCA represent all of the people in the community in its negotiations with the DUR, first and foremost those who are to be displaced by clearance, rehabilitation and code enforcement. We demonstrate to record our refusal to accept self-serving standards advanced by those who would turn Lincoln Park into a preserve for the well-to-do and profiteers.[85]

CCLP called on "less-well-off citizens" to join them in protest and to "take a hand in our own affairs."[86] Sixty people walked for three hours in front of the LPCA office as the board met.[87] Public protest did gain one victory. After the picketing, the board, by a vote of sixteen to fourteen, agreed to include a priority recommendation to the DUR for low and moderate housing.[88] Peaceful, persistent pressure worked.

Those seeking a more inclusive neighborhood now sought powerful positions on the Conservation Association Board. In January of 1967, Concerned Citizens ran James Reed as a candidate for the LPCA board of directors. Reed had a history of activism. He was named associate pastor of Trinity United Methodist Church in 1959, where he lasted only six months. Parishioners strongly opposed his attempts to have the church "identify itself with an emerging community organization." Superiors then re-assigned him to the Parish of the Holy Covenant on West Diversey where he embraced the poor, the gay community, and persons of color, among them Puerto Ricans.[89] Under him, in February of 1963, LPCA's Human Relations Committee called for a workshop to facilitate integration and, in 1965, he urged the group to reach out to the "Spanish Community."[90] Reed also appealed to LPCA as early as September 9, 1965, to fully examine educational and urban renewal issues. He urged the group to contact to the community, communicate clearly, and give "real representation" to neighborhood groups.[91] In October of 1966, Reed publicly criticized LPCA in the *Chicago Tribune* for failing to include low-income housing as a priority.[92] By 1967, the Mid-North Association was so concerned that members of Concerned Citizens, "who actually represent a minority of the area population," had essentially taken over the Human Relations committee of LPCA that Mid-North decided to increase its membership on that committee to check them.[93]

Reed's opponents foiled his bid for election by collecting proxy ballots. The true purpose of allowing such votes, as understood by LPCA office nominee and minister Larry Dutenhaver, was to allow members who were sick or away from town the opportunity to have a voice, not as a way to muster support against one candidate. Dutenhaver told LPCA he was "shocked and deeply disappointed" by the strategy to block Reed.[94] Reed's critics explained their position in a letter sent to members of LPCA in which they urged them to instead vote for his opponent. His detractors felt that he was nominated "only after extended controversy and by the slightest majority," and they took offense to his formation of Concerned Citizens and his open criticism of LPCA to the press. The writers, clearly understanding CCLP tactics, charged that, "one of [NSCM's] purposes is to infiltrate LPCA and its key committees" and disagreed with what they saw as the Concerned Citizens' emphasis on low- and moderate-income housing over "improved schools and every other important community goal." Finally, they did not "feel that it makes sense to elect as a director a man who will publicly attack LPCA, and work against it from the outside whenever it rejects his proposals."[95]

Two members of Volunteers in Service to America (VISTA) sent a letter to "All signers of the proxy letter" in which they, as "two relatively objective newcomers who took no part in the fight" defended Reed as even-tempered and diplomatic "rather than the wild-eyed radical and publicity seeker" critics portrayed. They also reminded those against Reed that he and Concerned Citizens picketed the December 1966 board meeting only after hours of debate led them to the conclusion that "all other means were exhausted in prodding the recalcitrant board into action on low and moderate income housing priorities for Phase II."[96] Reed told the Lincoln Park *Economist* he would not become involved in a proxy fight, as "that sounds more like a business corporation than a community organization." He also stated "LPCA should represent all of the people of Lincoln Park, those of low and moderate income as well as the comfortable and the rich ... LPCA should represent all racial and ethnic groups, not just one or two."[97] The two lost the election on January 23, which, to the VISTA volunteers, "may well have sounded the death knell to the LPCA as the true voice of Lincoln Park."[98]

Undaunted, Concerned Citizens clung to peaceful forms of protest, but their prose indicates a growing embrace of assertive ideas and tactics. In a 1967 position paper titled "Lincoln Park: Renewal or Replacement?" the group addressed low-cost housing in the area and encouraged the various neighborhood associations to consider it at the next LPCA meeting. Action Committee chairman Dennis Cunningham labeled Concerned Citizens "an informal group of Lincoln Park residents who are determined to do everything in their power to prevent urban renewal from destroying this community by forcing the poorest third of the population to move elsewhere because of a drastic increase in the cost of housing." He further stated, "We believe a crisis has been reached, and that the transformation of this community into a preserve for the well-to-do will soon reach the point of no return." CCLP argued that the renewal of Lincoln Park had become a "crisis" for the "one-third of the population at the lower end of the economic scale." Due to increased housing prices caused by renewal, that group would be forced to relocate, and (quoting the initial plan), "the cultural, racial, and economic diversity which gives Lincoln Park its identity is lost." Concerned Citizens called for a moratorium on relocating citizens; the immediate construction of low-cost housing (giving top priority to those residents whose housing would be replaced); and a "solid system" by which financing could be provided allowing for the construction and rehabilitation of the "necessary amount of two to five-bedroom family housing which will rent and sell for $50 to $125 per month." The group also offered suggestions as to how their changes could be implemented. It insisted that, "There is the system of below-market interest loan guarantees in the National Housing Act, almost every aspect of the Model Cities program, blanket mortgage plans such as the one worked out last summer on the West

Side, the rent subsidy plan for public housing, a not-for-profit community construction company, co-ops, condominiums, etc."[99]

Concerned Citizens again attacked LPCA for failing to represent lower-income residents, claiming only "lip service and tokenism." They rejected Project I as a "travesty" and claimed "The great majority of Negro and Latin American residents are being displaced, with more than 70% of them being relocated outside of the community. Many promising young artists have been forced to move." They then, in prose further indicative of a change in mood, claimed, "Radical action must be taken to save the Lincoln Park we know and love and wish to redeem." CCLP also accused the Chicago Housing Authority of withholding funds from housing programs and sought sweeping change in LPCA even though "the vested interest will not be surrendered, without a struggle." It also argued for "a militant and resourceful organization for the whole community." CCLP members promoted a more representative Conservation Community Council, and called for a reduction in membership dues, rescheduling of meetings so that more people could attend, open elections of officers, and for the CCC to be brought "under the complete control of the Association." The group concluded its address to residents with some additional assertive prose:

> We must not accept redevelopment plans which are predicated on profit-taking at every stage. We must not swallow expert nonsense about "increasing the tax base." We must question, resist, and overturn every rule, regulation, procedure, practice, prejudice, shibboleth and sweetheart deal employed by the traditional housing industry to divert the benefits of community renewal from the community. We must establish control over our own affairs which restores the government to its rightful role as the servant, not the master. It is well within our power to do all this. It is only a beginning.[100]

While offering fiery rhetoric, residents still continued their rational, steady approach to activism by gathering data on low- and moderate-income residents to expose the discrepancy between the rents they paid in relation to what they earned. In February and March of 1967, several members of Concerned Citizens polled 172 families to find out how much they could afford and the number of residents in their homes. They also asked them to sign a petition requesting that the city provide proper housing for people if their current homes were to be demolished under urban renewal. Seventy percent of residents polled resided in the southwest portion of Lincoln Park. Pollsters synthesized the results in a study that revealed the average rent paid was $75.40 and argued that families of four to seven members could afford about $78. They intended the study to inform city officials about the economic reality of the area, with the hope they could use these statistics to gauge how much rent these residents would have to pay in future developments.[101]

In June of 1967, CCLP produced another report. The group decided it would create a central office, survey the community as to how residents felt about Phase II and housing in general, and to "educate the community on urban renewal issues and possibilities for [the] area." They intended to survey Sheffield residents, and VISTA volunteers were to aid in gathering residents for survey distribution.[102]

CCLP published its newspaper the *Lincoln Park Press* shortly thereafter, and organized a picket line at the Conservation Community Council hearing on 221D3 housing to educate the community about issues such as welfare.[103] The *Press* began modestly enough; its first volume was simply typed, with "Donations Accepted" atop its masthead. However, suggesting the views of CCLP gained support from community members, over time the paper evolved into a publication that cost ten cents, one with pictures and advertisements for local businesses.[104]

In September of 1967, Patricia Devine began as CCLP's full-time coordinator with a small salary and a part-time, mostly volunteer, staff.[105] Devine came to Lincoln Park in 1964. Inspired by the Civil Rights Movement, she first became involved with the Parish of the Holy Covenant, and then NSCM. Learning of the impact of urban renewal on the Near West Side, she hoped LPCA would be a Back of the Yards–type group, but was disappointed that it did not, to her, represent small homeowners. She then joined CCLP to represent the "common" people of the neighborhood.[106]

In December of 1967, for the first time, Concerned Citizens of Lincoln Park considered splitting from the Conservation Association. Devine sent a letter to LPCA, members of CCLP, and "representatives of other Lincoln Park organizations." In it, she invited readers to an upcoming meeting of the Concerned Citizens' Steering Committee at which they would strategize for the upcoming LPCA board elections in January. Additionally, the group planned to discuss turning CCLP "into an independent, multi-issued organization for Lincoln Park." Devine credited Concerned Citizens members within the Conservation Association for swaying the board to allow for six new moderate-income housing sites to be developed but, unsatisfied with this, attacked LPCA for turning a deaf ear to the needs of the disadvantaged. She charged the association with becoming "more conservative in membership (white, middle income property owners, largely from the eastern part of Lincoln Park)" and of working to minimize the influence of Concerned Citizens. She also mentioned that CCLP's Steering Committee, in its last meeting, decided to reorganize Concerned Citizens as a broader coalition of groups, and to run Larry Dutenhaver for LPCA vice president.[107]

The Concerned Citizens of Lincoln Park began as a caucus group in 1966 during a time when activists nationwide began to embrace more assertive ideas and tactics. In just one year, CCLP moved from criticizing LPCA, to gaining influence within it, to breaking away. Concerned Citizens members used words like "radical" and "militant" after 1966, words that some Americans used to describe groups like the Black Panthers or Students for a Democratic Society at a time when activists across the nation, and in Lincoln Park, shifted tone and focus.

The Church of the Three Crosses

In this time of mounting tensions, Concerned Citizens found a key ally in the newly established Church of the Three Crosses. Members of the St. James United Church of Christ and the Second Evangelical United Brethren Church began drawing up a constitution and bylaws for the new union at a combined congregational meeting held Sunday, October 16, 1966.[108] They also wrote this constitution before the church even had a name and established procedures for holding meetings and voting. Much like the founding statement of NSCM, the church, in its bylaws, addressed its failure, asserting "We confess that we have allowed the political, economic, educational and social power-structures of the world to overcome us and we often respond in apathy and despair."[109] The organization only asked for 5 percent of a member's income as a tithe rather than the customary 10 percent, suggesting recognition of a low-income congregation. Members voted Larry Dutenhaver and Jerry Goethe as the pastors of the then-unnamed church. Dutenhaver, also on LPCA's housing committee, was one of the first area activists to become involved in both religious issues and urban renewal.[110]

The site of the new church itself was "under urban renewal."[111] By December of 1966 the church printed its newsletter the *Handclasp* in which it outlined that month's events, including separate services in both English and Spanish, and the hours of the Cellar coffeehouse, which was open every Friday and Saturday evening from 8 P.M. to midnight. It also announced CCLP's planned demonstration of the December 8 LPCA board of directors meeting. The church claimed, "The amount of low and moderate income housing which will be constructed in Project One is woefully insufficient." The letter did not distinguish between the Concerned Citizens and NSCM, portraying the groups as united. The writers announced

> We demonstrate to record our insistence that LPCA represent all of the people in the community . . . We demonstrate to record our refusal to accept self-serving standards advanced by those who would turn Lincoln Park into a preserve for the well-to-do and profiteers . . . We call on all the less-well-off citizens of Lincoln Park and all persons of conscience who understand that no good community can be built on the foundations of segregation—whether racial or economic or both—to join us in demonstrating to the LPCA, the DUR and the city at large.[112]

That the church newsletter used the phrase "preserve for the well-to-do" is further evidence of its close relationship to the CCLP, as the latter organization used that same phrasing.

Over the next year, members became bolder. At an all-church retreat held in September, James Reed, "challenged us to think of the church as 'guerillas.'" Rev. Steven Whitehead spoke on the topic of "Sheep and Goats." The group's Strategy Board, the official body of the church that met twice a month, at its August 28, 1967, meeting, heard from the suggestively titled Vanguard Ministry, which sought economic aid.[113] This group, headed by Whitehead, ran a bookstore and counseling programs and ministered on the street.[114] In order to publicize concerns over urban renewal, a full-page section of the October 1967 *Handclasp* titled "The time is *now* [emphasis in original] . . . To Voice the need for Low and Moderate Income Housing in Lincoln Park" highlighted the fact that over the summer, seven families of the congregation moved out of the area due to renewal. Three more would do so in the coming months. The authors also complained that rising rents forced "much of the diversity, both economic and racial, from our community," and that only eighteen units for families of low income existed.

The church credited Concerned Citizens and the Lincoln Central Association as working to maintain diversity, "thus creating a healthy community of the future which includes all kinds of families." It also urged readers to join with the Lincoln Central, CCLP, or LPCA to "bring about more inclusive planning in our area."[115] NSCM supported the church, commending it for facilitating the Hip Job Co-op and finding a space for it to operate.[116]

CHAPTER THREE

The Counterculture

"If there weren't any hippies on the street, we'd probably hire some."
—President of the Old Town Chamber of Commerce

Old Town

As the NSCM grew, between 1964 and 1967 in excess of twenty million dollars had been spent on new buildings in Lincoln Park and renovation as real estate values skyrocketed.[1] Under the General Neighborhood Renewal Plan, the first area targeted for renewal was the Lincoln Park area's southeast corner, home of Old Town, the Haight-Ashbury of Chicago.

The neighborhood was in transition as urban renewal proceeded in the 1960s. Of the nineteen census tracts in Lincoln Park, it contained the highest number of housing units, but also the lowest number of nonwhite residents and one of the highest concentrations of wealth.[2] Just as Lincoln Park residents had conflicting views of the neighborhood's identity, "Old Town" was an imprecisely defined area. The Old Town Triangle Association designated the neighborhood as between North Avenue, Clark, and Ogden, but residents also considered areas outside of this official boundary part of Old Town. One resident offered:

> Old Town is a community. I don't mean a neighborhood, which is merely a separate physical locale and of which there are dozens throughout Chicago. I mean a community in the sense that the common thread of its varied life, the principle of unity in all its diversity, is a kind of shared experience and shared outlook on life that reminds me of a small town, except that it's interwoven with so much that is cosmopolitan and sophisticated in Chicago.[3]

In the fifties and early sixties, Old Town had a reputation for being an artist- and family-friendly environment. By the mid-fifties, the neighborhood "was known as a place where artists and interesting people lived."[4] In

1957 the *Chicago Tribune* reported that the Old Town Triangle was an "art colony," a "melting pot," and a "village where the shoemaker's daughter goes to school with the celebrity's son and the retired coal miner wins garden prizes at the art fair." The paper compared it to Greenwich Village, but a local sculptor argued "The Triangle was never a Greenwich Village. It's more permanent, less pseudo, and non-Bohemian. This is a family neighborhood. Here artists are accepted members of the community, and even the beard wearers are good husbands and fathers." Some considered the area around North and Wells to be "questionable," but one policeman commented that Old Town was "a family neighborhood. They never give us any trouble."[5]

Old Town transitioned from artistic enclave to commercial success and hippie ground zero due to the area's reputation as progressive, the help of developers, and that Old Town's high rents made it a spot where those accepting of communal living could turn. In the early 1960s musicians, artists, journalists, and young singles, including students, moved to the North Side, forging what they saw as a "bohemian community" vs. the square world. As Old Town's middle class expanded, then, area entrepreneurs snapped up inexpensive commercial properties at the same time people bought up and flipped homes, creating a mixed zone of housing, commerce, and culture.[6] Wells Street, in particular, drew artists such as Joan Baez and Bob Dylan to coffeehouses.[7] They also played in bars like Mother Blues, the Hungry Eye, the Earl of Old Town, the Crazy Horse, and the Abbey.[8] Solidarity Bookshop, a store founded by anarchists and Wobblies, sold political literature.[9] In 1963 the *Chicago Tribune* reported on the neighborhood's transition from "a place which seemed inexorably sinking into decay" to one that "bloomed as a center of night-life." The neighborhood of "dingy discouraged houses by day, of complete somnolence at night" transformed to a spot "on weekends, at least" where Chicagoans flocked. Wells Street appealed to artistic types whose "small pocketbooks . . . prefer beer to whisky and cocktails."[10] A 1967 *Tribune* report highlighted the carriage lamps and cottages dotting the residential areas that gave the neighborhood a Victorian feel, and the section of Wells that attracted youth in crowds so large that "getting thru [sic.] this area is like running a gantlet." This eclectic mix could congregate in the middle of the street "highest in real estate value of all the shops on the strip" or at a place like the Chances R (south of North Avenue and, technically, outside of the "official" boundaries of Old Town) "where you can have a hamburger, drink a beer and agree that being able—and encouraged—to throw peanut shells on the floor is almost as good as finding a nickel cigar."[11]

In urban areas across the United States in the 1970s and 1980s, one of the first steps in the gentrification of a neighborhood was the migration of artists to the area.[12] For example, by the 1980s, the "culture industry" turned the Lower East Side into a chic part of New York city.[13] Drawn to cheap rents and burgeoning entertainment scenes, musicians, actors, and writers brought panache to neighborhoods and investment and rehabilitation followed. Artists were drawn to Old Town in the 1950s, and in the next decade the counterculture brought more people seeking an alternative to the mainstream.

Business owners such as John Moody and John Krenger promoted economic growth on Wells Street, attracted youth to the area, and were key in transforming the street into a commercial and artistic zone. One *Tribune* piece credited Moody, owner of Moody's Pub (also south of North Avenue) as "the cat who made Wells Street swing."[14] Krenger, a thirty-year-old marketing and sales consultant for Illinois Bell Telephone, first bought property in 1960. He turned two "broken down" buildings into livable spaces. This president of the Old Wells Association, "a group of merchants, property owners, and other residents dedicated to bettering Wells Street," was a "square" and no "artist or beatnik," yet, at the same time, he attracted them. After restoring his buildings, he placed an ad in the *Tribune* reading "Wanted: Students and artists with imagination. Do-it-yourselfers are welcome. Decorating allowances." Krenger's vision was twofold: to renew buildings in a way that restored their past glory and to turn Wells into, as the paper reported, "a quaint shopping area." Students and artists responded. Reactions were mixed as his personal campaign brought both more crowds and crime.[15] Wells Street housed 174 businesses by 1967, and land values increased four times over since 1955. The president of the Old Town Chamber of Commerce estimated that the land from Division to the north end of Wells to be worth eighteen to twenty-four million dollars, with the land in the center to be worth the most.[16] That year, retail sales on Wells Street were up 25 percent and grossed twenty million dollars annually.[17]

This sudden economic and demographic boom did not sit well with everyone. Those who shared the family-oriented vision of community outlined by LPCA began to question urban renewal efforts before the counterculture bloomed. Some worried over a tavern to be opened on North Wells on a lot designated for residential use. The OTTA feared that:

> A tavern at 1746–48 North will destroy the residential character of an area that is both presently and prospectively designated for renewal by the City Council. A tavern in that location would be the opening wedge in a series of developments which would drive out stable, long-term residents and their families and culminate in a string of eating, drinking, and entertainments establishments along that portion of Wells Street.[18]

In September of 1963, the Old Town Triangle Association held a panel discussion entitled "The Effects of the Wells Street Development on Family Living in the Triangle," attended by approximately three hundred people. The group's president offered that development in the area made it more like Greenwich Village, noted a "diversity that is nothing less than amazing" and revealed that twenty-three new saloons opened in the last eighteen months. However, he also complained,

> With all its good, Wells Street has brought in one bad element that Triangle families can do without. It's mostly the nighttime crowd—but only a part of it at that. It spills all over the Triangle. Parking is becoming impossible. Some mornings there are more paper cups with stale beer or old beer cans in sight than there is flora . . . This was the summer that indoor hootenanies moved outdoors . . . The weekend and night crawlers are in our midst and we hate it.[19]

Other panelists voiced their anger over tavern noise, hot rods, "unsavory elements" including "girlie shows," the "spiraling of residential rents, influenced by rising commercial rates." Another speaker noted that rents were so high only businesses dealing in liquor could keep up. While one newer resident was optimistic that undesirables would vacate within a couple of years, others discussed working with city officials.[20]

As thousands of people crammed into the streets of Old Town each weekend, Chicagoans wondered whether the neighborhood's identity was residential or commercial.[21] In 1965 the OTTA told residents, "don't hesitate to call the police about the high-fi [sic.] sets, folk singing fests and loud parties that run past a reasonable hour."[22] The *Chicago American* commented "Old Town, Chicago's never-never land of instant quaintness, may be killing itself with success." Another writer claimed "some keep their rents so high that only bars and restaurants can make it—and even they have a high turnover." The *Tribune*, in 1967, speculated that "The area might be limited only to professionals."[23] One urban renewal office employee commented that "With the price structure today, most families can't afford to live" in Old Town.[24] An area book seller and his wife "liked it better when it was simple" and another resident felt "utter amazement and disbelief." Some feared an increase in crime, and the district police captain increased the number of foot patrols on the street but commented that minors and cars clogging the area were his chief problems, although police arrested others for disorderly behavior. Despite the optimism of local businessmen, like the owner of the Beef and Bourbon restaurant, who predicted a "great future," others feared the negative impact of rent increases.[25]

Hip Old Town

Urban renewal brought prosperity to Old Town. With this boom in the 1960s came "hippies, pseudo-hippies, bikers, freaks, and runaway kids looking for a place to crash."[26] Between 1966 and 1968 countercultural enclaves grew in cities across the United States and beyond. In New York, the East Village became home to hips.[27] In Portland it was Lair Hill Park.[28] In Minneapolis it was Cedar-Riverside.[29] In St. Louis it was Gaslight Park.[30] In Los Angeles it was Venice Beach and the Sunset Strip.[31] And in Canada it was Toronto's Yorkville.[32] In Chicago it was Old Town. The media christened it the Chicago equivalent of Haight-Ashbury as early as 1966, and the area did in part model itself after San Francisco's hippie epicenter.[33]

Chicago's hip scene forces a reconsideration of the definition of "counterculture" and whether or not, as in some narratives, its character was defined in San Francisco and New York.[34] On one hand, the Haight was in some ways the model for Old Town's hip community. Old Town hips embraced the Digger idea of "free" and the Dutch anarchist group Provo. They even held a Be-In modeled on the one in San Francisco. However, their hip zone, unlike the Haight, was interwoven with commercial growth, so Chicago hips did not have their own reserved space in which to experiment. Hippies nationwide often "dismissed or displayed hostility toward Christianity as the old, irrelevant, and 'square' establishment religion."[35] Chicago's counterculture was unique in that it merged hip and minister as local clergymen walked the streets, hung out in coffeehouses and in the summer of

1968 planned for the Festival of Life. Police harassment here was almost immediate, making for another distinguishing component of the Chicago counterculture. Loitering Chicago hips were bad for business, and merchants who on the one hand benefitted from visitors there to see hips, on the other had no compunction about calling the police when hips interfered with the bottom line. The Haight inspired Chicago's counterculture, but Old Town was also a mix of teens and dropouts, ministers and full-time freaks (as hard-core countercultural members preferred to be called) in a zone of department stores and head shops, where anti-materialistic hips walked the same streets as businessmen, and blues music and psychedelic rock pulsed through the night air. As such, Chicago's fluid counterculture struggled to define itself in Old Town amidst debates over its nature from within and police harassment from without. The area also followed the national trajectory of the counterculture in that it grew between 1965 and 1967, but unlike Haight or the Village, hip did not decline as a movement by 1968. In Chicago, the counterculture only grew. The Chicago experience demands that historians reconsider the chronological framework and the ultimate meaning of the counterculture not as, in traditional narratives, a sideshow of the New Left but as its own movement with ebbs and flows in its development. From San Francisco to Portland, Minneapolis to Chicago to New York, the counterculture had regional distinctions as it grew nationally.

In Chicago, the subdivision of homes into apartments made Old Town, already known as a bohemian enclave, fertile ground for the counterculture. With Old Town rents high, hips willing to live communally and who had little interest in property ownership took root there. A local artist noted that, "By 1965 it was pretty crazy. By 1966 there were more airline stewardesses, advertising people. For artists the rents were too high." However, renovators developed older, dilapidated buildings and rented them out, subdivided into six or nine apartments. One property owner noted that one building was being rented "for $200 a month. It was a rooming-house. It had cockroaches, exit signs, linoleum on top of carpet on top of linoleum. There was a smell of opium." Conversions like this could be found in other areas of Lincoln Park. A Sheffield homeowner noted that, "The houses on Bissell had been converted to 'housekeeping rooms' with shared baths and a hotplate in each room."[36] One realty agent reported renting an apartment to one person and then, one week later, "finding ten hippies living in it." He claimed that this was the exception, but high rents did drive out families, leaving space to those who would share it.[37]

The first places Chicagoans could learn about the developing hip scene were mainstream newspapers. Readers of the *Lincoln Park Booster* knew about the upcoming Electric Theater, north of Lincoln Park itself, two months before it opened. The paper described the club's interior, replete with slide projectors and kaleidoscopes.[38] More importantly, underground newspapers defined and promoted the burgeoning counterculture.[39] Chicago's underground magazine *Seed* was first published in 1967. In its initial year, *Seed* reached "a few thousand" readers.[40] In time, the magazine boasted sales of forty thousand copies an issue.[41] It linked east and west countercultures via its membership in the Underground Press Syndicate and subscriptions to the Liberation News Service and the Resistance Press. *Seed* combined local hippie news with psychedelic art, cartoons, music reviews, personal ads, music gig announcements, and instructions on how to live the hip life (for example, each initial issue contained a section profiling a specific drug). Earl "the Mole" Segal first published it out of his head shop, the Mole Hole.[42] *Seed* staff lived primarily at the "core collective" of two houses and each earned fifty dollars per week.[43] They also gathered at Mr. Jeff's, a snack shop, where mail was delivered and meetings held.[44] One writer for the magazine described its readership as, "the usual blend of freaks, radicals, kids, sympathetic liberals, weekend hippies, curious suburbanites, and horny businessmen."[45]

Head shops, springing up across the nation, also promoted a sense of community among the counterculture. They not only sold drug paraphernalia but allowed likeminded individuals places to congregate, while at the same time generating a profit for hip owners.[46] For example, in Columbia, South Carolina, The Joyful Alternative Head Shop was both a unique expression of the local counterculture and tapped into national hip trends as defined by the Haight.[47] Such shops were often run by what Joshua Clark Davis terms, "Activist Entrepreneurs" dedicated to social and political change more than profit.[48] Chicagoan James Lato opened his Wells Street head shop after reading a *Time* magazine article about them in the spring of 1967 and then visiting New York to visit some.[49] Along with local church-run coffeehouses such as the Door and the Cellar, head shops provided congregational space to hips, occasional haven from cops, and commerce for owners. Taken together they reveal the blend of ministry, merchandise, and hip that were interwoven into Chicago's counterculture. While some in the pages of *Seed* painted a portrait of a hip scene truly at odds with the dominant society surrounding it, the Chicago scene was not characterized by a false dichotomy of hip and square, but uniquely mixed Digger-esque calls for "free" with hard work and interaction with mainstream society.

In some ways Chicago hips took inspiration from, and copied, Haight-Ashbury when creating a hip zone in Old Town. The Haight, arguably the birthplace of the counterculture, was a San Francisco neighborhood in decline that became home to a new generation of outcasts. Area freaks fleeing increased rents in the North Beach neighborhood found their way there in the early 1960s and created their own hip space in the city where they experimented with drugs, music, and sex in pursuit of a life other than that of the middle class.[50] By 1966, the Haight hosted a psychedelic shop, the *Oracle* (a hip underground paper), the Free Medical Clinic, and the Switchboard to exchange information on available housing, lawyers, and other services.[51] In January of 1967, Bay Area hips held the first Human Be-In at the Golden Gate Park in San Francisco, and that year some seventy-five thousand youth descended on the region as national publicity about the Haight grew.[52]

Chicago followed by appropriating some of the more well-publicized elements of the Haight. Borrowing from the language used in the original Be-In that called for a "gathering of the tribes," *Seed*, in its article "Tribes Assemble on North Avenue Beach," reported on Chicago's equivalent. Tipping its hat to the Bay Area event, the paper noted that, "On the fourteenth of May, the torch of love and eternal brotherhood arrived in Chicago, taken from the East and West coasts, and was planted solidly on the North Avenue Beach." The event lasted from 1 to 5 P.M., included kite-flying, balloons, and flowers, and ended peacefully after police ordered the park cleared.[53] The Vanguard Ministry even sent a minister to the Haight, "to see what structures are there to relate the church to the people in the streets."[54]

The theatrical troupe the Diggers was prominent in the Haight and inspired Chicago hips. Blending art and activism, Diggers eschewed capitalism and emphasized "Free," opening a Free Store in which items were given away and where everyone was the boss.[55] They also believed that people could better society, in wealth redistribution and in giving away as much for free as possible, ultimately building a collectivist world, one in which ordinary people, not the stodgy Left or others, would take leadership positions.[56]

The group also criticized and harassed area merchants for charging residents for goods and services. The Digger alternative was a series of Free Feeds in which Diggers gave away bowls of stew and soup made from donated, and often stolen, items.[57] In 1967, after publicly proclaiming the "Death of Money and Rebirth of the Haight," the group changed its name to Free City.[58] "Free" also took on the form nationwide of "Free Universities" on college campuses.[59]

The Digger influence on Old Town hips was evident early on. *Seed* offered a primer on all things Digger in its second issue, informing readers that Digger leader Emmett Grogan was busy developing branches in New York City, Los Angeles, Vancouver, and Seattle. Readers also learned of the Free Store in the Haight and the free feeds in the panhandle.[60] In May of 1967, under the headline "Diggers Started," readers learned of Old Town's Solidarity Bookshop that sought donations for free clothing.[61] Emmett Grogan stopped by Barbara's Bookstore in July of 1967, leaving a message ending "You are the Leader!"[62] But while Diggers in San Francisco heatedly criticized area merchants, Chicago hips refrained from such attacks. In the countercultural world of Old Town where hip and commerce were interwoven, *Seed* reminded readers that their Free store was "not the 'Hashbury' store" and needed help paying the rent as the local head shops that had helped so far could not do all the work.[63]

Old Town hips also took inspiration from the Dutch anarchist-satirical group the Provos, profiled in the first issue of the San Francisco *Oracle*.[64] In the late October edition of *Seed*, readers could enjoy both a poem titled "Provo," and learn about a new Old Town Free Store with, "free food, free clothes, free books."[65] In January of 1968, a group calling itself "Chicago Provo," announced it was starting the "Chicago Switchboard/Communications Company," like that in the Haight.[66] Through this, messages could be exchanged through the hip crowd, and readers could locate services such as medical and legal aid, crash pads, and the Hip Job Co-Op. *Seed* claimed, "The idea is to provide communication—instantly when necessary—in the hip and poor community."[67]

Developing and uniting a community founded on doing one's own thing was also difficult, as evidenced by *Seed* editors' repeated pleas for unity. One 1967 editorial claimed that "too much energy and talent is still being dissipated in pointless squabbling among the various anti-establishment groups . . . We don't care what name you go by whether it's 'Hippie,' 'Peacenik' . . . the important thing is that although there are minor differences, we're really all in the same bag."[68] One reader noted that, "I believe there are two basic elements to our hippy [sic.] community. There are those that are trying to change Mr. John Q. Public and those that sit home smoking their pot, dropping their acid, and putting the straight world down for not knowing where it's really at."[69] Another offered:

> My experience is mostly with people from Haight, and in comparison with the atmosphere in Haight, Chicago is an angry jungle of hard-face hippies. In Old Town hippies don't seem to know where they're at ... This is a very bad scene. I wish you people would please get *off* [emphasis in original] the Big Brother trip all the way and open yourselves up. Go to Haight and see what love is.[70]

Some readers complained that *Seed* sharply divided the world into the hip and nonhip, and *Seed* editors responded to such critics, and to those who claimed Chicago was poor ground to host a counterculture, by arguing that they witnessed "glimpses of a (so far) relatively dormant underground" but that they were "encouraged by the diversity" they had seen.[71] Even the Digger-inspired Free Store saw its share of internal bickering. In a story titled "Free Store: Fucked Up or Forward?" the magazine reported that the store recently survived a "power struggle" among those who volunteered to run it until the Chicago Provos settled things. In the wake of the clash, the store still needed donations and the magazine pled with readers to contribute.[72]

Chicago's counterculture was diverse enough to allow for argument about its true nature, but just how "counter" was it? *Seed* and local head shops are reminders of the counterculture's relationship to commerce. Thomas Frank has argued that the counterculture was quickly absorbed and packaged by ad men.[73] David Farber has rebuffed that claim, noting that many hip businesses blended ideology and capitalism into "right livelihood."[74] Consider that Chicago's Cheetah Club, with its dance music, strobe lights, and party atmosphere, was one of three Cheetah Clubs (the first was in New York City, another in Los Angeles) co-owned by Borden Stevenson, son of Adlai Stevenson.[75] The local Electric Theater was the latest development for the men who created the Electric Circus in New York City.[76] In San Francisco, hip storeowners earned the scorn of Diggers for not giving more money to community projects and free feeds.[77] In a Chicago undergoing urban renewal, the counterculture coexisted alongside Crate&Barrel. That store's owner welcomed the Carl Sandburg Village apartment complex, and a co-owner of Piper's Alley happily predicted that new high-rises would bring high-income shoppers.[78] The *Tribune* highlighted a fashion store in Old Town named "Horse of a Different Color" that was "a haven for seekers after today's 'with it' fashions."[79] This was not a sequestered zone like Haight or the Village, but a comingling of hip and commerce closer to Los Angeles's Sunset Strip where one could see bands, go for coffee, and buy both modern furniture and rolling papers.[80]

As hips struggled to define and develop themselves, Old Town merchants struggled with hips who on the one hand brought tourists, but on the other clogged streets while buying nothing. The president of the Old Town Chamber of Commerce saw promotional value in them, commenting, "If there weren't any hippies on the street, we'd probably hire some. Many shoppers come here because they like to see different types of people." The owner of the Chances R restaurant claimed "the long hairs discourage others from coming. A lot of merchants don't like them." Area merchants briefly discussed the "under 21, no-alcohol, coffee houses for teens at the south end of the Wells street strip" as a possible direction for the business sector. One, however, commented, "We want to cater to people in the early 20s and young marrieds [sic.]. The teen places are just not the way we think the street should go." Police Commander Clarence Braasch thought that hips were not too bad, as they obeyed police orders to disperse.[81] Deputy Chief Robert Lynsky, however, felt Old Town to be a "high crime" area.[82] After the riots in the wake of Martin Luther King Jr.'s assassination, one storeowner commented, "The store owners in this area are scared. We don't want our businesses to be looted. Many of us don't have insurance because this is a high risk area."[83] While this statement speaks to fears of Blacks, it also suggests that residents were weary in the late 1960s, and would keep an eye on any new area arrivals or changes to community makeup. Unlike New York City's East Village, where Blacks and Latinos were put off by hips rejecting things minorities sought like steady jobs and home ownership, in Old Town the tension was between hips and white businessmen who were okay with a hip presence so long as it brought in dollars, but when it threatened profits, merchants called the police.

And called they were. One last characteristic of the hip scene in Old Town was police harassment. *Seed*'s first issue reported undercover officers attending, then busting, a fundraiser held by a DePaul professor in his home.[84] That issue also charged that local merchants pressured the city into providing police harassment of hips. Asking, "Police trained by Former SS Officers?" and calling officers "non-thinking, gun-toting goons," the paper claimed that harassment was common in the summer of 1967.[85] Police cleared a park at Promontory Point at 55th and the lake, on July 4, 1967. At 5 P.M., officers demanded that a small group gathered for a Be-In cease playing conga drums and leave the park. Park goers refused to leave, instead surrounding the police cars. Officers called for reinforcements and the paddy wagon before arresting four, beating one.[86] One *Seed* reader noted, "This is not an isolated case: It appears the police have initiated a systematic program of harassment of hippies, Negroes, and progressive youth in general."[87] The magazine also offered advice in the articles, "If You are Stopped by the Police," and, "If You are Arrested."[88] *Seed* was so sensitive to police harassment that it ran the piece "Why It Didn't Happen Here: Cops Harrass [sic.] to Prevent Riots" that detailed police harassment on the West and South Sides, arguing that Mayor Daley's administration ordered it.[89] In late August of 1967, police raided an Old Town apartment that was a "gathering place for Old Town hippies," arresting six on drug charges.[90] One Chicago narcotics officer who investigated drugs throughout the city commented, "mostly we stay in Old Town. This is where the action is."[91]

Enter Yippie!

Chicago's hip scene was about to host one of the most infamous events of the 1960s. Abbie Hoffman and Jerry Rubin planned to bring a national protest to Chicago, but beyond that they didn't have much of a plan and they certainly didn't think of Lincoln Park. Then again, careful preparation and methodical planning were not their strong suits. What they did was create a national demonstration that Chicago residents organized. In doing so, they forced Chicagoans to band together and plan for a protest that would be seen as a turning point in the 1960s.

Yippie began in New York City on New Year's Eve, as Hoffman, Rubin, the *Realist* publisher Paul Krassner, and others got stoned in Hoffman's apartment and considered what to do about the Vietnam War and the upcoming 1968 Democratic National Convention.[92] In deciding to hold a protest and cultural event in Chicago, the group finalized discussions about demonstrating in the city first begun in December of 1967. At that time, peace activist Brad Lyttle called a meeting of approximately one hundred people in New York to discuss increased violence in demonstrations. Activist Ed Sanders recalled that as the group sipped coffee, one person asserted that the way to combat violence was to marry protest to a free music festival, like that of the 1967 Monterey Pop Festival in California. This spawned several additional meetings attended by Rubin and Hoffman.[93] Now, as the new year dawned, the two planned a combination of "pot and politics," for Chicago, an event blending culture and politics, rock bands, guest speakers, and fun.[94] In a New York press conference on March 17, the Yippies announced to the world that they would come to Chicago.[95] The group later invented the term Yippie, claiming that it stood for Youth International Party.[96]

Central to Hoffman and Rubin's protest style, and the countercultural movement in general, was spontaneity, theatricality, and a lack of leadership.[97] This allowed all participants to define and redefine the group and allowed for Chicagoans to take on key roles. Chicago pastor James Shiflett, who identified himself as a Yippie, defined a Yip as someone who "is determined to react to what he believes is a society based on irrationalities." He felt that the war in Vietnam and the leaders who designed it were irrational, and that Yippies used stunts as a reaction to this. He also observed that Yippie itself had no real leadership.[98] Hoffman and Rubin openly informed the media that anyone could be a Yippie, and eschewed formality, instead encouraging members to lead themselves.[99]

On March 22, the two met with activist Dave Dellinger and members of the umbrella protest group Mobilization to End the War (MOBE) at Lake Villa, a YMCA camp outside of Chicago. Neither Lincoln Park activists nor NSCM attended as this was a top-down attempt at planning by antiwar leadership rather than the grassroots effort it would become.[100] Participants agreed that Rennie Davis, who headed the Center for Radical Research in Chicago, Dave Dellinger, and Boston activist Vernon Grizzard would organize a protest. Planners envisioned numerous "Movement Centers," each with its own group and message spread throughout the area. The week would culminate with a Wednesday night march on the amphitheater as the Democratic Party, planners thought, would nominate Lyndon Baines Johnson (LBJ) for a second term.[101]

Hoffman and Rubin's attendance at Lake Villa was a rare appearance in Illinois.[102] Characteristic of its loose approach to protest, Yippie did not plan to land in Lincoln Park, but a hip resident there played an integral role in planning the demonstration the whole world watched. After the New York Yippies decided on their "Festival of Life," Krassner published an advertisement in the *Realist* in which he asked for someone in Chicago to serve as a local contact for demonstration planning. Old Town resident Abe Peck read the ad in February of 1968.[103] He then offered up an acquaintance's farm as an operational base. That same month, Peck met with Jerry Rubin and signed on as the Yippie coordinator in Chicago and the conduit between Chicago hip and New York Yip.[104] An NYU graduate, former Green Beret, and dropout looking for direction, he entered Old Town in 1967 during a trip across the United States in a VW van. A writer for the newly founded *Seed* gave him a place to stay. After a trip to California (and Tijuana), Peck found himself back in Chicago, selling textbooks, living in a shabby hotel, and frequenting the Headland head shop. In October of 1967, while in Headland, Peck learned of the upcoming protest against the Pentagon, which he joined, and on returning he began writing for *Seed*. He became increasingly involved in the publication as staff members struggled with continued police harassment.[105]

Yippie announced its initial convention plans for Chicago in an issue of *Seed* in which the magazine's writers again reminded readers of the oppression Chicago hippies faced. One article, "How to Think About the Police," decried them as brutal. The magazine also announced its "First Bust," in which police arrested one young woman for vagrancy. The *Chicago Tribune* also targeted *Seed*. The publishing giant bought *Seed*'s printing company and then dropped publication of the hip mag. Readers sent money and supplies, and soon the magazine reestablished itself.[106]

On March 25, the New York Yips met with their Chicago protégés backstage at the Cheetah Club in the Uptown neighborhood north of Lincoln Park during a benefit to raise money for *Seed* and Yippie. Present at the meeting was NSCM's Rev. Jon Tuttle who, like Peck, would prove instrumental in planning the festival. Tuttle and Peck worked together with Hoffman and Rubin to draft and sign the permit proposal asking permission to hold the festival at Grant Park, across from the International Amphitheater, miles south of Lincoln Park.[107] That week Peck, in *Seed*, optimistically promoted the upcoming event and listed the planned musical lineup.[108]

On March 26, Rubin, Tuttle, Hoffman, Krassner, and others alerted Chicago newspapers that they would hold a press conference the next morning in the *Seed* office. The conference was not terribly informative as Yip leadership had not yet decided on any agenda. With reporters in tow, the group marched to the Chicago City Council chamber downtown, where police met them and prohibited them from entering the building. They eventually met the mayor's aid, David Stahl.[109] He was to serve as a stand-in for the mayor, he claimed, because it would be inappropriate for Daley to meet with the likes of Yippies.[110] "Princess Rainwater" of Flushing New York presented a shocked Stahl with the permit request wrapped in a fold-up from Paul Moriat's album *A Picture of a Girl*. Next, Yips pinned a Yippie button on the mayor's aide, exited the building, and drove to the Chicago Park District Office where they held an impromptu press conference outside the building as they could not find the necessary park district employee with which to speak. From there, they proceeded to the Chicago Civic Center, where they held yet another impromptu press conference by the Picasso statue. Shortly thereafter, Krassner and Hoffman were off to the airport. For the next month there would be no word as to the permit.[111]

Daley Responds

As New York Yippies, despite their initial flashy arrival in the Windy City, were largely absent there in the summer of 1968, Chicagoans in Lincoln Park provided leadership. One New York Yippie later claimed that "We thought it would be up to the Chicago people from the newspaper the *Seed* and those identified with the Yippies to set up the communication centers, legal aid, hospitalization was anticipated for perhaps illness or sicknesses or accidental injuries."[112] What Yippie leaders did manage to do was bring a new, angrier rhetoric to a simmering area and provoke Mayor Daley into responding. Slogans such as "We will burn Chicago to the ground" and "We will fuck on the beaches" grabbed headlines, and police attention.[113] In January, Rubin spoke publicly, offering, "I support everything which puts people into motion, which creates disruption and controversy, which creates chaos and rebirth," and that "Repression turns demonstration protests into wars. Actors into heroes. Masses of individuals into a community . . . A movement cannot grow without repression."[114] Hoffman stated, "We do not wish to project a calm, secure future. We are disruption."[115] Unlike past disruptions in Lincoln Park that consisted of picketing and public outcry, Yippie made direct threats on personal safety, shifting the dynamic of conflict in the neighborhood from verbal disagreements over urban renewal to physical threats to the established order. Threatening to float ten thousand nude bodies in Lake Michigan and kidnapping delegates amused those in on the joke.[116] However, Daley wasn't in on it, and his police kept up on Yippie rantings in the news, accepting them as fact.[117] Hoffman and Rubin saw Yippie as a myth to which anyone could contribute meaning. Daley's contribution was to define the group as dangerous and increase the police presence in the Lincoln Park neighborhood.

The mayor's fears mirrored national concerns in the late 1960s. In cities such as Newark and Detroit and in Los Angeles's Watts, violence spawned by racial tensions erupted. Americans watched on TV as cars burned, smoke rose, and street melees unfolded on screen. President Johnson formed the National Advisory Commission on Civil Disorders (aka the Kerner Commission) to investigate. Chicago hosted violence on Division Street and its West Side in 1966 while 128 other cities faced disorder in 1967 alone.[118] To snuff such conflict in 1968, Daley dispatched his police months in advance.

As early as 1967, the Chicago police had increased patrolmen and the number of plainclothes detectives in Old Town.[119] During the summer of 1968 city hall adopted a twofold strategy against protesters: stalling their attempts to gain permits, and escalating police harassment of anyone who looked hip. Daley was not going to allow New York hippies to push him around. He saw protesters as a threat to the city and he viewed public space as a place in which citizens could congregate only if they followed his orders.[120] His press secretary later commented, "We didn't want hippies to come."[121] The mayor's desire to stand firm and not lose face clouded his judgment. As Mike Royko pointed out, Lincoln Park (the park, not the neighborhood) was a sheltered, out-of-the way area miles from the International Amphitheater. Surrounded by Lake Michigan on one side, buildings and traffic on the other, it would have been an effective place to contain a hippie presence.[122] Daley's foot soldiers in the Chicago Police Department also saw hips as some kind of threat, although they did not always know what kind, or who was hip and who was not. In general, they saw those on the fringe as "radicals looking to do harm."[123]

Seed dutifully covered convention news and cases of police harassment. By mid-March, *Seed* reported "several incidents lately of cops hassling our salesmen, holding them without charges, confiscating their papers." The next issue again detailed police harassment, but also advised readers abroad to plan their transportation, form their own guerilla theater groups, bring money, and "practice" agitating for convention week.[124] Peck then left town for the month of March and Stephen Treeman of *Seed* took over negotiations with the city for the permits required to hold the festival.[125]

Foreshadowing

New York Yippies failed to provide strong and consistent leadership in Chicago in the summer of 1968, but thanks in part to aggressive rhetoric, they did provide tension. However, Chicagoans acted to confront issues and plan for the Festival of Life as their attention shifted from urban renewal to surviving the festival. They rehearsed for August in April during the unrest following Martin Luther King Jr.'s assassination and during an antiwar protest on April 27.

On Thursday, April 4, Martin Luther King, Jr., fell dead to an assassin's bullet in Memphis. In response, protests occurred throughout the nation and on the West Side of Chicago. By Friday afternoon, thousands of Black youths left school and met at Garfield Park. Within hours, the destruction of property began. Daley mobilized the National Guard and issued his famous "shoot to kill arsonists" and "maim looters" order.[126] Authorities arrested 3,120 people.[127]

Chicago activists, attuned to protests in cities across the nation, had already begun to prepare for the possibility of violence. NSCM established the Summer Task Force in April of 1968 to plan for housing, food, and other problems anticipated for summer, and August in particular.[128] The task force offered up twenty-three different ways to prepare for the summer. Among them were education of youth and police, coordinating a planned April 28 demonstration to protest racism, and establishing legal, medical, and counseling centers as "We take the crisis potential of large numbers of youth seriously."[129]

Local groups then worked to provide aid during demonstrations. Armitage Church offered food. The NSCM Summer Task Force mobilized forces to distribute food and clothing via the Common Pantry for some 90 of the 120 hours of protest, and an NSCM delegation confronted police about their brutality.[130] The pantry and St. Theresa's Church were centers for food, clothing, and blankets. Students at McCormick Theological Seminary and the Unitarian Universalist Center for Urban Ministry raised bail. The group North Equal Housing arranged for housing for families that had lost their homes in fires, and lawyers dedicated free legal services as other residents contributed food, clothing, and money. The *Lincoln Park Press* ran a special "post-riot evaluation issue." In its front-page story "Law and Order . . . a cure for violence?" the paper attacked the city for indiscriminate arrests and poor jail conditions. It also detailed the bond-posting process some 2,800 adults and juveniles endured. As protesters did not expect mass arrests, they did not arrange for enough legal aid, and so the process was slow; some were in jail up to a day and a half before obtaining bail. This would prove a valuable lesson for August, when legal and other types of aid would be more readily available. The issue also covered the aid provided to riot victims by Lincoln Park residents.[131] An April 29, 1968, flyer titled "Community Needs to Meet the Urban Crisis" claimed that "If one would plot the riot areas during the past week, one would see that those areas which have strong community organizations did not break out in rioting."[132]

If the Daley administration's response to this unrest did not send a clear message to those planning to attend in August, its reaction to a Chicago antiwar protest on April 27 must have. Clark Kissinger envisioned a protest parade into the Loop that would also serve as a "trial run" for August.[133] The city's stonewalling of Chicago Peace Council leaders' attempts to secure permits for the gathering, followed by violence during the event, perfectly foreshadowed its tactics for the Democratic National Convention.[134] The attempt to gain a permit for the event met with resistance from city hall, which claimed the area planned for the protest needed repairs.[135] The Chicago Police collected information on the ACLU, warning the city's deputy superintendent that the group would seek an order allowing the protest.[136] As rumors swirled that the city would grant permits at the last minute, some 6,500 protesters gathered at Grant Park for a rally before the parade. After finally securing a permit to march on an assigned route restricted to sidewalks, the group rallied and then walked into the Loop, staying on sidewalks and obeying traffic lights as policemen attempted to hold things up. As the group moved into City Hall Plaza, it found that area roped off and the police moved in, ordering them to disperse. Police used force, and arrested eighty persons and injured another twenty. Civil libertarians established the Sparling Commission, headed by President Emeritus of Roosevelt University Edward Sparling, to investigate. The commission blamed the police for the violence, while the city blamed protesters.[137] Another march occurred May 4 at Daley Plaza, and while some 2,800 people attended with no permits, no police brutality ensued.[138]

The Free City Survival Committee

After April's taste of what could happen in August, Lincoln Park residents saw the potential for catastrophe and moved even closer to prevent one, taking leadership roles in festival planning. As Hoffman and Rubin traveled and made comical and well-publicized threats against the city, and in the face of police harassment and stalling by the city over permits, Lincoln Park residents from NSCM, *Seed*, and CCLP joined forces to form the Free City Survival Committee in May. As Chicago followed San Francisco in establishing a hip subculture, the Chicago Free City group evolved in the wake of the Digger Free City network established in the Bay Area by the end of 1967.[139] Free City really provided the infrastructure to the Festival of Life that prevented the week from becoming a total disaster. In some narratives of the 1960s, the counterculture undermined the more serious activism of groups such as SDS as stoned dimwittedness and radical talk displaced dedicated organizing.[140] In Chicago, a politicized counterculture combined elements of community planning and the hip scene to be the driving force preparing for a political and social protest.

NSCM's Jon Tuttle said Free City founders adopted their name, "because the name 'Yippie' was found to provoke police action" and that it "represented the non-conforming youths of Chicago and it took the responsibility of negotiating for the Yippie group in New York because of the need for weekly and bi-weekly conferences with city officials."[141] Peck said Free City wanted to accomplish more than just what the Yips intended in terms of protest, and that it was needed due to the more severe police repression hips in Chicago faced.[142] The group also handled negotiations with the city. In a letter to Stahl on behalf of Free City, Peck, apparently attempting to mend fences in the wake of Hoffman's and Rubin's March appearance, contritely wrote "let me apologize for the number of people at our first meeting. A committee (consisting of myself and two other members of Free City) has been formed for the purpose of such negotiations in the hope of streamlining communications."[143] Free City announced its presence to the hip community in a summer edition of *Seed*, indicating it intended to open a free medical clinic as counterculture activists did in Los Angeles and San Francisco.[144] Later, the *Liberation News Service*, a national outlet, hailed Free City as "a genuine community digger thing."[145]

The convergence of hip and minister was no small event, and underscores how seriously each group took August and how flexible Chicago's counterculture was. As early as 1967, *Seed* ran ads announcing the formation of groups such as NSCM's Vanguard Ministry, which wanted to "create channels for confrontation, dialogue, and understanding between the young adult, the church, and the community" through its workshop, free bakery, its aid to the local LSD Rescue group, and through its planned bookstore.[146] In doing so the magazine linked clergy with counterculture, and now the two came together in a move that might sound contradictory to some hips. By definition, the counterculture set itself apart from the community around it. Even the Diggers, perhaps the most organized countercultural group, established Free Stores and public events to liberate people from the dominant culture rather than work within it.[147] In Chicago, hips cooperated with allies in the clergy, and within the confines of politics and diplomacy, to move the festival ahead.

Additionally, splits occurred within the counterculture as a whole that impeded unification, making the creation of a hip-clergy-community confederacy in Chicago all the more distinct. Timothy Miller speaks to the eroding sense of countercultural unity when he addresses communes. He argues that even without solid statistics on the lives of hip communes, their "average longevity could not have been high" and that failed communes resulted from a lack of coherent vision going in, failure to enforce rules, or inability to change goals in response to changing conditions. Ironically, individuals drawn to communes were "terrible candidates for group living."[148] Chicago hips understood that August required an alliance to prevent open war and reached out to those they otherwise may have ignored. This union would prove key when the convention and festival began. David Lewis Stein realized how isolated the New York Yippies were as the convention dawned, writing, "We had established a beachhead in Lincoln Park, but that was all. We had no feeling for the life of the city and we could only guess at what the casual observers thought of us."[149]

Chicago hips, on the other hand, very much had a feel for the city. By March of 1968, NSCM relied on task forces to create shelters for the upcoming convention.[150] The ministry designated its Summer Task Force to handle the "Summer Crisis." The task force negotiated with churches and agencies for food, medical, housing, and refugee aid. In April, NSCM established a Racism Task Force. It talked to the police department about developing a racial sensitivity program, picketed to address the racism of white churches, and worked with the ACLU to "test . . . the unconstitutional ordinances passed by City [sic] which close the right to peaceful dissent." From May through July members helped mobilize youth in Lake View to "deal with police." The shooting of an area youth by police also occupied the force, which called for a Police Review Board to "deal with youth/police conflict." To aid this, the ministry's Racism Committee acquired materials from the Houston Police on sensitivity training for policemen.[151]

Concerned with what it called the "summer crisis," named its number one priority, NSCM selected Rev. Jonathan Tuttle as representative to Free City.[152] His appointment initially stemmed from an NSCM Ministry to Emerging Peoples with a focus on what it termed the Yippie/Hippie Community. The ministry intended to bring "conversation between the spiritual values of the Young People and the spiritual values of the Christian faith."[153] It was to be a way to deal with religious questions in the area, and an instrument to create self-help and support structures such as legal and medical aid, job help, and support to the Free City Survival Committee.[154] Like those in Chicago's counterculture, the ministry feared the worst in August. It asserted that the key issues facing the Yippie/Hippie community were of "survival" for pregnant women, against sexually transmitted diseases and drugs, arrest, the draft, as well as problems faced by runaways. NSCM planned to work with Free City, Head Imports, *Seed*, and the Yippies, arguing, "The whole question of Life Style is now being raised on the basis of survival." Tuttle, who one newspaper referred to as "the type of minister the hippies appreciated" alone served as staff.[155] He made his views against the war known to the hip community in 1967 when he announced, in an open letter to *Seed*, his decision to resist selective service, writing, "I hereby declare my solidarity with those actively engaged in the resistance. I pledge myself to seek to eliminate by all non-violent means including civil disobedience and violation of unjust laws to end, abolish, or destroy the system of military conscription in the United States of America."[156]

Tuttle was a blend of clergyman and Yippie who espoused what he called "The New Evangelism." He claimed that the church failed to reach out to people who saw it as an institution that, "celebrates its guilt and responds to grace with self-righteous pew sitting and dollar giving" and that most Americans saw it as "a self-righteous and virtually stagnant institution." His evangelism paralleled Yippie concepts, as when he claimed that it was a new and "highly experimental" process in which "Symbols and demonstrations have perhaps the most potential." Echoing the founding beliefs of NSCM, he argued that in order to convince the average person of the rightness of the Church, clergy must enter the community and interact with residents, and that by being dynamic, inspirational symbols they could convince others to follow. However, he departed from the group in his assertion that ministers must live as those they minister. Tuttle believed that a clergyman must eat, sleep, and breathe with those he wished to connect with, even to the point where "one is willing to and *does* [emphasis in original] run many of the same risks as those he is involved with." He wrote admiringly of the hippie community, as "persons of great vision and total commitment to a new and emerging life style, a life style in full accord with the limited vision of the content of the Kingdom possible to me here and now." He thought that by demonstrating an acceptance of their lifestyle it allowed him the credibility to disapprove of some actions as well. This new ministry would not only bring meaning to the unchurched, but also renew the church as laypeople and clergy recommitted themselves.[157]

In the spring of 1968, NSCM began a program in which it sent information to churches throughout the nation to persuade them not to come to Chicago. Tuttle drew up action plans, proposing that the organization establish food distribution centers and crash pads for sleeping during convention week.[158] The group was so concerned about the possibility for violence in August that in March it sent Tuttle to California to personally dissuade youth from coming in August "in light of potential conflict here."[159]

Yet while Chicago hips marched to their own tune when allying with the ministry, they took inspiration from the West Coast in holding rock festivals. Part of the growth of Haight-Ashbury can be attributed to the numerous concerts held there. Rock festivals were a new way to make the communal aspirations of the counterculture more effective as, "festival participants repeatedly emphasized an overwhelming sense of community that provided an impulse for continuing communal experimentation."[160] During the summer of 1968, Chicago's Free City held numerous gatherings in Lincoln Park, most of which required assistance from the city, and Dave Stahl, for sound equipment.[161] The events were to condition both police and community for convention week.[162] Rather than storm Lincoln Park, Free City actually asked for permission to congregate via letters to the city. Sometimes permission was granted in writing and other times not.[163] The group sent a professionally typed letter to Daley and William McFetridge of the Park Commission in which it requested permission to use amplified instruments in Lincoln Park on May 28 between noon and 5 P.M. The group stated that the purpose of this "Be-In" was "to channel activities in the Old Town area towards the recreational facilities that the parks offer. This will serve to lessen the congestion on Wells Street during Sunday afternoons."[164] Even in the face of police harassment, hips acted conciliatory and responsibly in their preparations.

Stalling

Despite the diplomacy and rehearsal Be-Ins, the city refused Festival of Life permits for Free City throughout the summer of 1968, while Chicago police harassed hips. Not that hips in other cities fared much better with authorities that summer. In Berkeley, officers and hips "began to hate each other" and launched into a "guerilla war."[165] In Portland, the police chief declared a "war on hippies" and ordered the city's Lair Hill Park to close at 11 P.M.[166] At Venice Beach and on the Sunset Strip cops targeted hips, harassing them on the street and charging them with loitering to clear them out.[167] New York Yips also felt the heat. Police busted their "Yip-In" at Grand Central Station in March, and in June police broke into Jerry Rubin's apartment, arrested him for possession of marijuana, and beat him.[168]

In the national narrative of the 1960s, 1968 has been noted as a turning point in US and, increasingly, world history, as students rioted not just in the United States, but in France, Germany, and Italy, and Soviet tanks rolled into Czechoslovakia to crush protesters.[169] In Chicago, 1968 was a turning point as well, but the change began before August. *Seed* writer Al Rosenfeld predicted a violent year, offering, "Be prepared, however, to cope with the harsh reality of violence. Don't let anyone tell you that your head is safe because it's an election year or because you happen to be young."[170] Another predicted a summer of police harassment and violence, arguing,

"In short, the police are prepared to wage war against the poor and oppressed of Chicago," and referred to officers as "Dangerous, and often sadistic."[171] Relations between grassroots activists and the city soured throughout the summer even as Chicago hips, ministers, and concerned citizens continued to reach out and work with city officials in a peaceful and organized manner in preparation for August. However, given resistance from city hall and the actions of officers on the streets, the picture of what August would be like was becoming clearer and clearer. If you were on the streets of Old Town in the summer of 1968, the forecast was bloody in a year of calamity and distress.

In spring Free City, in a request that again highlights its pragmatic and orderly approach, asked Dave Stahl to put in writing what they could do to cooperate with authorities during the August Festival of Life.[172] Stahl did just this, providing a typewritten list of eight major points. Point one was that Yips should self-police. Point two was "Obey our laws," namely those regarding curfew, drug use, indecent exposure, obtaining permits, and disturbing the peace. He also urged for open communication between the groups, and that they develop alternative housing plans for the convention as Grant Park was off limits.[173] Even with point-by-point, easy-to-follow instructions, the city did not believe that activists would obey, and continued its two-fold strategy of stalling and harassment. Resistance from the city resulted in a compromise of sorts: instead of Grant Park, adjacent to the convention, protesters could have Lincoln Park, secluded miles north of the amphitheater . . . or so they were told.

On April 25, Chicago police busted a Yip meeting on Clark Street, searched seventy people, and arrested eighteen on charges of disorderly conduct, resisting arrest, and drug possession.[174] According to one witness, police entered guns drawn, failed to state Miranda rights, and made arrests as hips made apple pies for their upcoming Apple Pie and Mother's Day Parade.[175] *Seed* got another dose of harassment after it announced a meeting to discuss plans for the "Apple Pie—Mother's Day Parade" event. Officers, who had a warrant for the host of the event for marijuana distribution, rousted the approximately forty individuals who gathered in his third-floor apartment. Six policemen, axes in hand, searched everyone in the room and found a "small quantity" of marijuana and LSD; they let some people go and held twenty-one others. Officers charged eighteen with disorderly conduct, and "keeping a disorderly house." That evening those busted posted bail raised by others.[176] Peck then called Hoffman in New York, informing him that the police had become "particularly vicious" and asked him to get in touch with Chicago city officials.[177]

Chicago Yips' next rehearsal for August was the Mother's Day Parade on May 13. Some three hundred persons attended the event, wandering in and out of Old Town. Tuttle performed wedding ceremonies, and Yips delivered a multitude of pies to the Chicago Police.[178] Shortly thereafter, blending counterculture and commerce, was a carefully planned Craft-In. Rules such as "No hassling of straights," and "Remittance of sales tax to the Survival Committee representative, with forms to be provided," reaffirm the more orderly form of commercial counterculture in Old Town.[179] Around that same time, Free City held a public sale along with other groups, advertising everything from hash pipes to stamp collections.[180]

On May 20, Free City held a benefit at the Electric Theater to pay off the fourteen hundred dollars in legal fees incurred from the apartment bust, but this only brought more harassment. An estimated 1,750 people attended. Peck watched as police gathered outside ready to enforce the 10:30 P.M. curfew for those under seventeen years of age and the midnight one for those under eighteen. Officers made their presence known, and kids began to "get up tight." When the police finally made their move, they arrested thirty-four, including the managers of the theater. Peck later noted that this was odd as, by law, the city was to notify a child's parents of a first curfew violation, not make an arrest. That night, police took all the arrested minors to the twentieth precinct house and booked them. Officers broke cameras and the band Canned Heat's amplifiers. Some partiers agitated for violence, but the majority of the crowd endorsed passive resistance.[181] Lincoln Park residents noticed and empathized. That night, Peck collected one thousand dollars from neighbors to pay for bail.[182]

A few nights later Peck met with Stahl at the *Seed* office under cover of darkness to continue permit negotiations. Stahl committed to nothing, offering "Gee, guys, you can't expect the mayor to allow dope and fornication in his front lawn." The only agreements reached were that they would not meet in the *Seed* office anymore, and that both sides would write up lists of requests they would share at their next meeting. Stahl also indicated that Grant Park was not a viable option from the city's point of view.[183]

Given continued police harassment, it was obvious some other plan was necessary. Police officers continued to target those with long hair, and one weekend officers arrested seventy-four persons on disorderly conduct charges, which they later dropped.[184] *Seed* distributors faced arrest, and later found charges against them dropped after the booking, message sent. On two consecutive nights in late May, tactical units swept through Old Town "to clear out loitering and loud-mouthed groups, some of whom have scared away customers in recent months," arresting sixty-five people who sat on doorsteps and congregated outside businesses. One sergeant noted, "Old Town was made for hippies and we don't want to drive them away but we don't want them bothering people."[185] Local Yips fought back by engaging the ACLU and appealing to attorneys and local residents. Still, fighting Daley intimidated some and one lawyer only agreed to help off the record, arguing, "I have to practice law in this town." Abbie Hoffman flew into Chicago to see what he could do. Chicago hips informed him that the Daley administration was more receptive to locals, and Hoffman flew back to New York.[186]

In spite of the pressure, Chicago hips continued civil discourse. After the Mother's Day and Apple Pie gathering, Free City sent a three-page letter to Stahl outlining its upcoming plans and appealing to him for assistance. Speaking directly to the harassment it faced, the group opened with, "It is unfortunate that our appearance and dress create as much animosity and discrimination as it does, particularly on the part of law enforcement officials, and we hope that you can help to minimize this discriminatory practice." The group informed him it was attempting to provide housing, jobs, and shelter for the "large numbers" of people coming to them for aid, and asked that the city help by providing necessary permits for gatherings, medical care via the North Side Medical Clinic, office supplies such as brooms and reams of paper, and inclusion in the Grant Park Summer Music Festival. Additionally, the group asked that youth not have to post bond when arrested by police. Free City also made known its neighborhood improvement plans for the summer, including "Sweep-ins" to clean up Old Town, plans for Sunday Park Festivals with free music, "Paint-ins" during which "walls, rocks and sidewalks will be designated beautification areas," and "Plant-ins" to replace glass and debris-covered vacant lots with flora. The group also sought to improve communication and understanding with the city, noting "We recognize that one of the causes of poor relations between our community and the police and city officials has been their misunderstanding of our life style. An open and free exposition of our beliefs and aspirations for the immediate future would do much to alleviate existing tension."[187] Such programs indicate that planners really felt themselves members of the Lincoln Park community, concerned with local issues ranging from litter to police brutality.

The city was not terribly interested. The end of May marked the first Be-In of 1968, but by June the Park District again attempted to block gatherings. One activist recalled that the district's attorney claimed that the city's insurance liability was a factor, and that the permits needed to be submitted by a certain time. By this point, Chicago Yippies had enlisted an attorney to work with Dave Stahl to get the concerts back on track.[188] On June 1 they held a "Bust-In" to protest the arrests made during the May sweep of Old Town, daring police officers to arrest them. Police ignored them.[189]

Neither the harassment nor the runarounds dissuaded hips from seeking the right to protest, and they still did so following protocol. On June 5, they held another meeting with the city, this time at a private home. They presented a list concerning summer activities and the festival. Stahl examined it and countered with a short, prepared letter that only indicated nothing illegal could occur during the festival. Tuttle was present and took issue with Stahl's treatment of the group; Stahl "felt bad about it and backed off." He then reiterated the city's point that Grant Park was out of the question. Al Baugher, part of the city's Commission on Youth Welfare, then appeared, and Stahl indicated that Baugher would be handling negotiations from now on: another stalling tactic. To Peck, from this point meetings became unimportant. Tuttle, however, wanted to move forward, feeling that the more planning Free City undertook, the better they could prevent violence in August. Baugher later escorted Free City members to Soldier Field, offering it up as a potential site, and took Tuttle and another planner to Navy Pier and the Edgewater Beach Hotel to inspect them as possible locations. Free City refused these offers, Tuttle phoning Peck in New York (where he was meeting with Hoffman and Rubin) to inform him that the Pier was so filthy it would take enormous amounts of time just to clean it. The group also feared that Soldier Field could entrap them should police attack. However, members did agree on Lincoln Park in part because, as Peck said, "we wanted to do a rural thing in an urban center."

In late June, the Free City Survival Committee met again to discuss plans for August. It was now that Peck, recognizing the warning signs, moved to cancel the festival as the city clearly was not going to cooperate. Those opposing him felt that events were already too far along to quit now and it was better to be as organized as possible rather than nihilistic.[190]

Residents of Old Town at North Clark Street. Chicago Public Library, 7233.

Displays such as this one, of the General Neighborhood Renewal Plan, communicated urban renewal plans to Lincoln Park Residents. Chicago Public Library, 3757.

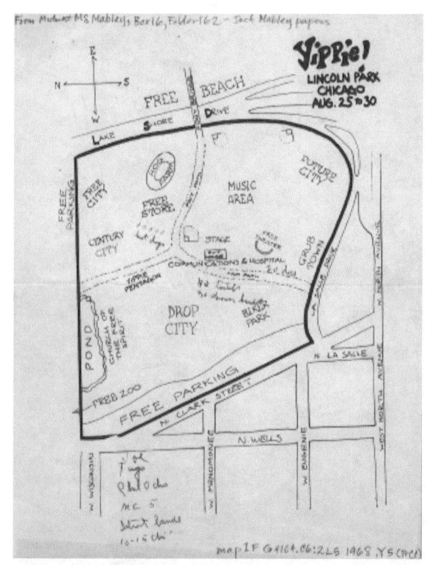

Map of the Yippie "Festival of Life." Newberry Library Website.

NORTH SIDE COOPERATIVE MINISTRY CONVENTION MOBILIZATION "HELP CENTERS"

North side Co-operative Ministry   281-0690   8:30- 4:30 p.m.
  contacts: David Doering, Owen Evans, Jonathan Tuttle
Jerry Jaecks, NSCM PEACE TASK FORCE: 353-6137 or 549-6996
Harry Sharp, NSCM SUMMER CRISIS TASK FORCE: 321-7168   GR28257

* Staff: Jonathan Tuttle: 549-1059, 935 6910
    David Doering: 248-7096, 281-0690
* SDS: 6663674 ((Joe or Wayne: 973-0759 or 927-3184)
* Mio Job Co-op: Dave Wyatt: 822-0651
  Coalition for Open Convention: 372-4172
  Coanon Amery: 327-0553
* Chicago Peace Council (Housing June Radke: 243-0022
* National Mobilization: Ag Winkler: 348-5157
          Office: 939 2666
  Laity and Clergy Concerned: 955-7965
* Newsletter: Cynthia Cusa: 248-8169
        Pat Divine (Concerned Citizens: 348-6842
  Church Federation: Douglas Still: Fr22427   Bruce Young: 477-2184
  LPCA: 477-5100
  Seed: (YIP) 337-2623   Daily Ramparts: 829-1381 243-1874
  McCarthy Headquarters: Hilton 922-4400, Amphitheater: 341-1825
  Medical Centers: Volunteers: Ruth Migdal: 248-3559 or Gr28257
    McCormick (North Side: 8:30- 5:50 LI94540, LI94541
    Belden and Halsted   5 pm - 8:30 a.m. LI93701, LI93702, LI93703,
    starting 5 p.m. August 24th   LI94540, LI94541
    St. Chrysostom's , 1424 N. Dearbourn,

    Church Federation, 116 S1 Michigan FR22427

    Trinity Chu ch, 125 E. 26th Street   (Father Lawrence)

HELP CORPS EMERGENCY (Food and clothing): RA6-0363

LSD Rescue : 642-7937, 664-1422
Cook County Jail: (Rev. Carolina Hampton, Chaplain): LA30101

Runaway Center: Grace Church 555 W. Belden : LI91002   Youth Influx: 664-1144
Reports on Police Behavior and Brutality: 252-6729 (Richard Rosenfield)

LEGAL AID: 641-1470, 641-1471, 641-1472 Mob: 243-2672

NSCM CHURCH MOBILIZATION CENTERS

  Armitage Avenue Church, 834 W. Armitage: LI95407 (BOSTON)
  Parish Of Holy Covenant 925 W. Diversey 348-6842 (HIGH SCHOOL YOUTH) 348-8578
  Church of Our Savior, 520 W. Fullerton LI9-3832
          (PEOPLE AGAINST RACISM: DETROIT)
  Wellington UCC, 615 W. Wellington WE5- 0642 (CLEVELAND)
  Church of Three Crosses, 1900 N. Sedgwick MI29232 (SDS)

  Messiah Lutheran Church, 3309 N. Seminary (Detroit People) 525-0605

Kitchens:
  St. Paul's Church, Orchard and Fullerton: DI83829
  Christian Fellowship, 912 W. Sheridan DI80770
  Parish of Holy Covenant, Diversey and Wilton 348-6842

Cars
  Messiah Lutheran Church: 525-0605
  Parish of Reconciliation, 1655 N. School 935-4341

Emergency Housing (only for emergency needs) (PLEASE CALL FOR RESERVATIONS)
  Parish of Reconciliation: 935-4341   Messiah Lutheran: 525-0605
  McCormick Seminary : LI93700   Lincoln Park Church: 248 8288

Flyer distributed by the North Side Cooperative Ministry. Lincoln Park Conservation Association Records, Box 79, Folder 16, Special Collections and Archives, DePaul University Library, Chicago, Illinois.

Festival attendees were surprised at the enforcement of the 11 P.M. curfew in Lincoln Park. ST-60004357–0008, Chicago Sun-Times collection, Chicago History Museum.

National Guard, NBC News truck in front of a demonstration outside the Hilton Hotel. Chicago History Museum, ICHi-065713; Peter Bullock, photographer.

Ministers from the Church of the Three Crosses set up the Tuesday night church service in Lincoln Park. Church of the Three Crosses.

Lots such as this were hotly contested in 1969. Chicago Public Library, 5956.

Protester being removed from Department of Urban Renewal Meeting. Chicago Public Library, 7654.

The Young Lords takeover of McCormick Theological Seminary. Collection on McCormick Seminary, Box 1, Folder 12, Special Collections and Archives, DePaul University Library, Chicago, Illinois.

Two buttons of Jose "Cha Cha" Jimenez. Grand Valley State University Special Collections and University Archives.

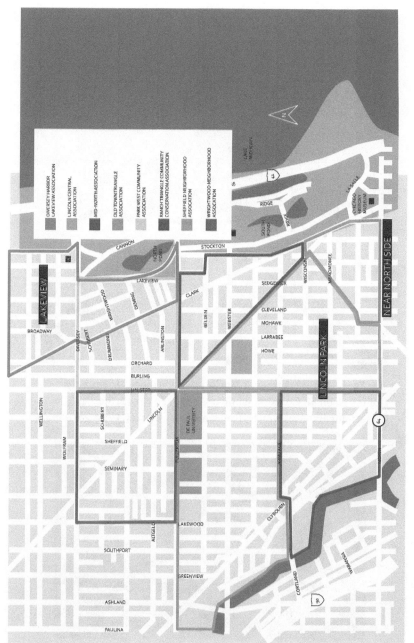

Map of modern-day Lincoln Park neighborhoods. Lincoln Park Chamber of Commerce.

CHAPTER FOUR

"Wear Some Armor in Your Hair"

"Chicago may host a Festival of Blood . . ."
—*Seed*

Urban Renewal 1968

While Free City planned, those promoting change in urban renewal also followed orderly paths to further their vision. James Reed ran for LPCA president again in January. He complained, "the present leadership has shown more interest in solidifying its control than solving the problems of the community" and called the group a "private club."[1] Again resorting to covert tactics to hinder their opponents, LPCA's Nominating Committee did not submit the challengers' slate. So, the candidates entered into the race via petition, in accordance with association bylaws.[2] Election results reveal just how little support the movement for broader inclusion had. Roland Whitman swept into office with 433 votes, trouncing Reed's 59. Dennis Cunningham took only 53 votes for first vice presidency, his opponent 432. NSCM minister Larry Dutenhaver ran unopposed for the second vice presidency and still only had 255 votes.[3]

While it tried to gain influence in the association, CCLP proposed its manifesto "An Action Platform for Lincoln Park," to LPCA members in January.[4] The group again berated LPCA for failing to serve low- and moderate-income families, while allowing land speculators to buy real estate with no resistance and focusing on "East side concerns as the trees in Lincoln Park."[5]

CCLP continued to draw attention to community issues via the *Lincoln Park Press*, but now reached out to the Puerto Rican community, largely ignored in renewal dialogue. The February issue gave page one coverage to area Puerto Ricans who it claimed were "exploited by weekly rents." It criticized LPCA for refusing to act on behalf of lower-income residents and for worrying about "eliminating voices of dissent from its board and committees," while "About 900 families have been ousted from the area through urban renewal clearance." The paper presented a "Demolition Scorecard" that counted 186 buildings demolished under Project I, but none built. It also listed 1,211 "Families or single residents displaced by urban renewal," 939 "families or single residents who had to leave Lincoln Park because of Urban Renewal," and 272 "Families and single residents able to remain in Lincoln Park."[6] CCLP called for residents to unify. Asserting that housing and education were the two "major" concerns, writers expressed concern that these matters were in the hands of the federal government, real estate agencies, housing corporations, banks, landlords, and the DUR rather than the rank and file of Lincoln Park.[7]

In that issue, only one letter to the editor, from the North Side Students for a Democratic Society chapter, appeared. In it, SDS singled out a local resident, and (after providing her address) lambasted her for racist practices as a landlord. It detailed her harassment of a Black tenant, charging that she at one point "took a police officer in" the renter's apartment as a form of intimidation and that her apartments were found in violation of Board of Health and Department of Buildings codes. The paper again promoted community by lauding the actions of neighborhood mothers who successfully petitioned to close off Bissell Street twice a week for a few hours allowing children to play. *Press* editors revealed that they ran an abridged version of this story in their first paper due to space limitations, but chose to rerun it in expanded form "Because we hope to encourage more local action by mothers of the neighborhood." The paper also noted that the frustrated CCLP began to shift tactics. Concerned Citizens now targeted the city's Conservation Community Council as the path to change rather than the privately run LPCA, calling for the "expansion of and free election of members to" the CCC.[8]

Keeping urban renewal and education front-page news continued in the next issue, which was part cheerleader, part attack dog. It criticized what it sarcastically dubbed an "open hearing" of the CCC, reporting that the majority of residents in attendance supported the addition of new sites for low- and moderate-income families. Additionally, Mayor Daley's representative at the meeting caused agitation when he suggested that only three of the new sites, rather than the six proposed by CCLP, be reserved for low-income housing. The *Press* reported that residents did not feel he had the "right to speak at a *community* [emphasis in original] hearing." The paper's editorial asserted that DUR planned to turn Lincoln Park into a place for upper-income residents only, and that "savings and loans, together with banks seem to be in collusion with real estate against individuals and families."[9] NSCM announced that its goal for 1968 was to gain more moderate- and low-income housing and officially joined Concerned Citizens of Lincoln Park. Dave Doering asserted, "we are basically trying to mobilize technicians and resources" for the housing fight and that the group in particular intended to provide aid to the counterculture.[10]

Feeling public pressure from this new, more assertive group, LPCA turned to its old ally, the city, for aid. When the LPCA board met on January 29, 1968, Roland Whitman read aloud a letter sent to Rev. Larry Dutenhaver in which he informed the minister that he knew of plans by Concerned Citizens to picket an upcoming fundraising luncheon. He then asked a fellow member to pass this information along to Mayor Daley.[11]

LPCA's board of directors gave some attention to community representation in LPCA at the May 8, 1968, meeting in a moment that again reveals how white liberals in the area remained unready for broader change. It accomplished little more than repeatedly offering the vague idea of opening lines of communication with other groups. The only motion passed was to "review point by point at our next meeting the 'Action Platform for Lincoln Park,' put out by the Concerned Citizens to start doing something about some of these things, such as low income housing for Project II, that we have been ignoring." The notion of taking CCLP seriously did not last long. At the June 26 LPCA board meeting, the group immediately struck the motion to address the Concerned Citizens Action Platform.[12]

A major showdown between members of the CCLP, LPCA, and NSCM occurred at a ministry open hearing on June 8. As the meeting began, NSCM members decided that their organization would further consider supporting local groups including the LPCA and Concerned Citizens, the Common Pantry, the Hip Job Co-op, and the Legal Aid clinic.[13] CCLP then presented a proposal for aid in which the group claimed that its mailing list had grown from two hundred to four hundred in the last few months. It also argued that with increased financial support from NSCM, the *Lincoln Park Press* would circulate to ten thousand people in the area.[14] Addressing urban renewal, architect and LPCA member John Alschuler urged NSCM to research and utilize existing housing programs, and outlined the types of programs already in place. He noted that "Past experience indicates that if RESIDENTS will ORGANIZE, determine FEASIBILITY and develop a specific PLAN FOR ACTION, the City and its sub-divisions

(DUR-CHA—CDA-FHA, etc.) will make every endeavor to assist them in accomplishing their goals [caps in original]."[15]

LPCA's president Roland Whitman then took the stage and blasted NSCM. Admitting he knew little of the group, Whitman asked those in attendance to convey a message to the heads of the churches of Lincoln Park. He indicated that many local ministers were "very uninformed, even misinformed" about LPCA's work. Furthermore, "It has become very fashionable among some of them to use the Conservation Association as a whipping boy, to dismiss it as a group of middle-class bigots which has no claim to play in any role of the life of the total community." He pointed out that NSCM members were "performing their tasks as part of and in furtherance of their vocations," while LPCA members went unpaid and thought, "appreciation of this point of difference should lessen the temptation toward sanctimoniousness." He then charged that financial contributions to LPCA by ministry members were "grossly inadequate" and that NSCM failed to "provide adequate staffing for the [food] Pantry, with the intolerable result that our staff was required to turn away hungry people." Next, he turned his attention to the issue of low and moderate-income housing. Refuting accusations that LPCA was indifferent to the plight of the poor, Whitman asserted that "LPCA is the *only* [emphasis in original] body in this community that has been willing to take the time and effort to develop and present to the Conservation Community Council a specific plan for increasing the amount of low and moderate income housing for Project I." And although NSCM members were on the LPCA sub-committee dealing with this issue, they criticized LPCA while their "participation was negligible. They attended virtually no meetings of the subcommittee." Whitman further defended LPCA by noting the Chicago Housing Authority leased housing program that, thanks in part to Conservation Association members, made funds available for three hundred rehabilitated leased housing units on the city's North Side (should the program move forward). He concluded his diatribe by suggesting, again, that NSCM members contribute more financially to urban renewal, and further offered that Lincoln Park churches could consolidate and turn some of their buildings into housing for the poor.[16] At the June 26, 1968, meeting of LPCA's board of directors, a motion to commend Whitman for his presentation passed unanimously.[17]

Whitman's, and his allies', anger was partially justified as some of them were coming around to the idea of broader inclusion of and aid to the marginalized. Various LPCA committees made their annual reports in February. The Planning Committee recommended that six sites be redesignated from private development sites to low or moderate-income housing units. The Human Relations Committee "studied ways in which the community and the schools can work more closely on youth problems, and sought assistance for displaced persons through Leased Housing."[18] On Monday nights in March, LPCA's office housed the Lincoln Park-Lake View Legal Advice Clinic, a legal counseling service staffed by attorneys affiliated with the Church Federation of Greater Chicago. Sixty percent of clinic clients spoke only Spanish, and in 1967 over 350 families obtained aid from this project.[19]

LPCA's endorsement of the *Alschuler Report* in late June would have been, in the board's eyes, conclusive evidence of concern for low-income residents as early as 1968. In May, an LPCA subcommittee on housing headed by John Alschuler, after studying the area for six months, proposed amending Project I to include more low-income housing, increasing it from one-third to two-thirds, along with building sixty middle-income housing units for a mix of low-, moderate-, and middle-income units. In June, the board unanimously *approved* the plan.[20] For CCLP members, however, the process moved too slowly. The years of resistance were too much, and instead of seeing this as a victory and a sign that the two sides could find common ground, the amendment looked to be too little, too late.

July

As the debate over urban renewal grew more heated, so did the debate over the Festival of Life. What began in a New York City apartment had, by July, become something to worry about in Chicago. While meetings with the city still occurred, Stahl missed half of them and Peck's Free City group became less interested in the convention as it was a "downer... You couldn't get near the Amphitheater anyway, we figured because the security would be so tight." By this time, he figured it would be better "to do something positive and to do our own thing and demonstrate our cultural alternative."[21] Free City branched out through the month. Now among its confederation were the Hip Job Co-op and other groups. Free City also ran ads in *Seed* asking for help with summer programs and announced that it intended to establish a free medical clinic, as activists in Los Angeles and San Francisco had.[22]

Peck now noticed a rift growing between Chicago and New York Yips, and between Hoffman and Rubin. The New Yorkers, especially Rubin, had come to view the convention as a more SDS style, antiwar protest rather than the cultural/political event Hoffman still envisioned. The Chicago Yips wanted, "nothing to do with the Convention, but . . . dug the idea of people coming to Chicago and grooving here." Communication between the two groups soon broke down, and Free City members began to question why they bothered to negotiate with the city. Still, the group, listening to Stahl's suggestion, submitted a second permit for permission to gather in Lincoln Park rather than Grant Park, Stahl persuasively arguing that guests often camp in the backyard rather than the front.[23] In the typed request, Free City asked permission to use the south end of Lincoln Park from 11:59 P.M., August 24 to 11:59 P.M., August 29 for "a five-day peaceful and joyous gathering dedicated to the sharing of life experiences." The group also, pragmatically, proposed boundary lines and requested assistance with sanitation and the needed permits to use microphones, bullhorns, "and other communications equipment necessary for information and the maintenance of order." In closing, they requested the use of Soldier's Field from noon to 10 P.M. on August 30 for a concluding rally.[24]

For Peck, one meeting in late July cemented his fear that the city would not really cooperate. He, Tuttle, and others met at the Chicago Police Department with the city's Al Baugher, deputy superintendent Rochford, police, and Commander Braasch and Sargeant Beutten of the Eighteenth Precinct. Rochford was concerned with drug use at the festival, and wanted to know if police officers arresting those smoking marijuana would create an incident. Stunned, Peck responded, "what do you want, a riot?" Aside from that, the meeting was professional but uneventful.[25] As things deteriorated, Free City again reconsidered its position on the festival. The group sent written notice that they intended to withdraw their permit request, argued that Free City had "no right to speak for a national coalition of youth" and indicated that another group that "could better represent the prevailing thoughts of people involved in the Festival" would submit a request.[26] During a press conference Peck warned, "If all you want to do is to lie in the sun and groove on life, stay away."[27]

August

In August NSCM, initially founded to reinvigorate religion on the North Side of Chicago, now secured kitchens, crash pads, and hospitals for convention week. The Racism Committee held a racism sensitivity work-shop and viewed films to increase racial awareness. The week before the convention, the Summer Task Force developed its medical corps, communication centers, and medical aid centers. It also designated emergency housing centers for Yippies and other young adults, developed legal resources, meeting spaces, food distribution, transportation, and contacted runaway centers.[28]

On another front, it was the charge of the Peace Task Force to "work within party and primary structures" to press the issue of the war at the convention itself. It endorsed no candidate, but sought to use "politics as education." It began planning its peace activities for August in April and examined the program of the MOBE and Laity and Clergy Concerned. From May to July, it met with those interested in protest to plan a peaceful demonstration and negotiated with the McCarthy campaign to help gain influence within the Democratic Party. By August it was involved with the pro-McCarthy group Coalition for an Open Convention. The force also transformed churches into workshop centers. Members appealed unsuccessfully to local politicians for talks the week before the convention. They also contacted convention delegates and developed their communication and mobilization centers at several churches, including Three Crosses.[29]

Jonathan Tuttle continued to build a support system among Chicago hippies, which included the Hip Job Co-op (sponsored by NSCM) that helped find jobs for the hip community.[30] From May through July he continued his negotiations with the mayor's office, worked with the Vanguard Ministry to develop a program for runaways, and sought to obtain resources and food for demonstrators. In August, he furthered his negotiations with the mayor's office until two weeks prior to the convention, when the latter called off talks. He also tried to develop a trusting relationship with the police at Yip events like the "Mother's Day Apple Pie March" and the "Bust in Old Town."[31]

In late summer, Yippies made contact with a resident who would prove key in re-defining the festival as a local protest. Around August 16 Yips ran into the owner of the Free Theater, Paul Sills, who gave them a key to the building.[32] Sills grew up in the theater and in Chicago.[33] Now a Lincoln Park resident and associate of NSCM's James Shiflett, he was interested in using his theater to connect with the community, and had been staging productions in it since 1965.[34] According to Sills: "The job of theatre artists is to unite the community with the celebration of its life ... Theatre in itself is absolutely meaningless. Theatre in the community is meaningful."[35] He had recently rented the Free Theater, a dumpy brick building on North Wells across from the park. Once home to Second City, it put on free plays, asking for donations. Sills initially declined Hoffman's request that the building, slated for destruction in coming months, be used to house demonstrators. However, he changed his mind days before the festival and allowed protesters to sleep in the theater and its courtyard, and for Yippie to place a mimeograph machine in the basement. Additionally, a local resident manned the door to negotiate with the police.[36]

Neighborhood Organizations and the Chicago Police

Other Old Town residents did not look forward to convention week. As the festival nudged hip and minister together under the Free City banner, it also brought LPCA members closer to the city and the Chicago Police Department. Much like the liberals of LPCA had a limit on the number of low-income houses they would tolerate, when it came to a political demonstration the threat of violence was the cutoff.

The Old Town Triangle Association and the Menomonee Club, a children's club, reported an increased hip presence and developed ways to combat it.[37] On July 29, 1968, the club's director wrote to the OTTA president about the "influx of youngsters into the area." He was most concerned with the boys employed by the Hip Job Co-op next to Menomonee that, he claimed, were "boys from the Cabrini homes" who were used as "pedlars [sic]." He asserted that they "roam the neighborhood . . . in a large gang." He also claimed that NSCM's Cellar "was holding itself out as a refuge for runaway hippies and any other teenagers that cared to drop in." On Willow Street, according to him, boys congregated, distributed the *Seed*, used "loud, foul and abusive language," stole bicycles, left bikes laying around, carried "dangerous objects (Hatchet, Hoe, etc.)," and harassed residents.[38] An Old Town resident wrote to "vehemently protest the influx of 'hippies' into the residential side streets . . . that we have relegated Wells Street to the barefoot set without protest should indicate how we, the people who live here, feel about the renaissance of that tourist attraction." This agitated resident argued that the St. James Unitarian Church set up a "hippie haven for runaway children" on North Park Avenue. While arguing that Old Town "is, perhaps, one of the most liberal-oriented of all the areas of

Chicago," the author also asserted that "this invasion should not be allowed, even here" and urged the association to take steps to close down the St. James coffeehouse and the church itself.[39] Other residents began to target the St. James as well, arguing that urban renewal legislation be used to deal with it. One person requested that OTTA discuss the St. James at an upcoming meeting, as not only did it sponsor loud rock bands, but attracted hippies. He closed with a suggestion: "As I recall, St. James was originally not in the GNRP [General Neighborhood Renewal Plan], but saved at the request of its pastor to be used for religious purposes. Since it is no longer needed, can't Urban Renewal be asked to take another look?"[40] The above letters, along with another dated July 29, 1968, also protested the NSCM's free STD clinic (sponsored by the Chicago Board of Health in cooperation with the Free City Survival Committee and the Vanguard Ministry, the Hip Job Co-op, and *Seed*) at the Church of the Three Crosses.[41]

As the festival loomed, these residents wanted more direct action on their behalf. In the first week of August, the OTTA's Special Committee on Neighborhood Problems, formed "to keep the Old Town Triangle area free from unlawful and destructive activities brought to our attention by letters and phone calls from residents commencing early in August."[42] On August 5, O. M. Forkert of the OTTA met with the building commissioner to discuss building violations at 240 W. Willow and the Cellar at 1718 North Park. Witnesses reported people moving used mattresses into the Cellar, and charged that someone illegally opened up the addresses of 1740–1742 North Park. Additionally, Forkert met with Commander Braasch on the sixth to ask him to check up on the Cellar and 240 W. Willow. Forkert wanted to know from where *Seed* got its money, and promised to investigate. The committee viewed urban renewal law as a way to block hips, and it discussed "trying to reach DUR with pressure and request for inspection to Fire Department on properties: 1740 N. North Park Street," along with some houses next to a grocery on Menomonee, and a stretch of unpaved street at Sedgwick and Menomonee. The group also intended to contact LPCA about the street. One member planned to speak with the commissioner of health about the Cellar and 240 W. Willow. The group also discussed the use, "if necessary," of its "newspaper contacts" and possibly "*Time* and *Newsweek*" to make hip lives difficult.[43]

Forkert followed up with Braasch by reminding the commander he left with him "copies of 8 documents concerning the lawlessness created by the shameful activities of the hippies." In this letter, copied to Mayor Daley and

Police Superintendent James Conlisk, he also reported that witnesses saw the delivery of mattresses "to the hippie hangouts at the addresses which are available from the letters given you yesterday. It is obvious that this is for the housing of these people during the Democratic Convention." He also suggested: "There are health and building code laws which prohibit such 'mass' sleeping practices, and we hope you will put an end to these activities as well as the criminal matters submitted to you yesterday."[44] Forkert was even more direct with the Building Department commissioner in a letter he copied to Daley, and Alderman George Barr McCutcheon. Reporting the same addresses that he had to Braasch, Forkert noted

> It is obvious that this is for the housing of hippies during the Democratic Convention. We request that you at once pull the violation files on these buildings and ask your Assistant Commissioner, Mr. Fitzgerald to inspect them with your task forces since there are obvious violations with our city's health and building codes. I would appreciate having a brief report on this to submit to our Board of Directors on August 15th.[45]

In September of 1968 the OTTA proudly reported its August actions to members, indicating that "arrests were made and the rash of many unlawful activities was diminished."[46] However, hips and ministers were quicker than authorities and dodged their attempts at capture and eviction. The chief of inspections reported to the building commissioner that "there was no evidence of any mattresses or sleeping accommodations" at the Church of the Three Crosses. In a blatant lie, NSCM's Rev. Whitehead informed him that the church wanted "to have no part of any of the so-called 'hippie' or radical groups connected with their organization." Nonetheless, the inspections chief alerted a police sergeant in the Eighteenth Precinct, who stopped by the church twice weekly on rounds, of the possibility of sleeping accommodations there and informed him that he should contact him if this proved true. Despite the reporting, the zoning administrator found no problem there.[47] The chief code enforcement officer echoed these findings, indicating that in his inspection of five addresses he found "no evidence of any extra mattresses or sleeping accommodations." He noted that 219–25 West Wisconsin was "Converted to a low rental rooming house. It is a possible center for hippies." Another property was vacant, and "these two buildings would possibly make ideal hangouts for undesirables. However, there was no sign or evidence of activity on August 13, 1968."[48]

Old Town residents were not the only ones investigating hippies. The Chicago Police Department's Red Squad also prepared for convention week in August, increasing the number of undercover agents on the street and communicating with intelligence groups throughout the nation.[49] The group's surveillance and harassment techniques varied, from crowd reconnaissance and photography, "electronic eavesdropping," paying off informants, undercover infiltration, and, in a moment worthy of Ian Fleming, made its headquarters in the fake corporation Midwest Continent Import and Export located on Navy Pier.[50] The squad had an agent in a high-level MOBE position, and CBS news reported that one in six demonstrators during convention week worked for the government. Even Jerry Rubin's bodyguard during the week was an undercover cop.[51]

Chicago/New York Split

Despite harassment, Free City continued attempts to obtain permits for the convention and endured obstacles from the city as Chicago activists grew distant from New York Yips.[52] Hoffman and Rubin were largely absent from Chicago until August but, in response to Peck, they and Krassner flew in to meet with Stahl. Their continued presence, however, was nonexistent. Hoffman, who put in more appearances than his colleagues, arrived in the city at the beginning of August.[53] Rubin hitchhiked there just days before the convention.[54] Weeks before it, Hoffman contacted Chicago attorney Dennis Cunningham, having obtained his name from Paul Sills, and enlisted him to represent the Yips in permit negotiations with the city.[55] Cunningham was a committed activist, having attended law school with the intent to represent those in the civil rights movement.[56]

Peck's personal relationships with Hoffman and Rubin deteriorated as he now saw the violent possibilities encouraged by the two, especially Rubin. Additionally, the two warred among themselves as to the direction the convention should take. Hoffman and his faction of New Yorkers favored a cultural event, while Rubin and his cohorts stressed violence and political protest.[57] In early August, Peck wrote "A Letter from Chicago," published by Liberation News Service and *Seed*. In it, he criticized Yippie for a lack of leadership, vision, and philosophy. He listed the reasons why there should not be a festival, including the fact that Free City only had "$25 in the bank."[58] He also highlighted the differences between

New York Yips who wanted to "shit all over the Old Men" and Chicagoans who sought a festival characterized by "fun and frolic." He concluded by warning "If you're coming to Chicago, be sure to wear some armor in your hair." Peck informed Hoffman of his ill feelings prior to publishing the letter.[59]

Part of this concern came from the fact that Chicagoans could not nail down Yippies' plans. Free City wanted a set itinerary from the New Yorkers, and when Hoffman finally presented one (the New York Yips previously claimed they needed to keep things "flexible"), Peck and others who wanted fun, not blood, found it to be more politicized and potentially violent. He claimed that it "freaked out Free City" as "suddenly self defense classes were a major activity."[60] Peck again wanted to pull out of the festival, but felt damned either way: if Free City backed out, it gave the city a green light to brutalize protesters; if it remained allied to the New Yorkers, it appeared to sponsor an event in which its members did not believe.[61]

On August 5, Peck and head-shop owner George Sells again met with members of the police department and Al Baugher. Peck detailed what was required for convention week. The park commissioner indicated that the city could install one or two toilets for the festival, and Peck was incredulous. A city official Peck did not know then informed the commissioner that demonstrators planned to sleep in the park. The commissioner then claimed he was unaware of this, and said that the city would have to reconsider the entire application. His feigned ignorance also stunned Sells who, several weeks before the convention, urged readers of the *Los Angeles Free Press* to come to Chicago, believing that the city would allow visitors to sleep in the park. In response to stalling tactics, Sells and others backpedaled, sending some 180 letters to underground papers warning potential attendees of violence. Peck felt things were coming to an impasse, as a key city official such as the park commissioner knew so little of their plans at this point.[62] He called Hoffman in New York that night, informing him that the city pretended not to know the Yips wanted to sleep in the park. He also detailed the harassment *Seed* faced, including the recent breaking of its front office window. These things made him nervous enough to consider withdrawing the permit, and he asked that Hoffman join him in Chicago to talk to city officials.[63]

Deputy Chief Robert Lynsky later offered that the Chicago Yips withdrew their initial permit request because locals knew "out-of-towners were going to come in and take over and that there would be danger of violence and destruction in the Park."[64] With less than three weeks to go until the convention, the New York and Chicago Yips met in the hot, cramped *Seed* office while "several large men parked outside" watched on. As tempers flared, the group called SDS's Tom Hayden to mediate. Evaluating Peck, he turned to Rubin and uttered "CIA."[65] Peck filled Hoffman in on police harassment, including repeated visits by Chicago's Red Squad. The groups finally decided to file a new permit, signed half by Chicago activists, half by New Yorkers. Tuttle signed, Peck did not. On August 8, the New York Yips and their Chicago allies filed the joint permit with the ACLU indicating they would take the city to court for nighttime usage of the park.[66] The Yips had their day in court on August 22 but, on learning that the judge was Daley's ex-law partner, withdrew the suit.[67]

The Free City Survival Committee published this statement in *Seed*:

The word is out. Many people are into confrontation. The Man is into confrontation. Nobody takes the Amphitheater. Cars and buildings will burn. Chicago may host a Festival of Blood . . . There will be ample opportunity to disrupt the Democratic Creep-Follies. There are many reasons to disrupt the Death Gala. If you feel compelled to cavort, then this is action city. There is no reason to wear flowers for masks. If you want to go up against the wall, then come.[68]

Countdown

Hoffman and Rubin's threats to put LSD in the water supply, kidnap and seduce delegates, and float nude bodies in Lake Michigan during convention week were the first public gauntlets thrown down in the Festival of Life.[69] Daley, then, posted guards around the Chicago water supply. Now, as the convention and festival loomed, tensions heightened. On August 18, the Intelligence Division of the Chicago Police Department began surveillance in Lincoln Park. Undercover police photographers snapped pictures of leaders, or those they suspected as being leaders. Undercover agents mingled about the crowd. On August 20, officer Robert Lynsky requested more manpower in Lincoln Park, and the result was that the Chicago Police Department increased officers' shifts from eight hours to twelve.[70]

Chicago residents caught between Yippie rhetoric and police intimidation continued demonstration planning. Free City worked with the Student

Health Organization in asking the director of Medical Care of the Chicago Health Research Institute for sanitation facilities. The group also sent a letter to Dave Stahl and the Chicago Board of Health listing health requirements.[71] The Church of the Three Crosses responded positively to MOBE's request for housing, asking that there be no cooking in the church, stipulating that it could only be used in the afternoons and early evenings, and that seminars held there be for the use of the community as well as out-of-towners.[72] Approximately two weeks before the convention, the MOBE assigned Students for a Democratic Society members, who began arriving there the Friday before the convention, to the church. The church was set up for business: typewriters sat on tables, literature sat neatly stacked, and a mimeograph machine stood in the corner.[73] Ministers opened its doors for sleeping when it became apparent that there were not enough homes in the area to accommodate the students.[74]

Monday the nineteenth, Rev. Larry Dutenhaver closed the Church of the Three Crosses at 10 P.M. As he locked up, he noticed SDS registration records. However, the next day on opening the church he found empty beer cans and figured someone had slept there. When, a couple of hours later, someone discovered that SDS records were missing, its members quickly proposed that law enforcement officials had broken in and stolen them. Dave Doering felt that, as the sound of conversation differed from that in the past, the police bugged NSCM phones, specifically at Bethlehem Church.[75]

In the week before the convention, North Side residents "began to panic," and frightened parents sent their children out of Old Town, but NSCM worked to calm fears.[76] The ministry held meetings Monday, Wednesday, and Friday evenings to "orient community people on what to expect." The group did not want residents to board up their homes in fear that that would "clearly escalate the upcoming confrontations."[77] The first meeting NSCM held was on the nineteenth, and covered "Orientation to the Y.I.P. Convention" from 6:30 to 7:30 P.M. On the twenty-first, the group covered "Orientation to the National Mobilization," then "Orientation to other groups" on the twenty-third. Daily meetings through the thirty-first followed. NSCM encouraged "cool" people to aid them, and organized a survival training program in Lincoln Park for Tuesday.[78] Crash pads began to open on an as-needed basis. Numerous flyers circulated from various sources as to where one could find legal aid, LSD rescue, a car, medical aid, or a place to sleep.[79] That same week Ruth Migdall from MEDICS, an "independent group of persons with medical concerns [who] assist at such things as riots," arrived and began to set up medical centers. NSCM's Summer Task Force set up six mobilization centers, and "some ten to twelve" churches opened their doors. The task force also had three people working on housing for Black challenging delegations.[80] Pat Devine recalled that some Lincoln Parkers had their own demonstration plans to highlight urban renewal during the Democratic National Convention, and as such were somewhat opposed to the larger protest about to unfold.[81]

LPCA also understood that convention week would be problematic. Executive director Jay Ridinger encouraged President Roland Whitman to send representatives to NSCM's Yip meeting.[82] LPCA's Youth Committee chairman met with MOBE members and offered no formal proposal as to how LPCA should handle the arrival of protesters and discussed what would happen if the city denied them permission to sleep in the park. Board members then moved to contact the city to urge it to allow protesters "to use the Park facilities beyond the curfew hours so that they are not forced to sleep in the streets here in Lincoln Park." Later that day, LPCA telegraphed the city, encouraging officials to let protesters sleep in the park. This was no embrace of protest, but more an attempt to contain members to the park area rather than have them wander the streets of Old Town.[83] The telegram sent to Stahl, Daley, and others argued that allowing members of Yippie and MOBE to use the park was necessary "so that these people will have a place to sleep and will not be forced to walk the streets at night."[84]

Adding to the tension, police shot and killed hippie Dean Johnson on the early morning of the twenty-second at North and Wells. Officers claimed he fired a weapon and fled the scene. Many suspected otherwise. To Yippies, it was if a "brother" had died.[85] A protest occurred without much planning, but the funeral some had discussed for Johnson failed to materialize.[86]

National Protest, Local Protest

In the last week of August, residents who peered out of windows now saw uniformed soldiers. On the twenty-third, day five of a searing heat wave, five thousand Illinois National Guardsmen arrived at Chicago armories. By midafternoon, the city sealed all emergency doors at the federal building and posted guards at all main entrances.[87] By the twenty-fourth, a seven-foot barbed wire fence surrounded the amphitheater as fifteen hundred police moved around it. The Chicago police even sealed manhole covers.[88] Daley placed twelve thousand officers on twelve-hour shifts, to be joined by six thousand army troops, six thousand Illinois National Guard, and approximately two hundred undercover agents.[89]

His concern sprang in part from fears that Black neighborhoods would respond as they did in April after King's assassination. As the convention approached, the media speculated about this possibility, one journalist chronicling the "black mood" and the "white mood."[90] However, no Black organizations intended to get involved with what they saw as a white protest. Some Blacks stayed away voluntarily, while others, like Jeff Fort of the Blackstone Rangers, heeded police harassment in the weeks preceding the convention and left town.[91] On the first night of protest, some Blacks in attendance tried to persuade others to go home.[92]

The first appearance of signs reading "Park Closes at 11 P.M." days before the convention stunned residents who stayed for the festival, but they were determined to hold their ground as the national protest over the war spawned a local protest about park access. Dennis Cunningham's wife felt that those resisting the police did so to claim the park as theirs, and many of those yelling "to the streets" and "the park is ours" were long-time Lincoln Park residents.[93] Throughout the week, protesters frequently chanted the slogans "The Park Belongs to the People" or "The streets belong to the people."[94] While some waved Vietcong flags and talked about the war, to some residents the fight was about who controlled space. Others worried that locals might attack those in the park.[95] It was all about the park for the police, too. Some officers were surprised that they actually had to enforce the law, as they had rarely done so before, save to break up romantic couples.[96] However, deputy chief Lynsky later offered that by not clearing the park it would be interpreted as a "sign of weakness" by demonstrators.[97]

In the years before the convention, activists in urban renewal, the ministry, and the counterculture worked at times with each other, and often parallel to one another to promote their visions of community. Now, convention week brought them together as they focused not on urban renewal but on surviving the Festival of Life. Hippie, minister, and concerned citizen rubbed shoulders, conversed, fled with, and aided each other. Lincoln Park resident John Schultz wrote that, "no one thought anymore in terms of civil rights and liberties. We thought in terms of citizens' protection and a citizens' underground, and the makings of it were showing fast in Lincoln Park."[98] Even Chicago newspapers, notably the *Tribune*, ignored LPCA and NSCM and instead focused on violence and the behavior of protesters.[99]

Flyers distributed during the week highlight the degree to which the confederation of local groups moved together under one umbrella. Some listed various "help centers" set up by area organizations. One handout listed Rev. Doering's and Tuttle's phone numbers, along with phone numbers for SDS, the Hip Job Co-op, the Common Pantry, MOBE, *Seed*, LPCA (inexplicably), along with churches, medical centers, the LSD rescue center, legal aid, kitchens, and places to find cars. Another listed aid centers, churches, and *Seed*, but also the Free Theater and the Cellar. Yet another offered Concerned Citizens along with the theater and SDS's Church of the Three Crosses location.[100] At the onset of the convention these groups, on paper at least, stood united.

Word of mouth and the underground press further helped connect demonstrators.[101] *Seed* employees, including Peck, worked furiously to get the latest issue out. In the "Chicago" edition of the *Realist*, Hoffman still promoted the idea of a large, successful rock concert."[102] Yet *Seed*'s special convention issue reflected both tension and a sense of wonder regarding the impending event. The colored convention guide offered a map of Lincoln Park and accompanying "Yippie plans" devised by Hoffman. Grounding these whimsical offerings in reality, it also ran the columns "What to Do in Case of an Arrest" and "How to Survive the Streets." The latter offered festival-goers tips such as sleeping on roofs to avoid harassment, renting a garage for housing, and offering labor at places like service stations in exchange for bathroom usage. *Seed* also advised readers to avoid hotels and motels from which police could roust them, and to bring gear such as boots, medical kits, condoms, fatigues, rain ponchos, and vitamins. In addition, the Free City Survival Committee informed readers that it would help demonstrators find housing, and provided a phone number to call.[103]

In contrast to firm local leadership was the uneven guidance from national leaders. Bedlam characterized Friday the twenty-third as New York Yips pulled public stunts and bickered. On that afternoon, the Yips released their presidential candidate, Pigasus, and police arrested Rubin for disturbing the peace.[104] Dennis Cunningham attended a chaotic meeting at the

Free Theater that day. He later told investigators that to anyone who witnessed it, it would have been "ludicrous" to believe that this group could disrupt the convention.[105] More practically, members of Free City met with Congressman Sidney Yates on the twenty-third and asked for his help in opening the park. Yates's attempt to involve a local politician failed. This did not surprise Free City, as the group was only there as a "last futile gesture" anyway.[106]

Hoffman, Rubin, and Krassner also made a futile gesture: they decided not to encourage people to stay in Lincoln Park past curfew. They printed leaflets requesting residents leave the park at the theater.[107] Locals ignored them, as the event now became their protest in addition to Yippies'.

Aside from the drama surrounding Pigasus, the week began with residents observing and waiting. On Saturday the twenty-fourth, the day before the festival "officially" began (or as close to official as Yips could get), the park looked more like a church picnic than a protest. Hoffman, however, viewed things differently. On the same day he helped organize a "hash cookie production line," he called Cunningham around 1 P.M. to tell him people and police were arriving at the park, and that "shit was about to happen."[108]

This was not the only time Yippies in Chicago worked to provide drugs. Robbie Lieberman has rightly called on historians to better examine the role of drugs in the 1960s, and the festival was hardly a drug-free zone.[109] According to Paul Krassner, on the weekend prior to the convention, Hoffman and others worked on "Yippies cigarettes" lashed with hash oil, and a more powerful, incapacitating honey laced with the same oil. After having ingested the latter Krassner, in Lincoln Park, held "on to the grass very tightly so that I wouldn't fall *up* [italics in the original]."[110] One wonders what kind of leadership Yips on honey (or other substances) could really provide. Peck later revealed that "When police and reporters couldn't find key Yippies, they suspected covert activity; often, though, their disappearance was due to complete stonedness."[111]

That afternoon around three hundred to four hundred persons played music, danced, and waited for something to happen. By about 4 to 5 P.M., a "substantial number" of those in the park were residents, but it was not always easy distinguishing a local bystander from a protester. By 5 P.M., the number present tripled according to Cunningham, who noticed a "brief, but not serious," argument between older residents and young people, but other than that he thought things were calm. Even the police were mostly relaxed. That evening Cunningham, after stopping by the park and the theater, attempted to inform Commander Braasch "that as far as the long-time residents of the community were concerned, it was o.k. for the yippies to stay in the park over night"; unfortunately, he could not reach him.[112]

On Saturday, Rubin and Hoffman, again accepting the probability of violence, agreed that people should not be encouraged to demonstrate in the park past curfew. Rubin drafted a leaflet in which he pointed out that, as an out-of-towner, he had little right to fight the police. Other Yip leaders produced similar leaflets and drew up a list of churches at which to crash.[113] That evening Lincoln Park hosted approximately one thousand to two thousand protesters who sat around, smoked pot, played guitars, and chanted "Om" as directed by poet Allen Ginsberg. The protest that organizers once hoped would host half a million people now attracted a fraction of that, suggesting that both the summertime cooperation between some residents and the police and the efforts of the NSCM and *Seed* to dissuade demonstrators was effective. A New York peace group that chartered two hundred buses for the Pentagon demonstration of 1967 needed only five for Chicago.[114] National organizers like Tom Hayden lamented the low turnout.[115] Police that night entered the park unmolested, put out the bonfire with cold water, and cleared the area with minimal disturbance.[116]

Sunday the twenty-fifth marked the opening of Yippie proceedings. That day the hot weather broke. The rest of the week was sunny, with temperatures in the seventies.[117] Neighborhood citizens, some with children and baby strollers, came out to hear music and look around. Paul Sills, his wife, and their two young daughters arrived to watch events and the music planned for that afternoon.[118] The MC-5 were set to perform, but police refused to allow the Yips to use a flatbed truck as a stage. As the band played loudly on the grass, someone cut the electricity. A scuffle ensued, and around 5 P.M. police arrested several taunting protesters.[119]

That evening, police implemented the rarely enforced curfew, beating unarmed protesters and journalists for three hours until the park emptied. Hundreds yelled and picked fights with policemen as they moved into the streets, and another thousand who sat in the park faced police nightsticks. Some one thousand tried to move south toward the Loop, but about one hundred policemen repelled them at the Michigan Avenue bridge. Other protesters clogged the streets, causing a traffic jam until dispersed by officers.[120]

Amidst the gas and batons, a few laymen and clergy present passed out brochures detailing the resources they had gathered. They also came to the aid of a Chicago resident as police clubbed him.[121] About fifty to seventy-five people stayed in the Free Theater that night.[122]

On Monday, while the mellow daytime park environment continued for some who played bongos, napped, read newspapers, and chatted about how determined they were to stay in the park, the violence of Sunday shocked a wider group of Lincoln Park residents to take more direct action.[123] Concerned Citizens' Monday, August 26, edition of the *Lincoln Park Press* sported the slogan "People First" and offered "Lincoln Park Area Becomes a Police State" as its headline. Noting that none of the groups using the park, including Yippies, community organizers, and McCarthy volunteers posed any threat to the area, it claimed that people desired to sleep in the park as "hotel space is not available and few have any money . . . Many area residents have offered their homes to the young people, and churches have opened their halls. Still, thousands remain homeless." The paper also alerted readers to where they could find ten Movement Centers in and around Lincoln Park and highlighted a case of police harassment in which a police officer ordered some thirty to forty activists making signs for a neighborhood unity march to line up for a search. In the process of frisking these people one officer threatened to crack the head of one man while shoving his pregnant sister. Even in the midst of the struggle for the park, the issue of urban renewal was not totally forgotten by CCLP. Some planned a unity march set for Thursday, August 29, "against realtors who are getting rich off of the community, and against the Department of Urban Renewal which is destroying many homes." The paper encouraged readers to "Bring your family, noise makers, and hot dogs. We will end the march with a picnic."[124] This protest was not part of any plan made by the Yippies or MOBE. Instead, some residents used the momentum of the festival to launch yet another, albeit minor, attack on urban renewal.

With violence now a reality, members of the local clergy, including Rev. Reed, Doering, and Dutenhaver, met at a nearby church at around 11 A.M. to discuss what they saw Sunday night and improvise their next action. The potential for more bloodshed concerned them, and they decided to meet again at 9 P.M. at the Church of the Three Crosses to discuss minimizing it. A failed attempt to open McCormick Seminary also fueled discussion. Its refusal to allow protesters inside prompted at least one pastor to feel it betrayed the religious community, and that it "was a classic example of the church turning a deaf ear."[125] Throughout the afternoon other people lit fires in trashcans, erected a small barricade, and sat around.[126]

NSCM officials then stepped up their involvement in the festival by meeting with police and youth to discuss restraint. Clergymen were now willing to get physically involved in potential melees, wanting to act as "buffers" between officers and youths.[127] NSCM called a meeting at its offices at 6 P.M. at which members agreed on the buffer strategy, as many felt that telling demonstrators to go home simply would not work. Larry Dutenhaver later said that they wanted to be a "presence," and members distributed mimeographs informing people where they could find medical help and shelter.[128] They then met at the Church of the Three Crosses at 9 P.M.; about forty to forty-five people were present, half of them were clergy in clerical garb while laypersons wore white armbands adorned with a cross. Around 9:45 P.M. they went out in groups of four to five.[129] That night Movement Centers endured stink bombs and police raids. In the Free Theater, residents and Yippies monitored police radios.[130]

Monday night was chilly, so some who gathered at the park lit fires in trash bins. The atmosphere was calm, and those who advocated violence seemed so out of place, one resident felt they had to be undercover police there just to start trouble.[131] At 6 P.M., two hundred police officers arrived at the park in four buses to reinforce units already present.[132] Perhaps a bit late, Yips held a meeting at 10 P.M. that evening in the Lincoln Park Hotel to discuss "how to survive" Chicago. Hoffman gave a public speech against both violence and the city, and as time went on tensions built.

Some park protesters began erecting barricades made of picnic benches and trash barrels between themselves and police. They overturned picnic tables, placed debris-filled trash cans atop them, and lit them on fire. From 10 P.M. to 11 P.M. protesters stared at the police from behind twenty- to thirty-foot-long, flaming barricades.[133] Abbie Hoffman moved throughout the crowd, urging people to leave.[134] Locals readied themselves for authorities. The police made two announcements to abandon the park, then fired tear gas canisters.[135]

At the corner of LaSalle and Eugenie a group of ministers convinced officers to let them cross the "no-man's land" between cops and kids. Their buffer idea instead turned into intervention as they became "chaplains, medics, and support troops for the young warriors."[136] Badge-less police chanted "Kill, Kill," as they moved in to clear the park, but ministers were able to minimize additional violence by restraining some Yips from throwing rocks or bottles. However, they could not stop the police and faced occasional clubbing themselves.[137]

Lincoln Park residents again proved instrumental. Larry Dutenhaver followed police, wrote down badge numbers, and intervened in beatings. In Old Town he watched as officers ran north on Clark Street, clearing pedestrians. He ducked into a doorway to avoid them, emerging when they passed in order to follow. When they stopped, he noticed a young man lying beneath them, his head bleeding. As the police stood there unconcerned, Dutenhaver asked to be let past their line to assist the boy and was refused. He then demanded to see the sergeant, whom he then showed the bleeding youth. Dutenhaver was then able to find a medic to take the boy to a hospital. Cops called him an "SOB" and a "fucking fake," and invited him to "give us a target."[138]

The Monday night gassing brought Old Town citizens "out of their houses, coughing and gritting their eyes, angrily."[139] Protesters fled into Old Town, zigzagging in and out of bars and restaurants, through alleys, homes, and churches. About one thousand swarmed the neighborhood, some ducking back into the park, forcing policemen to repeatedly reform their lines.[140] Cunningham, his wife, the Sills, and other neighborhood residents quickly retreated to a local bar for "several drinks." Stepping outside, they were swept into the crowd's movement. They kept moving to avoid police, and Sills became separated from his wife. He went to find her and the others kept moving until they found safety.[141] As the police moved through Lincoln Park's main streets in unmarked cars, protesters scrambled to find shelter. One demonstrator recalled:

> The kids were huddled inside the apartments, the head of the apartment welcomed freely others. They were all crowded in. There was an element of fear. People didn't want to be in the streets. There was some apprehension at the police coming up into the apartments which, as I was coming back down the steps, was confirmed. Police came in through the doors and started dragging kids out that were standing in the hallway without allowing anyone to make an explanation... Many of these were from the Chicago area or the suburbs and not really a part of the hard core Yip or Hip that had come to Chicago, but merely those who were coming in for the fun, though they were at this point mad at the police and certainly

much more willing to accept the SDS or Hip and Yip lines. There was an almost universal reaction, "why the beating, why can't we stay in the park tonight?"[142]

This same person later proceeded to the Church of the Three Crosses, where people tried to ascertain who was injured and hospitalized. Clergy observed events and tried to help victims to aid centers. One seminarian suffered a skull fracture, and another was gassed and wounded. Ministers and residents finally decided to meet again on Tuesday to discuss the violence.[143]

Activist and comedian Dick Gregory later commented, "If you were in the streets, and if you moved, you were a Yippie," and Dutenhaver saw residents of Clark Street beaten by police while sitting on their porches.[144] Others made their way to shelters rather than hotels, as hotels not only charged money, but managers refused service to hippies.[145] Some fifty persons a night crashed at the 57th Street Friends meetinghouse, which one activist called "one of the most active centers throughout the week."[146] Medics set up a hospital in the basement of the Free Theater. The tired and injured filled it to capacity on Monday night. Protesters avoided the courtyard, feeling it unsafe, but the beer garden next door found use as a sort of hospital.[147] One young woman, the victim of a police beating, commented, "Those cops don't realize that I didn't want violence . . . but now that I've been clubbed, I can't wait to get my hands on them."[148]

On Tuesday, more clergymen from a wider variety of denominations involved themselves with the festival.[149] NSCM, at a 10 A.M. meeting, decided to get the community together to meet with Commander Braasch and to hold a nighttime church service in the park to consist of songs, prayer, and preaching. The eight-foot cross from the Church of the Three Crosses would accompany them.[150] To aid needy demonstrators clergy planned to march alongside police as they cleared the park. Cunningham and Sills had had enough. They learned of and attended the morning meeting held by the clergy, and, with ministers, set one for 4 P.M. with Commander Braasch and Deputy Chief Lynsky at the Cultural Arts Center (used as police headquarters) to discuss harassment.[151]

Tuesday afternoon the scene at the Free Theater reminded Abbie Hoffman of Valley Forge, as demonstrators (some bandaged) huddled over fires cooking hot dogs while others slept, quietly chatted, and played folk songs.[152] Parents wandered through the park trying to find their runaway children.[153] Still, residents determined to take action and that afternoon, in the words of Sills, "the community was welded together."[154] At 1 P.M., about one hundred residents met with members of NSCM to debate future action.[155] At 4 P.M. residents, now calling themselves an Emergency Committee, met with Braasch. All types of people, artists, lawyers, clergymen, formed the group, including "the monied, the artistic, teachers, ordinary citizens" who told Braasch that "they were not afraid of people with long hair" and that they wanted an end to police harassment. They wanted to patrol the park themselves, only calling the authorities when necessary. When denied this, they asked if the police would at least walk more slowly during sweeps.[156] Cunningham argued that residents felt no threat from the youth present, just the police. Sills asserted that if the city allowed the community to police the park, there would have been no problem.[157] They also told Braasch they knew he could not authorize police removal from the park, but asked that he make this request and informed him they would return to see him that evening. They made little progress. Lynsky informed them that the park would be closed again that night, but allowed several ministers to ride along with the police as observers.[158] Braasch tried to counter residents, informing them that protesters had damaged his car and that he had received word that protesters meant to harm the police. When told that the ministers were to conduct a service that night, Braasch asked, "Am I to understand that the ministers will act in civil disobedience of the law?"[159] When the meeting was over, residents gained little more than the right to observe officers. Someone announced, via microphone, the churches that would be open for crashing.[160]

The increased pushback from the city resulted in increased resistance from residents who, despite what Yip leaders and the police wished, dug in their heels. So upset were some that they came to the Church of the Three Crosses to report police beatings they witnessed, in addition to providing food, housing, cars, and other help.[161] Others supplied food and hiding places, and accompanied wounded kids to local hospitals, claiming that their injuries were the result of domestic accidents so as not to attract police attention.[162]

On Tuesday from 8 to 10 P.M. citizens, galvanized by the events of Monday night, held what Cunningham called a "town meeting" on the steps of the Academy of Science at which various persons spoke. Then a delegation, including Sills, met at the Cultural Arts Center with Deputy Superintendent

Robert Lynsky who commented that "there was no professionalism any-where anymore" and that he realized "there were a lot of sadists on the police force." He also told them the police would remain in the park. Minis-ters then told him they would be holding a worship service.[163] Sills later noted, "It was the only town meeting of a spontaneous nature I've ever encountered."[164]

Tuesday night's service was the most important moment of neighbor-hood autonomy and unity during convention week. Police cars drove slowly by the Church of the Three Crosses with windows open, rifles and pistols held out. The helicopter light shining down, probing the neighborhood from above, also reminded protesters of a powerful police presence.[165] Face-to-face interactions changed, too. On Monday, dressed in a suit, one demon-strator received no problems from the police as he worked a bread line. On Tuesday, now clad in a pith helmet, jeans, and boots, police arrested him for begging while he attempted to use collected funds to purchase food from a local restaurant. Officers forced him Into a car in which they beat him be-fore releasing him.[166] Jon Tuttle received word that the police had switched to "federal streamer" gas, more potent and powder-based, allowing it to stick to grass, skin, and clothing rather than dissipate into the air.[167]

In the face of this intimidation, ministers held their community church service that night. Approximately two hundred Clergy and Laymen en-tered Lincoln Park carrying the large cross as some two thousand people joined them. The ministers carried it over police lines, set it up, and ex-plained the program to bystanders at around 11:30 or 12:30.[168] The clergy moved Sills, who, along with others, was not sure if death for these minis-ters was imminent or not.[169] The service began and some kids liked it, and many either did not care or were put off. According to one demonstrator, "though the ministers were trying to move the kids' energy into more pa-cific directions and wanted to act as a buffer between the kids and the cops, the demonstrators unconsciously used the ministers as a way of holding a large group in the Park for confrontation with the cops after 11 P.M."[170] Still, no one offered an alternative protest or dramatic gesture, so all eyes were on the ministers.[171] As the police moved into position, an announcement rang out for everyone to sit down and lock arms, and protesters instructed each other how to combat the effects of tear gas.[172] People again erected barricades between themselves and the police. Officers then made two an-nouncements to clear the park.[173]

In a moment symbolizing both the local *and* national meanings of the protest, some demonstrators took the cross, and a Vietcong flag, and marched toward the police, now readying tear gas. One NSCM minister told those assembled, "We are not going to run. Our strength is our common cause."[174] Police moved in and the crowd scattered into Old Town. Someone yelled "The police have tear-gassed the cross of Christ."[175] Some made their way to the Church of the Three Crosses, where drivers waited to ferry them through the area.[176]

Dutenhaver walked the streets, monitoring police. At about 1 A.M. he witnessed officers beating a young man and attempted to intervene. Without warning, the policeman with whom he spoke shoved him into oncoming traffic. Dutenhaver avoided cars and returned to the officer, pointing out the traffic, but the officer blocked him from the sidewalk. Meanwhile, a squad car arrived and took the youth away. Dutenhaver took down the number of the car and one officer's name.[177] Other ministers helped as best they could, grabbing the wounded and washing tear gas from their eyes.[178] Tuttle watched police beat a man, then drive off, leaving him in the street. The minister then helped him to a hospital.[179] The assault on Tuesday's church service further galvanized residents. One MOBE member claimed that after the violence of Tuesday some "85% of demonstrators were willing and did in fact refer to the cops as pigs on Wednesday."[180] Tuttle noticed that one resident assembled a pile of bricks on the sidewalk, ready to be used as projectiles.[181]

On the now infamous night of Wednesday, August 28, when Chicago Police officers clubbed and gassed protesters on television, Abbie Hoffman was in jail, having been arrested that morning.[182] By then, though, his presence was unnecessary, as Lincoln Park residents had assumed leadership roles in the festival. Clergy held a staff meeting Wednesday morning. It was thought that Grant Park, miles south of Lincoln Park, was now the center of attention, and Dutenhaver searched in vain for the cross (aided by an apologetic Braasch). In an afternoon meeting with residents, Braasch invited Sills, Cunningham, and anyone else in the community who wished to ride along with the police.[183]

That evening activity had moved to Grant Park, and the hip presence in Lincoln Park diminished. Clergy decided to send about seventy-five ministers to the former to serve as buffers.[184] Clergy and Laymen Task Force members in Lincoln Park walked and rode with police, helped the injured, "put down violence by youth gangs coming into the area" and cleared the park, helping people to emergency housing centers and McCormick Theological Seminary, which now opened around 2 A.M. to house protesters. Others worked the convention, talking to delegates. Some hips tried to dissuade local gangs from becoming violent, and other clergy worked with National Guardsmen to open up communication and stem violence.[185] By 8 P.M. the action moved downtown, as maybe five thousand protesters faced police clubs near the Hilton Hotel near Michigan and Balbo while chanting "the whole world is watching."[186] At 11:30 P.M., Cunningham, Sills, and two others, after initially rejecting the idea, boarded a bus loaded with policemen and National Guard and rode with them, observing. The police mainly ignored them, and the one time they entered the park they found no one there.[187] Tuttle returned from Grant Park to Lincoln Park at around 11 P.M. He watched local teens throw bottles as police cleared the area. Many who would have been in the park were at the Conrad Hilton or had already found shelter.[188]

Immediate Aftermath

On Thursday the "Yippie show" at Lincoln Park was over, and by mid afternoon Old Town was business as usual.[189] Television crews interviewed leaders to get their reactions to the battle on Michigan Avenue. Dick Gregory attempted to launch a march on Thursday afternoon, only to face tear gas.[190] A little after midnight on the twenty-ninth, the Democratic Party officially ended its convention.[191]

On Friday, Hoffman was on a plane out of Chicago.[192] MOBE closed its national headquarters in the city.[193] Others who came from out of town returned home.[194] On Friday, ministers held an "Evaluation and Review" and collected testimony concerning police brutality at Sills's Theater.[195] By this point, officers outnumbered demonstrators in Lincoln Park.[196] One hundred ninety-two policemen experienced some form of injury, and the Medical Committee for Human rights reported treating 425 injured, and an additional four hundred suffering from mace or tear gas. Police arrested 668 protesters.[197]

Ministers found their influence and credibility strengthened due to their actions during convention week. One resident felt that the image of the clergy was as improved as the Police Department's was damaged. As various denominations mingled with demonstrators, helped them, and suffered alongside them, people saw them as relevant. Police conduct also, one demonstrator claimed, "radicalized" the community.[198] The Three Crosses' Jerry Goethe found that community members volunteered their homes after watching incidents of police brutality, while one youth was "glad to see the church in the street."[199] The *Christian Advocate* editorialized that, thanks to media coverage, most Americans saw the "bricks, bottles, billy clubs and tear gas" surrounding the event, but were ignorant of the efforts of the clergy, who it praised, commending the ministers for riding in squad cars throughout the night and marching with police as they gassed crowds, "talking, explaining, being intermediaries, helping with hurt or frightened policemen."[200] NSCM president June Alder wrote to the editor of a local paper, thankful for an editorial that commended NSCM for its actions during convention week. She claimed that churches housed and fed young people, but that "many church members as well as clergy were present with the young people and the police, attempting to exert a calming influence."[201]

The underground newspaper the *Rag* commented "America exposed herself . . . Chicago is merely a domestic version of our foreign policy."[202] The efforts of the city of Chicago to disperse protesters did not contain them, but unleashed them. For Lincoln Park residents, the Festival of Life was yet another grassroots battle for self-determination. Peck felt that the rioting was based on "the idea of territoriality, i.e., that the Park belongs to the kids, was crucial."[203] The New York Yippies brought a divisive event to an area already divided, but Chicago residents rose to guide the festival before, and during, that infamous police riot.

CHAPTER FIVE

1969

"There's been a definite shift since the Convention. A lot of kids are
concerned with Revolution. It's heaviest amongst the younger kids.
People are rapping, people are thinking about projects."
—*Seed*

What demonstrators at the Festival of Life did not know was that
the last week of August of 1968 was in some ways the first week
of 1969. Unlike the city's West Side where, "Residents got on with
their lives, returning to work and school . . . Community groups that focused
on local problems continued on as before, with little noticeable change in their
agendas" after violence, in Lincoln Park the atmosphere changed as antipathy
some held toward city hall and the police now crystallized.[1] The violence of
the protest set the tone for the next year and initiated a marked shift in the area,
much as the nation's political climate changed after Chicago.

The *Chicago Tribune Magazine* offered a portrait of two Lincoln Parks in
1969. One, a friendly, family-oriented area. "Where else in a big city in the
United States can you walk down the street and know all your neighbors?
Where else will neighbors come over and help you move plaster out of your
home, each bringing his own 50 gallon drum—this happened to me," asked
LPCA executive director Pat Feely. Pat Devine, however, offered "As a matter
of survival, people who are threatened are forced to take radical action."[2]

A 1969 poll further revealed divisions in the area. Thirty-four percent of
those polled believed that LPCA accomplished the most in terms of urban
renewal, as opposed to 11 percent who voted for CCLP. However, when
asked if LPCA represented all of the residents of the area, 37 percent voted
yes, while 47 percent voted no. While those polled felt that urban renewal
forced many residents to move, 30 percent felt renewal efforts provided a
"reasonable amount of housing for low income groups," while 12 percent
said no (the remaining 56 percent did not know). Lastly, some 83 percent

indicated that more control and planning for renewal should be handed over to local residents, as opposed to 10 percent who voted no.[3]

The year 1969 was also contentious nationwide. Abbie Hoffman, Jerry Rubin, and six other supposed leaders of Chicago demonstrations faced trial for conspiracy to incite a riot. Later that year the Mỹ Lai massacre made headlines, and instead of peace and love the Hells Angels brought violence and death to California's Altamont Speedway. Charles Manson's "family" slayed actress Sharon Tate and friends in her home, re-igniting fears of the counterculture. In October of 1969, in Chicago's Gold Coast neighborhood, some two hundred members of the Weathermen (the usurper of Students for a Democratic Society) stormed the streets, smashing cars and destroying property.

Days after the festival, urban organizers continued the fight against urban renewal and now for the first time openly joined with persons of color. Some planned protests at the Department of Urban Renewal for both August 27 and the 29.[4] CCLP announced that a Unity March would be held on September 5, "of Latins [sic.], Blacks, and Whites in the neighborhood against the realtors who are getting rich off the community, against the department of Urban Renewal which is destroying the neighborhood and against the police who are harassing the people." Puerto Ricans from the neighborhood's west side, heretofore largely absent from urban renewal debate, planned for the march to occur after a rally with the hope that hundreds, if not a thousand, people would join. CCLP called on residents to distribute leaflets, make posters and phone calls, and prepare food for the picnic following the march. Pat Devine claimed that in the last week, incidents of police harassment in the neighborhood increased. She cited two episodes in particular. In one a police officer, at gunpoint, ordered forty to fifty people (many of whom were from poor families) making signs for the Unity March to line up. When he found nothing, he left, commenting, "he controlled the corner, not the residents." Then on Thursday, August 29, CCLP received word from the police and realtors in the area that if they held the March that day, they would be "met with guns."[5]

Those promoting a more inclusive neighborhood were not inaccurate in noting the racial bias in urban renewal. Of the 2,097 structures cleared under Project I, 230 were commercial, 102 were industrial, 521 were unclassified residential, but 1,244 were residential. While Latin Americans made up 7 percent of households, they occupied 11 percent of all structures cleared under Project I. African Americans were only 1.8 percent of the area's population, but their homes comprised 40 percent of cleared houses. Sixteen percent of Asian Americans were forced out.[6]

After Daley's election in 1955, the Chicago Housing Authority turned into a "bulwark of segregation in Chicago."[7] CHA erected 15,591 family housing units between 1957 and 1968, and 14,895 of these were high-rises. These units, combined with the Dan Ryan Expressway completed in 1967, segregated Black residents. By 1968, 91 percent of public housing units, according to the city itself, were "in areas which are or soon will be substantially Negro."[8] Those who wanted more low- and moderate-income housing feared a conspiracy between residents and city hall to wall up Lincoln Park and, as Bill Gleason commented, "The aldermen had largely succeeded in their containment policy."[9]

The increase in community engagement in Lincoln Park also followed a nationwide trend in urban, grassroots activism. In the late 1960s urban renewal programs in low-income neighborhoods caused what Daniel Bell called a "Community Revolution."[10] A new kind of "militant community activism" began as new, angrier leaders stepped up to take charge of their neighborhoods. In Boston's South End, white ministers, Black social workers, Puerto Rican organizers, and white professionals united to combat the Boston Redevelopment Authority. The South End Tenants' Council, the Emergency Tenants' Council, and the Community Assembly for a United South End spurred people to attend urban renewal committee meetings, occupy a building, and seize a parking lot. Such activism created a new "political space" that forced city politicians to deal with new leaders.[11]

Free City

At the same time, teens still came to Old Town and ministers continued to counsel them. Some kids ran there to escape poor home lives, others to experiment with the counterculture. As at Haight-Ashbury, speed and crime seeped into Old Town, according to the Vanguard Ministry's Rev. Stephen White. However, the network of churches there reached out to many, providing a way to offset creeping problems.[12] By 1970, according to one pro-choice activist, "The churches were very busy in those days. Every group under the sun was meeting in a church basement somewhere."[13] One reverend spoke of the community he was trying to create as an "extended family," one that was "a combination of old fashioned, small town rooming house" that addressed community issues.[14]

Seed reported on renewed divisions in Old Town after the batons and tear gas of August brought so many together. Peck wrote of the area as host to "several species of human being." While "original Old Towners" lived on the 1800 and 1900 blocks, "the 1700 block is the DMZ, the buffer between Old and Freak." South of that were the tourists and teens. Peck also noted the hypocritical business owners who on the one hand loathed hips, but also feared the money the hip scene generated vanishing. One person noted the split between the "acid-grass people" and "speed freaks" who lived "separate lives." Peck also claimed that Wells had no "structured haven" for hips and that "there's nowhere to go unless you know someone with a crib." Despite what the magazine claimed—that in the wake of the convention more people talked of revolution—traditional forces and high prices had driven off youth. Peck lamented "the street seems to be dying."[15]

Police harassment, however, was not dying. *Seed* experienced police persecution in January of 1969, when officers arrested Peck and three others on charges of obscenity.[16] The next month officers arrested eight people inside of Doc Gandolf's [sic.] General Store (both store and coffeehouse) for possession of drugs and other drug-related crimes, charging sixteen others with disorderly conduct. Soon after, the store lost its lease.[17] That same month, the president of the Mid-North Association sent the latest issue of *Seed* to the CPD's Community Service Officer, noting that it "surpasses any past issue in vulgar and obscene articles."[18]

In the wake of the festival and in the face of increased repression, the magazine underwent a significant shift: it now reported on more than just the counterculture, and offered the idea of a united "Free City" as it addressed urban renewal. In 1969 it began running a "community" section, and highlighted "Free City" services such as mechanics, banks, legal aid, furniture dealers, and medicine. These were not entirely free, but places open to trade, donation, and volunteerism.[19] The paper that was once primarily concerned with explaining and exploring the counterculture ran stories about local housing issues along with pieces about music and drugs. Molly, a pregnant student in search of an abortion, found the abortion service Jane's number through an ad in *Seed*.[20]

This Free City took direct inspiration from the Digger publication the *Digger Papers*, manifestos and other pieces in Krassner's the *Realist*. *Seed* specifically quoted the August 1968 *Digger Papers* piece "The Post-Competitive, Comparative Game of a Free City," in a tour-de-force issue that, over several pages, explained Free City in general, and in Chicago.

The issue served as a primer to creating a Free City in Chicago, instructing readers as to how to apply the guidance provided in the *Digger Papers* to the area by supporting businesses already part of Free City, and encouraging the creation of more. "The Digger Papers suggest a minimum number of organizations that can act in concert to construct a Free City . . . What is the goal of a Free City? The goal is to allow every brother and sister to have what he needs to do everything."[21] *Seed* offered ideas on where to find merchandise, mechanics, food, legal aid, furniture, schools, and other goods and services including "hustles" that instructed readers on how to rip off local businesses.[22] These were categories first mentioned in the *Digger Papers*, and while *Seed* kept the headings, it then inserted in the magazine places in Chicago where such services could be found. Additionally, the paper reported on police harassment faced by the local gang the Young Lords, the urban renewal efforts of the Appalachian, white gang the Young Patriots in Uptown, and on Tuttle's continued ministry.[23]

However, the issue also *omitted* the following from the *Digger Papers* "Free City" essay:

> By now we all have guns, know how to use them, know our enemy, and are ready to defend. We know that we ain't gonna take no more shit. So it's about time we carried ourselves a little heavier and got down to the business of creating free cities within the urban environments of the western world.[24]

Even after the chaos of 1968, Chicago hips found guidance from the Diggers, but they were not about to mention guns or violence . . . yet. Theirs was still a fragile counterculture interwoven with the clergy, entertainment, and commerce and so they, as they had in 1967, followed the Haight's lead but also adapted it.

Guerilla Ministers

As part of this Free City network, NSCM continued its overtures to Latin Americans, demonstrating an increased focus on ethnicity. By this time, five churches in the ministry were Spanish-speaking, and members felt that

NSCM would be best to deal with issues relevant to Latino residents, as "The church is the only Spanish structure in our community and would act as base." NSCM also sought funds to establish another coffeehouse for teens that would focus on problems among Latin Americans.

NSCM also sought continued funding of Tuttle's efforts. The group recognized that his strength lay in his ability to connect with hips and argued, "He is very able in relating to this 'fringe community' into exposure with the main stream of America to raise concerns about the war and its implications." NSCM repeated its longstanding emphasis on diverse, new approaches to problems, arguing that individuals like Tuttle represented new ways of interacting with the community. The bearded, six foot six- tall, long-haired Tuttle moved between some twenty-one churches and held "office hours" in Lincoln Park on Sundays, providing aid and counsel to kids with drug problems.[25]

Despite efforts to move forward, the NSCM-funded coffeehouse Alice's Restaurant finally closed. Enough residents complained about the noise and clientele that the building owners refused to renew the lease. Rev. Doering argued that its closing put two hundred to three hundred youths "out on the street."[26] *Seed* claimed, "it symbolized a kind of liberated zone within a city of increased repression."[27]

Dave Doering was a changed man after the festival. Now, he sought to place the issue of white racism more centrally in NSCM discussions. The ministry had long been concerned with racial issues, even discussing the use of "Guerilla Theater" to address racism as early as June of 1968, but now Doering sought to move it into a more prominent position.[28] Claiming "The Black man (and hippies, and youth and others) are now beginning to raise the question of survival as an issue," he highlighted tensions in the United States, noting that "the right wing is on the move in society as well as the church," he argued that the latter had dropped civil rights as a priority approximately two years ago in favor of concerns over urban renewal and the Peace Movement. He called upon white readers "who believe in radical new understandings of love, forgiveness and reconciliation" to pay more attention to racism.[29]

Doering continued to promote his vision of a more racially diverse community the next year. In February of 1970, *Christian Century* published a piece in which he advocated a more tolerant and united Protestant front. By that time some Protestant churches across the nation discussed coming under one large umbrella in a movement called Consultation On Church Union, which stressed acceptance and diversity. Doering explained NSCM to readers, highlighting the thirty churches and eight denominations that composed it in 1970. Central to his vision was that the church needed to relate to everyday life ("what does baptism mean to an unmarried welfare mother or to an abandoned suburban housewife?" he asked), and that hopefully the new movement would allow "blacks, Indians, Orientals, whites, the Spanish-speaking, young and old, conservatives and liberals and radicals to sit around the Table of Christ."[30]

His post-festival philosophy was most clearly outlined in an essay titled "The Mission of the Church: A Position Paper Relating to Issues, Needs, Target Groups and Target Structures" that echoed C. Wright Mills more than the New Testament. Doering argued that, "Man in a mass society is quite often man without voice and without a community. Man is lost in a mass society, under the pressures and demands of mass production." He feared that the Church was one form of mass media that, due to its impersonal nature, repelled people rather than assisted them in finding a home within. He specifically stated that the poor and elderly as well as young people, divorcees, or those in nontraditional homes felt alienated from modern religion. The Church's response to these people, he argued, had been to try to "force the outdated 'middle class family media' on the church-goer, to go where the media fits its content (mainly in the suburbs), or to ignore the mass majority who do not 'fit'." This forced those who could not find identity in the church to turn to "the local bar ... a teenage gang ... in the Peace Movement, in the civil rights movement, the SDS, the communist party, in an LSD group." He condemned the ministry for propagandizing and encouraging conformity, and asserted that it must change to provide people with "freedom and enough information, knowledge and support that self determination becomes possible."[31]

The self-determination Doering mentioned was central to his new ideology, and he advised that therapy groups, language courses, and other tools and resources be made available for members to achieve this. He argued that the Church should examine those places where people currently find identity "whether it be in a civil rights group, a Viet Nam Peace demonstration, or a homosexual bar." Then, "key to the mission in the world must be that of acceptance ... an openness on the part of the church to all kinds of new styles of life ... new forms of identity and role." If the Church accomplished this, it could free itself of the "media bind ... where the world can receive the word in new ways (so) Christian values can come alive and inform life styles where life is possible both in the church and the world."

Recommending a more confrontational approach to change, he offered that to make the Church more significant it needed to minister to all groups and "sub-cultures" using "invasion techniques ... infiltration, 'lobbying,' confrontation, opposition tactics." He was skeptical of government, and insisted that the Church should not sell the style of life promoted by authorities, but instead a Christian life to make the world more loving and forgiving. A man who once fought for a position of influence in the LPCA now, after August of 1968, spoke of self-determination and confrontation.[32] His views had clearly shifted after the festival, and he was not alone in this.

The Lincoln Park Town Meeting

While NSCM, active in the community since the early 1960s, shifted focus and tone after convention week, other area residents, run-of-the-mill liberal Lincoln Parkers, now assumed more active roles in the area. In the aftermath of police brutality, police conduct was now a community concern. The group that finally settled on the name Lincoln Park Town Meeting (LPTM) grew out of the Emergency Committee meetings held during the festival. LPTM's approximately 125 members agreed to serve as "watchdogs" over the police. It sought to educate residents about their legal rights, observe officers, investigate complaints, and see that action would be taken. LPTM met at the Church of the Three Crosses and initially did not allow police to attend.[33] One minister commented, "The community itself became radicalized when people saw police chasing demonstrators ... People began having community meetings once a week in the old Second City building after the Democratic Convention ... Often two hundred people would come. There were people sitting there spying on us. It was a real fellowship time."[34] Paul Sills helped found the group while still producing plays.[35] *Seed* derided them as "a bunch of scared citizens who banded together during the Convention" but also detailed a meeting LPTM had with Police Commander Braasch.[36] While it took a swipe at the new organization, that *Seed* covered LPTM's meeting at all was another change from its previous focus on countercultural issues.

LPTM's main goal was to curb police brutality. It organized police observer groups to follow officers throughout the neighborhood, and a community review board heard resident claims regarding harassment and shootings. Policemen, including Braasch, began occasionally attending meetings. He claimed residents misunderstood the police, and used meetings to size up the group.[37] By this point he needed any avenue to communicate with Lincoln Park residents and improve his department's image; in February of 1969, some three hundred residents protested police harassment, squeezing into the East Chicago Avenue police station. For over an hour, they hurled accusations at Braasch and charged that police murdered a neighborhood youth.[38] Further changing the atmosphere, less than two weeks later the Chicago police announced an increase in foot patrolmen in Lincoln Park.[39]

LPTM was active throughout the summer of 1969. Every month members held a business meeting the first Wednesday, its Town Meeting Forum the third Wednesday, and its Police-Community Relations Committee met the fourth Wednesday. The latter formed two subcommittees, one to look into establishing a bail fund, and the other to prepare position papers on police functions.

Meeting members also interacted with the Black Panthers. Lucky, a Panther, spoke at one meeting. The police arrested him and seven other Panthers earlier that day, but he emerged from jail and informed meeting members of his arrest and future Panther plans. Some members disliked hosting the men, but Lucky returned for the next meeting on June 18. There, he informed residents that the Panthers were not terrorists, emphasizing their free breakfast for children program and planned free medical centers. He also offered the group's aid to the Town Meeting.[40] The support of the Black Panther Party for the Town Meeting was certainly a new important development in the struggle over community identity in a post 1968 Chicago. Even in the avant-garde world of Haight-Ashbury, hip was largely a white affair, but the diversity of activists in Lincoln Park grew.[41]

Continuing the face-to-face activism residents engaged in during the festival, during a July 4 peace march in Lincoln Park, nine LPTM members acted as police observers. The police viewed the demonstration as important enough to send Lynsky and Braasch. Later that month in a moment that again highlights the new concern over race in the area, LPTM heard from Edward "Buzz" Palmer, Executive Director of the Afro-American Patrolmen's League, formed to combat police brutality from within the CPD. He claimed the league represented some 35 percent of Black policemen of Chicago, and warned that Chicago's Black community verged on eruption.

In August, LPTM decided to write Daley to encourage him to retain Black activist and Lincoln Park resident Dick Brown on the Conservation Community Council. It also contributed twenty-five dollars for an LPTM–police joint-sponsored outing for poor children.[42] Attention to police may have had some effect on a Protest March held September 28, 1968, and a Peace March was held April 5, 1969. Neither faced attack by the police.[43]

The Concerned Citizens Survival Front

In the spring of 1969, a local paper incorrectly reported that members of LPCA and CCLP had reached an "entente," making LPCA "a more reliable instrument for community activity."[44] However, by March of that year, Concerned Citizens turned inward, changing its name to Concerned Citizens Survival Front of Lincoln Park (CCSF).[45] Those active in CCSF met in February to decide who could join the new organization. Members were mainly white and Latino poor and working-class residents who felt "directly threatened by urban renewal, speculation, welfare, police and other local and national problems."[46] The first meeting was set for April 14, to be presided over by NSCM's Rev. James Reed, convenor of the organization. Pat Devine designated herself as staff. By this point, both Reed and resident Dick Vission thought LPCA a lost cause. Vission felt that the group's membership was so white and middle class that it was off-putting to persons of color or the poor, and Reed noted the lack of a Spanish-speaking staff and the use of parliamentary procedures to keep poor voices silent as deterrents to joining it.[47]

The Neighborhood Program adopted by the Survival Front outlined new goals and, tellingly, what "defense action" it would take. One central objective was "to make the Lincoln Park neighborhood a place where poor and working people of all races, cultures and family size can live cheaply and well, and have power to control the community. TO ACCOMPLISH THIS WE ARE FIGHTING FOR [caps in original]" low rents and adequate housing, an end to evictions, construction of new homes and recreational facilities for low- and middle-class residents, and "community control of all services." To gain control, CCSF sought a federal injunction against the forces of urban renewal, and planned to stop the city's Conservation Community Council from meeting until low-income residents had representation in the group. It vowed to "send ultimatums" to urban renewal agents and promised "that serious action" would be taken against them if they continued evictions, rent raising, and failing to provide adequate housing for the poor. CCSF also determined to distribute leaflets, work with small local business owners and, reflecting fears shared by LPTM, to "initiate legal protection for neighborhood people from all forms of harassment by police and others." To place economic control of the community into the hands of tenants, CCSF sought to establish rent control, and begin tenement management via a "Neighborhood People's Corporation." It would also use this entity to build housing, train residents to work for the community, and "spin off" other businesses such as a cooperative credit union, a day care center, and cooperative stores.

The use of language such as "cooperative" and "people's" reveals the turn to the left organizers took, and an emerging bunker mentality in CCSF's plans for "defense." It called for a "force of people always on call" to protect residents from evictions, rent increases not approved by the community, and "police harassment." It also sought to establish a "list of community enemies who are trying to push people out of the neighborhood." Finally, it called for "militant action in defense against urban renewal, realtors, and institutions which work against poor and working people." Members hoped to educate residents about their legal rights, welfare rights, first aid, and "our own historical, cultural and political-economic heritage."[48] Mention of a shared heritage placed all residents of Lincoln Park, Black, white, Puerto Rican, and poor, under the same umbrella.

CCSF viewed police and neighbors with suspicion, and was as much a guarded leftist group as urban renewal organization. Its headquarters on Lincoln Avenue featured pictures of Malcolm X and Fidel Castro on the walls. Dick Vission commented that due to the twenty-four-hour surveillance the organization was under, "we have to be suspicious of everyone the first time they walk in here."[49] Those barred from CCSF membership included "Property owners who refuse to rent their property to low income families; members of the Democratic and Republican Party machine organizations; representatives of city agencies; the police department and other related agencies; members of property owners associations, etc. who refuse to push as first priority the purposes and programs of this organization."[50]

The Young Lords

The Puerto Rican population in the United States had been building since the end of World War II, but until 1969, Lincoln Park activists did not directly include Puerto Ricans in urban renewal planning. Distrustful of established community members, CCSF's sensitivity to class and race accompanied an alliance with the Puerto Rican street gang The Young Lords which, due in part to police violence during convention week, transitioned from a gang to a politicized neighborhood improvement group. The Lords, really just kids with no experience in local politics or training in community organizing, brought with them a penchant for public outbursts.

Lords' anger, however, was not without foundation. Urban Renewal greatly affected the Puerto Rican population on Lincoln Park's west side, located mainly on Armitage Avenue near Halsted.[51] Seven percent of Lincoln Park residents were Puerto Rican, and by 1967 the first phase of the GNRP displaced about four hundred low- and moderate-income families, many who were Puerto Rican or Mexican.[52] To some Puerto Ricans, already forced out of the Near North Side in the 1950s to make way for Carl Sandburg Village, the urban renewal fight of the late 1960s was round two.

Fighting for turf was nothing new to them. Puerto Ricans who came to Chicago continued a postwar migration initially bound for New York City. The US Commission on Civil Rights reported that some 61,000 Puerto Ricans lived in the New York City area in 1940. By 1960, this number reached 612,574, then tapered off.[53] In the 1950s, the US government and private agencies recruited Puerto Ricans for seasonal and contract labor. "Operation Bootstrap" was designed to export the Puerto Rican lower class to the United States for labor, which would also allow the middle class of the home island to lower its amount of poor.[54] Chicago-based recruiters targeted Puerto Ricans for labor, and as word spread among the Puerto Rican community (both in New York City and back home) that work in New York was drying up, more Puerto Ricans headed for Chicago.[55] In the 1960s they moved from the West and South Sides of the city to the North, where they initially found cheap hotels and rooming houses, and where they were just two or three train stops from service jobs in the Loop.

The city of Chicago, however, wanted to control Puerto Rican settlement to avoid the development of predominantly Puerto Rican neighborhoods that evolved in New York City. The director of the Commonwealth of Puerto Rican office in Chicago, in collaboration with the Welfare Council of Metropolitan Chicago, encouraged widespread Puerto Rican settlement over the city rather than in one concentrated area. City officials feared not only the establishment of Puerto Rican barrios, but the creation of any meaningful bonds between Mexican and Puerto Rican Americans that could threaten the white power structure of the city.[56] This planning, however, failed to guide settlement and Puerto Ricans found themselves in Lincoln Park, the same neighborhood that the Daley administration and its allies envisioned as a white bedroom community for downtown workers.

A 1966 copy of the *Mid-North News* reveals the separation between white and Puerto Rican Lincoln Park. It announced an upcoming meeting of a talk to be given by two VISTA volunteers working the "disadvantaged western sections" of Lincoln Park, where "you will hear much interest about this group which is strange to most of us because of the language barrier," and that the VISTA volunteers "have fascinating stories to tell about unknown regions nearby."[57] In the early 1960s in the Sheffield neighborhood, a Puerto Rican block on North Clifton caused "concern" among residents, so much so that "at both steering committee meetings and general block meetings, if the subject of Puerto Ricans is brought up, the meeting progresses no further."[58]

In such a divided climate, a street gang served its members by offering an "alternative" culture that both reflected community values, and provided a distinct support system.[59] Nationally, gangs made headlines in the 1950s, even spurring Congress to investigate "juvenile delinquency" depicted in Hollywood films such as *Rebel Without a Cause*.[60] In Lincoln Park in 1960, while over ten thousand white youth between ten and nineteen lived there, less than five hundred Puerto Rican children of that same age lived there, so gang membership was, to some, a way to stay safe.[61]

Gangs in the postwar era were not typically on the front lines of urban renewal. Seven Puerto Rican men formed the Young Lords in 1959, but it took the leadership of chairman Jose "Cha Cha" Jimenez to turn it into a political organization in the late 1960s.[62] Urban renewal moved his family four times during his childhood and he rose to the rank of Lords chairman by age seventeen. During and after a stay in jail before the Democratic National Convention he was influenced by the works of Martin Luther King Jr. and by Black Panther Fred Hampton.[63] When Jimenez shifted the gang to the Young Lords Organization (YLO), he modeled it on the Panthers, including the use of berets and dividing the group up into divisions, designating field marshals, and adopting a 13-point plan like the Panthers.[64] YLO soon offered free breakfast programs for poor children and monitored the police.[65] Jimenez delegated leadership, figuring that YLO could continue if he was arrested if responsibility was already meted out.[66] In fact, in YLO's first newspaper, they reprinted the Panthers' original 1966 13-point plan, and claimed, "Y.L.O. stands for an end to police brutality and mistreatment; adequate housing for all; decent jobs and living wages for all; community control of the schools, the police, and all other institutions in our community; an end to the colonization of Puerto Rico and all other Third World countries which are politically, economically, or militarily controlled by the U.S. and the U.S.S.R."[67] In outlining the paper's goals, the group claimed, "In order to develop a Movement, we shall have to develop militancy and consciousness among the people.... Our task is now to 1.) define revolutionary goals 2.) recruit individuals to our cause and train them as educators and protectors of the people 3.) develop the correct strategy for educating the masses and enlarging our fighting organization and 4.) connect ourselves with or develop fighting groups in different areas of the city."[68]

The Lords turned their attention to urban renewal as early as 1967 when they opened their café, Uptight #2 and, similar to what the Black Panthers created in California and elsewhere, offered service programs to the community, including a drug education program.[69] After the 1968 Democratic National Convention, though, renewal became central to Jimenez and YLO.[70] The Festival of Life brought Jimenez face-to-face with CCLP's Patricia Devine. He and his friends arrived in Lincoln Park as spectators on a "field trip" as part of an ex-offender program.[71] Some of his colleagues talked with women on a street corner, including Devine who accused one gang member of working against his own people. Jimenez took offense, and called Devine a communist. She replied that she was proud to be one. He and his friends returned to her apartment where she and Jimenez talked until morning.[72]

By early November of 1968, Lords associated with the gangs the Blackstone Rangers and Disciples.[73] They negotiated peace among nearly all Latin and white gangs, and even inspired the Latin Kings to establish a breakfast-for-children program. Jimenez also sought to forge a group similar to the LSD (Lords, Stones, Disciples) alliance between the Vice Lords, Blackstone Rangers, and Disciples.[74] He met with Fred Hampton in December of 1968. YLO then allowed a branch organization to grow in New York, which then spread to other cities on the East Coast.[75]

Membership in the "Rainbow Coalition" of the Panthers, Lords, SDS, Uptown's Appalachian Young Patriots, and middle-class Rising Up Angry brought YLO, and Chicago's North Side, more deeply in touch with national protest movements in the tense and occasionally violent post-1968 years.

This was an alliance of Blacks, Puerto Ricans, white working-class youth, and transplanted Southerners, one that was unprecedented in postwar Chicago.[76] The coalition reached out to gang members, students, the young, and the nonwhite throughout Chicago. Additionally, Patriots leader Bob Lee spoke at the Church of the Three Crosses.[77]

Confrontation

Finding a place for Puerto Ricans in Lincoln Park became a priority for YLO after the festival. While first-generation Puerto Ricans were more likely to want to return to the island, second-generation kids like Jimenez instead wanted to claim space in the United States.[78] To do so in Chicago, Jimenez would also ally the Lords with CCSF. The former first began to make their anger known via public protest during Conservation Community Council meetings, and reacted to recent police violence by joining with Pat Devine and Richard Vission in a march down Halsted Street.

YLO protested renewal throughout 1969, believing its most effective tactic would be causing enough trouble to force a response from politicians and others in power.[79] Much as the Black Panthers had adopted a "strategy of confrontation," so did the Lords.[80] YLO became known for, and expert at, stopping meetings. Lords wanted, as one said, "to destroy . . . a system created by white people."[81] In January, YLO disrupted a meeting of LPCA's Common Council held to discuss bids on vacant land and the use of pre-fabricated housing. The real issue to Lords, however, was representation on the Conservation Community Council: eight of the nine members were white professionals. The quorum necessary to start the meeting failed to form when a DePaul University friar walked out praying. Lords angrily approached the front of the room, stating they should fill in for the missing council members. Shoving followed, then chairs sailed through the air, windows were smashed, the bathroom floor was flooded with water, and the urban renewal displays were destroyed. The editor of the underground newspaper *Fred* commented, "The situation in Lincoln Park has obviously gone beyond negotiation."[82] Police charged Jimenez with mob action, to which he later pled innocent.[83]

It was a difficult year for Jimenez. In February, police arrested him (for the second time in two weeks) as he picketed the Wicker Park welfare office. He and others had been at there all day demanding emergency aid for welfare recipients previously denied it. As tensions mounted in the late afternoon, someone tipped over a coffeepot. Jimenez restrained a case-worker from shoving a welfare recipient, and police charged him with mob action. This allegation stemmed from a warrant issued over his involvement on January 21 of the "destruction" of the Lincoln Park Urban Renewal Service Center. In that incident his bail, set at ten thousand dollars, was quickly met thanks to contributions. Protesters gathered around the District 19 station holding Jimenez to demand his release. While in custody, officers found two outstanding warrants from 1966 and 1967 for assault, and he was served them, but again bonded out in no time.[84] Jimenez was not the only YLO target of police. In September of 1969, officers arrested four Lords for disorderly conduct, claiming they refused to leave private property after a meeting near Armitage Avenue Methodist Church.[85]

By that point YLO needed legal representation. In the summer of 1969 Dennis Cunningham, along with fellow attorney Jeffrey Haas, opened up the People's Law Office and represented not only YLO, but Fred Hampton and the Panthers, members of SDS, and antiwar protesters.[86] The office was another indicator of the changed climate in Lincoln Park after the festival. The attorneys placed a four-foot-high, hollow wooden barricade in front of the office's glass windows and filled it with cement to stop bullets. They also placed a three-foot-high steel gate in-between the inner office and outer door; to enter, the receptionist had to buzz the person in. They had a built-in gun cabinet stocked with a shotgun and a 9mm pistol. Law office staff trained with the weapons.[87] This was done on a shoestring budget as, according to Haas, "We began operating on the Marxist principle 'From each according to his ability and to each according to his need.'"[88]

Furthering concern over police, on May 4 of 1969, an off-duty officer shot and killed Young Lord Manny Ramos while he attended a birthday party across the street from the officer's home.[89] Media coverage of the event brought YLO more into the spotlight and further politicized the gang. Jimenez cited the murder of Ramos as the moment "that I became a real revolutionary. Instead of going out and killing a pig, I saw the need to sit down and analyze the ways of getting even. Not with a gun. It wasn't the right time. It still isn't. We have to educate people before we think about guns."[90] The day after the incident, YLO and other groups, including the Panthers and SDS, held a rally at the corner of Armitage and Halsted.[91] YLO and around one thousand people marched to the 18th Street police station demanding an investigation, which police assured them was underway.[92] *Seed* reported on the shooting and inquest, offering a full-page memorial to Ramos and a story written by CCSF's Dick Vission.[93] The jury at the coroner's inquest took just over four minutes to pronounce the shooting as justifiable homicide, but the Lords and *Seed* remained skeptical.[94] Additionally, Armitage's Rev. Bruce Young began "Concerned Churchmen Against Police Violence" in response.[95]

Days after the Ramos incident, Lords seized property, a shift in tactics that gained them some short-term victories. Members stormed McCormick Theological Seminary, occupying the president's office, in order to protest its lack of action on behalf of the poor in renewal. Armed with walkie-talkies, they barricaded the doors and held a press conference demanding funds from a national conclave of Presbyterian ministers meeting at that moment in Texas. They also charged McCormick as being a silent partner of the city, and demanded $601,000 in funds. They held out for five days until McCormick's board agreed to their housing demands, pledged to join the school to community groups, publicly stated it opposed racist urban renewal practices, and allowed its facilities be opened to the public.[96]

McCormick's seminary chief, Arthur McKay, listened to the demands and later defended YLO and his decision not to call in police. On day two of the takeover, McKay met for two and a half hours with the Lords. He told the *Chicago Tribune*, "We refuse to regard these people as anything but our friends and neighbors. We consider this a peaceful demonstration. We believe that the channels of communication have to be kept open and that this does not necessarily close them."[97] In a talk he later gave to area business leaders in which he claimed calling the police would have led to rioting, he offered, "There are gangs and there are gangs. It's a great danger to freely categorize groups—not all people fit into the old stereotypes." He argued, "The problem facing us is to energize the moderates to respond to this way to situations of confrontation. If the only alternatives are what the hardcore right and left wing have to offer, I'm afraid we've got nothing to look forward to but civil war."[98]

In June, Lords and their allies took over the Armitage Avenue Methodist Church, angry that for the last six months their pleas that its basement be opened as a day-care center went ignored. They were also upset that the church would not rent or sell to them to achieve that goal.[99] Church officials asked the police not to get involved.[100] While the community was stunned, Rev. Bruce Johnson, a supporter of the group, allowed YLO use of what was to be called the "People's Church." Fifteen percent of that congregation reportedly fled as the church was rechristened.[101] Lords minister of information Omar Lopez recalled that the Cuban population, in particular, was not fond of the new People's Church and left.[102] *Seed* ran an article soliciting materials and aid for the new day-care center.[103] The Lords also ran a free breakfast for children program out of the church, and a health clinic.[104]

The church takeovers happened as tensions escalated on the street and in community meetings. The May 1969 meeting of the Conservation Community Council continued the shift toward a more combative atmosphere, and marked the first of two turning points that summer. Council meetings had been contentious, but now they became, to some, scary. As the May 20 meeting of the council approached, CCSF issued a flyer in which it asked that the city agree not to approve new demolition until it erected low- and moderate-income houses. The group also asked that residents sign petitions and attend the 7:30 P.M. meeting. Additionally, it disseminated the names and addresses of council members and urged that residents contact them directly.[105]

CCSF members and others then attended the May meeting of the council, insisting that it could not continue until the poor were more adequately represented. YLO and other groups lined the wall, demanding the resignation of current council members. Council member Dick Brown agreed with their insistence, introducing motions asking specific members to resign.[106] For their actions at the May 20 meeting, Devine, Vission, and Jimenez faced jail.[107]

The July 29, 1969, meeting, held this time at Waller High, attracted approximately five hundred people, and was the second summertime turning point.[108] That night council members met to discuss, among other items, Site 19, approved for "commercial recreation" that the council now considered using for a tennis club. The meeting began about twenty minutes late, and "Several audience members, generally appearing to be part of the welfare mothers—young militants coalition, declined to occupy the audience seats, preferring to sit, stand and crowd chairs upon the stage in front of the committee."[109] As council chair Lyle Mayer began the meeting, shouts from the audience erupted. Amidst the noise he reminded crowd members that speakers from the audience must submit a written request to the chair for permission to speak. Dick Brown then seized the stenotype machine, moved to the rostrum, and pulled Mayer away from the microphone. A fight erupted as police officers stationed at the back of the room moved forward, but by the time they reached the stage the scuffle subsided. For the next hour members of CCSF, YLO, the Young Patriots, SDS, and the Black Panthers, all of whom spoke periodically, took over, denouncing the tennis club and demanding rights for the poor. Brown offered to end the protest if the council agreed not to meet again until an advisory committee "representative of the community" was appointed to monitor the council.[110] LPCA's Stephen Shamberg pointed out that voting on this would, either way, end the meeting as the council could not move if it passed, and Brown would not allow the meeting forward if it was rejected. After this motion was voted down eight to four, Brown went to the podium. He then tried to move the PAC (Project Area Committee), a group of those affected by removal, to oversee building in their areas.

As Mayer tried to turn off the microphone, another audience member leaped on stage and over a table, followed by more from the audience. Someone threw a chair at Brown, and the meeting adjourned.[111] Lords demanded Site 19 be reserved for a "People's Park."[112] Brown's opponents flooded the Department of Urban Renewal and Daley's office with demands for his removal from the CCC.[113] Brown, however, claimed that he did not seize the microphone but just sought to restore order.[114]

The *Lincoln Park Booster* ran editorials on the events of July. In response to six men being indicted for their actions at that meeting (one being Brown), the paper denounced violence as a legitimate response, but admonished Lincoln Park residents for doing little else to combat displacement caused by renewal. The paper reported that one of the four men charged with mob action during the July 29 meeting received five years' probation.[115] This unnamed person received testimony on his behalf by LPCA executive director Pat Feely, who informed the paper that the other three men "haven't seemed receptive to establishment-type help such as his group could offer."[116] Dick Brown was under indictment for battery due to July 29.[117] However, in light of another arrestee's guilty plea, he felt a guilty verdict for him would be inevitable.[118] Criticizing the tennis club idea and comparing the area to Berkeley, *Seed* observed that, "The neighborhood is tense. The merchants, the cops, the sanitation department, the landlords and city hall are putting the people up tight as is."[119] Shamberg claimed that many Conservation Community members "have said they are afraid to go to any more meetings in the community in the absence of police protection . . . We will not allow hoodlums to take over our meetings and prevent members of the council and others from the community from speaking."[120]

Lords and their allies employed a confrontational strategy again in September at a Conservation Community Council meeting at Waller High. Members of CCSF, YLO, NSCM, Lincoln Park Town Meeting, and others took over for over two hours, demanding reform of council membership and new plans for low-income housing. The council ended the meeting by resolving to gain permission of Vine-Orchard residents prior to allowing demolition in that area.[121] One hundred policemen lined the Waller High School auditorium, and when the CCC's Marvin Rosner's motion that all but ten officers leave was defeated, he and councilman (and LPCA member) Malcolm Shanower left. In their wake, Dick Vission called for more representative membership on the CCC, and that the council was "declaring all out war on the poor people of Lincoln Park." LPTM's attorney said public housing subsidized by the Chicago Housing Authority was the only solution to helping the poor.[122] By 1969 Vission also claimed that among LPCA, "There was really no ideological orientation except property. Their ideology follows their pocketbooks."[123]

The confrontational push to gain seats only succeeded in driving the council behind closed doors. Rev. James Reed requested that council members meet with CCSF and others. As before, he asked that there be no new demolition (in the Vine-Orchard Area) until new housing was established for residents. Additionally, he requested that city plans for the next phase of development, Project II, be stopped until western residents could complete their own plan.[124] Council chair Lyle Mayer, however, had a different idea: he wanted the council to meet privately. Writing on behalf of the group, he suggested it meet in public only when it planned on taking deliberate action and indicated that members decided that they should meet together prior to public meetings to clarify agenda items. He offered that these meetings would smooth over public ones as they would eliminate time spent explaining items to members and asked the group's council if "executive sessions" or council "workshops" would be permissible under law.[125] These would allow members to simply avoid dealing with disruptive area residents they wished to avoid and table open discussions of renewal.

The Poor People's Coalition

Ducking behind closed doors, however, failed to deter those fighting renewal. They next formed the Poor People's Coalition (PPC). It evolved out of the Independent Precinct Organization, originally formed to take aldermanic seats in 1969.[126] PPC was in contact with NSCM, YLO, CCSF, LPTM, and others. These groups allied to demand that the city's Conservation Community Council, in a legally binding manner, compose itself entirely of poor and working-class people, divided equally in terms of ethnicity. They also demanded an end to demolition in Lincoln Park until low-rent housing was built and that future demolition and construction would be carried out only by "companies that will hire poor people, of all races and cultures, through the facilities of the Poor People's Coalition." A few weeks after their demands went out, the group did get an audience with the CCC, but the latter would not consider any of the demands, only agreeing to meet again to discuss matters. The allied inclusive groups clearly did not have faith, stating "We have thought that the CCC was a farce for a long time—that it represented only the rich and not the poor working class. We still think so."[127]

PPC then took inspiration from California activists by seizing an open lot. In October of 1968 some in the Berkeley area began to fight for a "People's Park." In April of 1969, California hips united with activists to build one. Some envisioned it as a symbol of hope, and to others it "could lead to a community willing and able to defend its turf." Without permit or permission, activists claimed the land, and in May of 1969 a riot ensued as they battled the police.[128]

Lincoln Park activists followed suit. In June, CCSF promoted the idea for a People's Park mentioned by YLO earlier, handing out leaflets to solicit materials from the community.[129] Authorities relented, and volunteers established a temporary park at the corner of Halsted and Armitage. The gang Comancheros was particularly active there, clearing it of garbage and erecting swings and slides.[130] In a month, with little money or firm commitment from activists, the park suffered.[131]

Still not defeated, CCSF and its PPC allies adopted a new tactic to secure their vision: incorporation. They formed the Poor People's Coalition Development Corporation to bid for cleared land that they would then develop. The corporation obtained startup capital from McCormick Theological

Seminary, and Lincoln Park resident and architect Howard Alan drew up a building plan, consulting with poor residents on its design. As a result, Alan proposed including a terrace that would allow residents to interact, thus bolstering the sense of community.[132] This perfectly legal approach resonated with area liberals, including a former city development and planning commissioner. The president of McCormick publicly supported the Development Corporation, as did one Alderman, who enlisted a prominent city architect to endorse the plan.

By January of 1970, their plan was in place and the Conservation Community Council voted eleven to two to recommend it to DUR. Only LPCA president Peter Bauer and the Ranch Association president opposed.[133] Some council members claimed the Poor People's group intimidated them. Others denied this, but the result was that neighborhood groups moved to block the plan. The Lincoln Central Association gathered some thousand signatures in protest and sent them to the mayor and the Department of Urban Renewal board. LPCA protested via press conferences, and by direct contact with the city. These groups favored the bid submitted by the Hartford Company, which included only 15 percent low-income housing (in most other respects, the plan resembled PPC's). The Department of Urban Renewal listened to LPCA and its allies rather than the CCC. On February 11, the DUR board met for five minutes at city hall, and voted to accept the Hartford bid, overturning the initial recommendation by the CCC. Police arrested two CCSF members as they moved to the front of the room.[134]

A PPC member then rushed the board. Police subdued him and charged him with disorderly conduct, resisting arrest, and assaulting a police officer as he screamed, "Come with me!" to Lords in the crowd. The city claimed it overturned the initial Conservation Community Council eleven to two vote in favor of PPC's bid explaining it did not want to set a precedent by awarding the disruptive coalition.[135]

PPC did not back down. At a press conference, Dick Brown and six others threatened to resign the Conservation Community Council if the coalition failed to win the bid.[136] Brown and others then decided to wait to resign until the City Council acted, as now the ACLU was investigating the February meeting at which the Hartford Company won the bid.[137] In June of 1970, residents asked the City Council's Housing Committee to reconsider the Hartford decision. LPCA's Pat Feely argued against the coalition's plan, insisting that the experimental nature of the building the group proposed was "at the expense of the civility of the community."[138] That month the City Council finally gave the Hartford Company approval to develop.[139]

Then, in July, activists set their sights on the Orchard-Willow Vine block, proposing modified plans calling for 280 units in one high-rise. Dick Brown promoted this plan, and those who were fearful of the man who jumped the stage now saw value in a "buffer between the ghetto and Lincoln Park." Former PPC opponents favored it, and it passed despite opposition by Alderman Singer and Conservation Community Council members. After this victory Brown finally resigned from the council in December.[140]

Violence

While activists took over community meetings and tried to work within the system to obtain and develop land, to some, violence became synonymous with Lincoln Park. Bombings, stabbings, and random acts of aggression linked to the Lords and their allies delegitimized them in the eyes of many. And it was not just the liberal, established whites of Lincoln Park who charged confrontational activists with violence. George Peters, owner of the long-running LSD rescue, accused YLO of intimidation, theft, and the rape of a girl in 1969. Lords, fearing that his business on Armitage would bring more Red Squad investigators, asked him to leave the area. *Seed* first attacked Peters, claiming he pressed the girl into making false accusations. Soon after, the magazine backpedaled, offering, "Other sources indicate that this is true and that the Young Lords' and Comancheros' discipline had broken down and some of them were vamping on the LSD Rescue people."[141] One resident commented, "Gangs would come singing loud, threatening down the street. I remember times when shots were fired. We were scared, afraid to go out for groceries. There was one kid found dead in an alley. The hippies accused him of being a narc ... One night I heard someone screaming, 'I've been stabbed.'"[142]

One target of attack was the Republican George McCutcheon who replaced "Paddy" Bauler as 43rd ward alderman.[143] One September evening someone firebombed the offices of both Alderman McCutcheon and Alderman William Singer, and the Feedstore restaurant. McCutcheon accused YLO, claiming it targeted him after he refused to allow them to close off the street in front of Armitage church for a party. The group denied involvement.[144] McCutcheon also said he received threats on his life from

Lords leaders.[145] Hitting back, Rev. Bruce Armstrong, of the Armitage United Methodist church, met with McCutcheon and criticized him for blaming YLO. The alderman countered by telling Armstrong his church was being "taken in" by the Lords, who he claimed to be responsible for community violence.[146] In October, the city helped a bit with the People's Park, although rumor had it that city officials ordered that entire area cleaned only in response to the bombing of McCutcheon's nearby office.[147] The bombings came just four months after James Mosberg, director of the Ranch Triangle Association, found a bomb in his mailbox. He also claimed to have received threats via telephone and postcard, and found a dead rat on his doorstep.[148]

The day after the bombings, LPCA sent a press release denouncing the attacks to the papers, TV, and radio stations, stating that the group, "emphasizes once again the state of anarchy and revolution openly advocated by some militant and dissident elements in the Lincoln Park Community." Noting that recent CCC meetings, "have been disrupted by threats, violence, and physical assault on its members. Such incidents are intolerable and have reached emergency proportions," the group asked that citizens and businesses "condemn these terror tactics," while additionally requesting that police and government agencies "investigate and vigorously prosecute this blatant assault on our citizens and democratic institutions." All seven neighborhood organizations signed the release.[149]

The neighborhood made national headlines again in late September when someone fatally stabbed Rev. Bruce Johnson and his wife in their home. No one was charged in the murders.[150] Armstrong was stabbed eighteen times, his wife Eugenia nineteen, in addition to her skull being bludgeoned. The church's membership had, according to one person, declined to less than a dozen, in part due to his support of YLO.[151] A memorial procession began at CCSF's office two days later, and NSCM planned a memorial service at which Jimenez spoke.[152]

A week later, in October, the Weathermen staged their National Action, coined the "days of rage" by the media. Lincoln Park was yet again in the spotlight as Weathermen, many of whom stayed in the area, rioted through the Gold Coast.[153] On October 7, Weathermen began to check into area churches and seminaries, and by the eleventh just under three hundred people were arrested for disorderly conduct or mob action, and rioters smashed more than eight hundred cars and six hundred residential store windows.[154] Tuttle appealed to NSCM to supply housing to protesters.[155] McCormick Theological Seminary offered shelter, and the police raided it.[156] Clergy were assured that things would be nonviolent, and felt misled when they turned destructive.[157] *Seed* feared that this violent action would convince the public that repression of activists was warranted.[158]

Cunningham's People's Law Office handled the cases of Weathermen charged with crimes. Weatherman Cathy Wilkerson slept in Dennis and Mona Cunningham's attic on a sleeping bag while other Weathermen met in the home, crashed there, and, to Mona's annoyance, raided the fridge.[159] Mid-North board member Peter Bauer warned other board members that "SDS has elected Chicago to experiment tactics [sic.] in the Lincoln Park area and that we are dealing with revolutionary anarchists," and felt, "we must get the silent majority out to back the Council otherwise in the next 6 months we will get rapid deterioration."[160]

Chicago media and the police only added to the tension. Newspapers regularly reported on the Black Panthers and gang violence while State's Attorney Ed Hanrahan made speeches and radio broadcasts about the latest indictments of gang members.[161] He also declared a war on gangs in the spring of 1969.[162] In a moment that sent shockwaves throughout the Black Power and antiwar movements, on December 4 Chicago police officers on the city's West Side, armed with a map of the building provided by an informer, entered the apartment of Black Panther Fred Hampton in the middle of the night, shooting him to death.[163] The Panthers publicized the killing, opening Hampton's dwelling to the media, and to visitors, who lined the block waiting to see the hundreds of bullet holes. To preserve evidence, the Panthers removed the apartment's door frame and Hampton's bloody mattress and stored them in the home of Rev. James Reed, who also helped gather bullet shells.[164] Later, an investigation would prove that all but one of the shots came from police weapons as part of a COINTELPRO operation.[165] Jimenez was part of the honor guard at Hampton's funeral.[166] In time, Hampton's family sued Hanrahan. The Ranch Triangle Conservation Association, however, had a different issue with him. The organization wrote him in December of 1969, insisting that "more effective and conclusive action be taken, particularly in the case of gang leaders."[167]

CHAPTER SIX

Confrontation and Gentrification

"There are other areas in the city where poor can live. LPCA wants an integrated community only to a degree and there already is a black community on the edge of Lincoln Park. There is also a Latin population, but the Young Lords do not represent that community."
—President, Park West Association[1]

Reactions

The new, confrontational, behavior of Lincoln Park activists angered and repelled community members, including liberal LPCA leaders who, by 1970, actually agreed to increase the allotment of low-income housing in urban planning, having approved of the Alschuler plan as early as 1968 that increased the ratio of low- and moderate-income housing to 2/3 rather than 1/3.[2] However, what happened next in Lincoln Park was not the backlash historians have asserted occurred on the national scale as the Silent Majority retaliated against protesters.[3] They now objected to the tactics used by their opponents as they finalized their vision. Whereas police violence garnered letters of support (and gave birth to grassroots groups such as the LPTM, Free City, and CCSF), violence, or the threat of it, committed by residents, including those of color, drove the more established liberal whites of Lincoln Park even closer to authorities.

In the wake of the riots surrounding the Democratic National Convention, the Daley administration claimed to have received one hundred thousand letters, of which 95 percent supported the police, and some Americans began to sport "Support your local police" bumper stickers on their cars.[4] Gallup Poll numbers indicate that 56 percent of Americans approved of Daley's handling of Chicago, while 31 percent were against.[5] The Chicago Association of Commerce polled two thousand area businessmen, 69.3 percent of whom thought the police handled things "about right," while 4.5percent felt them "too brutal," and 16.2 percent found them too lenient.[6] For his part, police captain Robert Lynskey praised the "professional manner" some three hundred of his officers showed at Lincoln Park on August 26, 1968.[7]

Even though LPCA openly opposed high-rise public housing (construction of which would end with the *Gautreaux* ruling), the new wave of disruptions angered members while they, and the city, began to *accept* some broader inclusion after the convention.[8] In January of 1969, CCSF's Dick Vission asked the city to reserve land for residents. By March the city complied, diverting land set aside for use by Augustana Hospital.[9] LPCA encouraged Daley to make the Conservation Community Council more representative of Lincoln Park by naming four new members. The mayor named one Puerto Rican and two African Americans (including Richard Brown) among the four. Richard Vission, however, called the new appointees "a joke except for Pat Creer and Dick Brown" and claimed, "The people who are being hurt have no representation."[10] In late April 1969, the city's CCC approved a "resolution that no additional sites requiring the demolition of residents be approved by the council until low and moderate income housing is constructed in the Lincoln Park area." This decision came prior to a study, conducted by NSCM's Larry Dutenhaver, of potential new sites for low- and moderate-income housing.[11]

LPCA also made public its intent to raise the number of low- and moderate-income homes in planning. Director Pat Feely feared that increased property taxes in 1971 would discourage lower-income families from moving to the area, as LPCA policy involved "encouraging as many prospective low-income tenants as possible to own their own property."[12] The liberals in the LPCA and CCC were indeed bending.

OTTA's concern for the future of the area, however, took on a racial overtone. Touting the services LPCA provided, it turned to a scare tactic, noting that "The December Newsletter from the LPCA shows that the total population for our area dropped from 97, 873 in 1930 to 67, 804 in 1970! Where have all the people gone? Well, mostly they have been bull-dozed right out." After breaking down the population by white, Black, and Other (including Indian), the organization offered, "In other words, the general population, based on the last census, decreased by 22%, the white by 33%, and the Black increased by around 300%."[13]

The city looked into any potential threat, no matter how banal, those promoting a different vision posed to the neighborhood. The CCC investigated the People's Park. In its "Special Secret Report," two members detailed their findings after mingling with, they sneered, "the Peoples people." Condescension permeated the account, as investigators reported their discoveries concerning which colors represented which group (e.g., Purple Beret for Young Lords) and general activities in the park. The report commented on the woman "missing a couple teeth in front" to whom she spoke, as well as the "overweight young man," riding his bike. The writers ended the report with a snide "Wear your button, visit site 19, and dig, man, dig."[14] One Mid-North member wrote to the commissioner of the Department of Urban Renewal about the park. Noting that a recent attempt by CCSF to solicit funds was possibly illegal, he offered that he was "certain that the funds collected will be used to further the revolutionary aims of the Young Lords, Young Patriots, Black Panthers and other groups operating in the Lincoln Park area." He suggested that the city investigate if it was possible to grant them the land, offering, "Let's beat them to the punch and take the 'thunder' out of their action. It is my feeling that they will fall flat on their face if they try to operate a playlot. But, let's give them that opportunity if it is legal and within the city's budget to do so."[15]

In addition to secret investigations, LPCA openly lambasted the PPC. Association president and local attorney Stephen Shamberg called the May 1969 CCC meeting a "turning point."[16] It became contentious due to what LPCA referred to as "another attack on the democratic process led by persons one writer aptly characterized as 'pseudo-revolutionary middle-class totalitarians.'"[17] Shamberg denounced the disrupters, arguing their complaints did not justify their actions.[18] In a letter written to LPCA members, he condemned protesters at the meeting, but also agreed with their agenda. He wrote of both public housing and privately owned housing for the poor as "miserable" and that the promises made by authorities "illusory." Additionally, he offered that the "complaints of many members of our community about urban renewal are justified" but argued that their conduct was not. He concluded by asking that CCC members continue to attend meetings in large numbers to curb this.[19]

In a response to the July meeting, Shamberg thanked those who turned out to "support the democratic process." He argued that protesters attempted to subvert democracy, and in doing so threatened to inadvertently undo urban renewal once and for all. He quoted an editorial in the *Chicago Daily News* that "If duly elected boards or appointive councils are not

permitted to perform their function, democracy is destroyed. And if dissident groups who demand a 'voice'—but are really insisting on having
things their way or else—persist in such methods defense tactics will have
to be devised." He painted a grim picture of a future threatened by radicals,
and insisted that "Our government must not be allowed to avoid providing
low income housing because of the intense bitterness that is maturing in
our community."[20] He also considered filing civil and criminal complaints
against protesters, and claimed that members were afraid to come to meetings without police protection.[21] Shamberg, a thirty-year-old attorney, had
previously worked with the Neighborhood Legal Assistance Center helping Cabrini-Green residents file suits in court against landlords. His sym-
pathies lay with the poor, as when he told the *Chicago Tribune*, "We must
not allow any further demolition until new low income and moderate
family housing is constructed . . . If our council is prevented from meeting
by physical violence or meets only with uniformed police present, we will
lose our power to make decisions."[22]

Nineteen residents who attended that contentious July meeting echoed
Shamberg's belief that the cause of neighborhood diversity was just, but
confrontational tactics inexcusable. They expressed their "sincere desire"
to work with the PPC, but claimed to be put off by its behavior. The signa-
tories supported CCC's Lyle Mayer and condemned the "manner in which
some of the residents conduct themselves" and the "wanton destruction" of
private property in the area. Similarly, a group of residents sent letters of
support to Alderman George McCutcheon and the *Chicago Sun Times* editorial director, agreeing with the views of CCSF, but denouncing their actions. They expressed outrage at fellow residents who got away with
breaking the law, creating a spectacle, and in the end harming law-abiding
neighbors.[23] In another letter, LPCA members defended themselves and
invoked the language of Richard Nixon, indicating that they were not "fat
cats" but were "the working class in Lincoln Park" and a "silent majority
who work for Lincoln Park instead of talk." They expressed their outrage
with the slow movement of urban renewal and the lack of promised loans,
and reminded "you who call yourselves dissidents" that without LPCA
"Lincoln Park would have been bulldozed from end to end and you would
have another Carl Sandburg Village."[24] A local pastor denounced the actions of Dick Brown, offering, "His words are not our words, his ways are
not our ways," but urged the community to act on behalf of those in need,

pleading, "Let there be public hearings in every street and block before one more house is leveled or one more family removed or one more dollar made."[25] Members of the IPO expressed their belief that "direct physical attacks cannot be tolerated" and also criticized the DUR and renewal as being poorly planned and a source of neighborhood tension.[26] In September, the Old Town Triangle Association wrote to the DUR's Lewis Hill disagreeing with the methods used by the "protesters" but also restating that group's opposition to the displacement of residents before alternative housing became available.[27]

Confrontational behavior also irritated Mid-North members. In regard to meetings addressing land being taken from Augustana Hospital and redistributed for housing, the *Mid-North Association* noted "practiced debaters and agitators," who were "becoming good pupils in the art of intimidation."[28] After the July LPCA meeting, Mid-North's president sent telegrams to Daley and Commander Braasch decrying the outburst. She informed Mid-North members of what happened and offered that she, and others, wanted reassurances from the city "that *all* [emphasis in original] citizens' rights to peaceful assembly will be protected by whatever means necessary." She also met with community leaders and planned to work closely with neighborhood presidents of LPCA, the CCC, and the Eighteenth District Police to "bring about the necessary cooperation and protection to insure our freedom from threats and violence in the future." Additionally, she asked that Mid-North Association member Peter A. Bauer distribute his first-hand account of the events of July 29.[29]

The more combative atmosphere was enough for the Mid-North Association to request, and get, police surveillance of its president's home during a meeting of the board held there in August.[30] In an attempt to better the images of those allied with LPCA and rally support against the forces of disruption, Mid-North's Peter Bauer wrote a letter in early August in which he sought to clarify "misleading news reports" about the July meeting. He claimed that the meeting was "almost immediately overtaken and *no* [emphasis in original] testimony was heard on any items on the agenda." In addressing the tennis club issue, he asserted that the media left much out and that Project I designated the site for some kind of recreational sports facility. He insisted that other ideas for the land, including those allowing free or low-cost use of facilities, were not widely reported. He noted eight disturbances that year, and claimed that "citizens with whom the militants disagree have received threatening phone calls, have been threatened with arson, or have had their names, home addresses, and phone listed under 'Community Enemies' in a local revolutionary newspaper." He encouraged residents to provide evidence to the state's attorney, attend CCC meetings, and speak out against violence and "terrorist tactics."[31] The police announced they would be present at council meetings. More than one hundred officers attended the next meeting as members again avoided allowing low-income high-rises.[32]

In an executive session meeting behind closed doors, the board of directors of the Mid-North Association discussed the July 29 LPCA meeting. One member feared that, according to area residents, Mid-North and LPCA were seen as linked to DUR. He suggested Mid-North write a white paper to outline the group's position on housing. Members agreed that a stand on low-income housing should be prepared and sent to Mayor Daley and Lew Hill of the DUR. On the other hand, the group also planned to limit admission to its upcoming September 8 meeting. That gathering would be limited to members only, and "Green cards will be given members as they check in" before watching televised footage of the July 29 fracas.[33] They also requested police surveillance and protection for that meeting, writing directly to Commander Braasch.[34] The Mid-North Association also stated that "We strongly oppose and disapprove of the street gang tactics, personal threats, planned disruption of public meetings, intimidation of businessmen, institutional take-overs, and particularly the continuing cooperation of the Armitage Avenue Methodist Church, by the Young Lords Organization, Comancheros, SDS and their affiliated gangs and groups. We further openly express our support and cooperation with law enforcement agencies, the LPCCC, the LPCA and our neighborhood associations, and will continue to abet their efforts by signing complaints and communicating incidents which are detrimental to the welfare of our community."[35]

Additionally, the Ranch Triangle Conservation Association appealed to the Department of Public Works to help clean up graffiti, as "The scrawlings of different gangs combined with Leftists inspired Revolutionary slogans has a very depressing affect [sic.] on an area in which DUR and homeowners have spent so much money and effort to make Lincoln Park an outstanding community."[36]

Going beyond holding restricted meetings and calling the police, some LPCA members (believing that NSCM members radicalized the CCSF) formed the group UPTIGHT ("United People to Inform Good Doers Here and There") to cut off funds to the suspected ministers.[37] Members claimed that, in the wake of the YLO June takeover of Armitage Avenue Methodist Church, the neighborhood lived in fear. In addition to community and school board meetings facing disruption, UPTIGHT spokesman Harry Port claimed vandalism in the neighborhood increased. Residents testified at a meeting in the Chicago Temple, First Methodist Church, that armed gang members patrolled the church and threatened people.[38] Rev. Shiflett accused OTTA's Peter Bauer of using UPTIGHT to "exploit the divisions in our community" and convince suburban Methodists not to contribute to the Armitage Methodist Church and Holy Covenant, both with supposed ties to activists.[39]

In the early part of the decade, the LPCA worked with the Department of Urban Renewal to create a renewal plan for the area. When the Festival of Life loomed in 1968, some members appealed to the police for aid in thwarting it, and then for protection in its aftermath. Now, LPCA leadership turned to the US Congress for assistance in combating the "radical" members of the grassroots movement for a more inclusive neighborhood. Members of LPCA corresponded for some time with the Senate Internal Security Subcommittee, and finally in August of 1970 the subcommittee called LPCA executive director Pat Feely and board member Harry Port to testify about activism in Lincoln Park. The two presented testimony with help from Chicago Red Squad files.[40] Shortly after the takeover of Armitage and the Days of Rage they decided to assemble a committee to track community activism. They offered Congress a timeline of neighborhood activity from September 1968 through June 1970, and specifically named Patricia Devine, Larry Dutenhaver, Dennis Cunningham, James Reed, James Shiflett, Stephen Whitehead, and Dick Vission as members of CCSF. They expressed concern that YLO allied itself with the Panthers, noting times when Lords spoke out against the murder of Fred Hampton. Both claimed that the parent group for the Chicago Left was NSCM and that CCSF aided the Weather Underground. They also argued that a storefront law office (most likely the People's Law Office) supported by McCormick money housed the Left.[41]

Reed denied the charges, accusing Feely and LPCA of trying to "create a white, upper income slice of suburbia in the Lincoln Park area."[42] He then abruptly revised his statement, insisting that NSCM provided aid only to certain programs that leftist groups undertook. A bail fund existed at one time, he maintained, but it no longer did. In addition, his group only gave between two and three thousand dollars to others. He also insisted that NSCM "has never taught revolution and opposes violence."[43] Reed publicly decried violence and criminal action, and advocated for "the participation of all people in their efforts to secure better education, legal services, and good housing" while attacking LPCA's attempt to create a "pseudo-liberal, high-income, upper middle-class slice of corrupt suburbia."[44]

In August of 1970 Marjorie King, former SDS member and leader of the group Women's International Conspiracy from Hell also testified to the Senate subcommittee, claiming that Reed appealed to her for bail funds when she handled such money for SDS. She also asserted that certain wealthy Chicagoans financed activism. For example, one paid Lords members one hundred dollars an hour to serve as waiters at her parties, donated thousands of dollars to activists, and maintained apartments in Old Town for those in need of shelter or on the run from authorities. YLO's Mike Soto testified that Reed was a "big instigator" and that CCSF was "one factor of violence in our community."[45]

The *Christian Century* lashed out at the hearing. Harkening back to the days of Joe McCarthy, the magazine called Feely's and Port's appearance a "parody on congressional hearings of 20 years ago." It revealed that Feely obtained NSCM budgets and other information used in testimony as vestryman of his church, which belonged to NSCM and reported that the neighborhood had been divided for some time, spurred on by LPCA action. It also argued that the men's testimony brought more polarization to Lincoln Park. It claimed that those accused were not offered the opportunity to cross-examine witnesses, but that NSCM was considering petitioning the subcommittee in order to testify.[46] NSCM wrote to LPCA's board of directors for clarification regarding Feely and Port's testimony. Calling the charges they leveled "entirely erroneous and in many respects slandered," ministers asked for a written reply (to be delivered within fifteen days) addressing if and to what extent the two men represented LPCA, if the group endorsed their charges, and for a copy of the year-long study the two mentioned in testimony.[47] The impact of the hearing, according to Doering, was that the ministry lost about half its members.[48]

And yet even with pressure on the movement for broader inclusion, some Lincoln Park residents still called the area unsafe at night.[49] Chicago police now worked even more closely with neighborhood groups to stem violence and weed out dissention. LPCA's Feely remained in touch with the police, even contacting them in regards to the political background of a local theater owner (most likely Sills).[50] Neighborhood organizations had productive working relationships with the police for years, but this relationship became closer in the early 1970s. Police officers appealed directly to Mid-North members about vandalism, and the prosecution of "hard-core gangs."[51] In January of 1971, Eighteenth Police District commander John O'Shea spoke to the Mid-North Association about patrols in Mid-North, Cabrini-Green, and ways residents could help the department.[52] By March of 1971, the district commander reported to Mid-North's Executive Committee that "renewed activity on the part of the Concerned Citizens . . . was to be expected in the spring. Dick Vission and [Weather Underground Organization leader] Bernadine Dorhn have returned to the area with imported assistants from New York. They can be expected to renew their activities in the community as soon as the weather becomes warmer."[53]

The Chicago Police and FBI provided additional strain on the movement for broader inclusion. Red Squad members confronted the parents of one of Dennis Cunningham's clients, warned them that he was a "known subversive" and advised them to find another attorney. Unmarked cars sat parked in front of his office, drivers often verbally harassing clients.[54] In fact, the Red Squad was so interested in activity in Lincoln Park that officers even had substantial files on the Old Town School of Folk Music.[55] The FBI's COINTELPRO "sabotaged" the establishment of the Rainbow Coalition among SDS, the Black Panthers, the Young Lords, and the Young Patriots.[56] Dick Vission stated that he and Dick Brown were held for three hours by Gang Intelligence Unit members when they appeared in court to ask for a bond reduction on their July 29, 1969, arrests.[57] Squad cars parked near Lords standing in front of the People's Church, and officers frisked members to intimidate them.[58] Officers tailed Lords so often that, as one later recalled, "You used to get to know the people that were following you."[59]

Serendipity City

The movement for a cosmetically diverse Lincoln Park, begun in 1948, weathered public criticism and picketing in the 1960s. Having also survived the Festival of Life and its aftermath, this movement for the most part realized its original dream as the 1970s unfolded. One renovated brick home in Sheffield valued at $16,000 in 1964 sold for $29,000 in 1970, then for $35,000 just one year later. A Young Lord said that, "By 1971 it [the Sheffield/Lincoln Central area] was beginning to change a little bit. Most of the hippies by then were going to the coast. Latino families were being pushed out. One building on the corner of Armitage and Halsted was remodeled about two years ago—seven Latino families were pushed out. Old white ladies couldn't afford to live in the area either."[60] A Mid-North Building owner offered, "I don't like the classier aspects of the neighborhood. I don't want it to turn into a suburb. As it changes from a lower middle class to upper middle class the neighborhood tends to lose services, to become car oriented, lose its local orientation." A developer in Old Town noted, "When I first moved in everybody took boarding houses and converted them into flats. In the last three or four years it has changed so that people are converting now to single family residences . . . They are wealthy, young people. Many have kids that they sent to private school."[61] A store owner shared that he had to stock more "gourmet" items on the selves, and switched from Schlitz and Hamm's beer to imports.[62]

In 1972, the 43rd Ward Citizens Committee published the second volume of *Serendipity City: A Selective Guide to the Best in Shopping, Dining, Entertaining, and Existing in the Lincoln Park Neighborhood*, a document that speaks to the effectiveness of the GNRP. Noting that Wells Street, the epicenter of Chicago's counterculture, also used to be its locus of antiquing, the guide claimed that North Clark Street, Lincoln Avenue, Belmont and Diversey still had shops, with another four on Broadway, sixteen on Clark, one on Geneva Terrace, and three on Sheffield. The publication also boasted of twenty-one thrift and other shops, twenty-six home furnishing stores, sixty-six pubs, fifty-five boutiques, and ninety-three restaurants, including six Mexican, two Indian, two Middle Eastern, five Italian, ten Japanese, two Korean, seven Chinese, two Czech, one Swedish, four German, and five French among them.[63]

The food may have been diverse, but throughout the 1960s and beyond Lincoln Park remained a predominately white enclave. In 1960, approximately 1.5 percent of the population was African American, and 2.5 percent Puerto Rican. In 1970, 7.2 percent of the population was African American, and 4.6 percent were "other nonwhite." In 1980, 8.6 percent of the population was Black, with 8.1 percent nonwhite. The white population,

88.6 percent in 1970, dropped only to 83.3 percent ten years later.[64] In that year, homes in Lincoln Park were worth on average $123,700, whereas the number for homes across the city was $47, 200.[65]

By the early 1970s, attention turned to high-rise development. One OTTA president lamented Wells Street's continued existence and questioned "whether the new high rise residents will be a plus or minus to our community."[66] OTTA worked to block the development of high rises. Some feared their encroachment since the late 1960s, while businessmen felt new buyers in the area would be beneficial.[67] LPCA's Roland Whitman and the CCC's Lyle Mayer moved against a high-rise development on North Wells.[68] From 1971 to 1974 Old Town residents fought the development of two high-rises, succeeding in securing a revised plan for low-rise commercial and apartment buildings.[69]

However, by 1974, high-rise condominiums, either converted from other buildings or built anew, spread in Lincoln Park and surrounding neighborhoods. A shopping center and apartment complex sat at the corner of Clark and Wells.[70] A high-rise on North Lakeview Avenue offered ten different floor plans, and views of Lincoln Park and Lake Michigan.[71] Lincoln Park West was now home to a thirty-eight story building its architect boasted was cutting-edge.[72] Another twelve-story conversion in Lincoln Park West, its developer anticipated, would attract "young executives who work in the Loop and don't want to live in the suburbs."[73] On Fullerton avenue, just west of Lincoln Park, was a thirty-story high-rise of glass and steel.[74] One Mid-North Artist commented, "By 1970 it had turned quite a bit. Houses were selling for $55,000 to $60,000 which we thought was a lot of money. I remember when people were paying $30,000 to $40,000."[75]

Lincoln Park's struggle to define community identity in the postwar years also had an impact on the city of Chicago as the urban renewal plan devised and executed there was part of a pattern of development. Hyde Park-Kenwood preceded Lincoln Park and established the practice of fusing influential residents with government to further renewal. Lincoln Park, along with the Uptown and West Town neighborhoods, followed suit.

In Uptown, local leaders in business and government formed the Uptown Chicago Commission in 1955, similar to LPCA, that prepared a renewal plan in 1957. Unsuccessful in getting it passed in that year, in 1960 the commission took up a community study published in 1962, one that Larry Bennett called a "city within a city" plan similar to Lincoln Park's

GNRP. And, as in Lincoln Park, in Uptown those who felt marginalized by renewal lashed out by interrupting Uptown Conservation Community Council meetings in 1968 and 1969.[76] Marketers even promoted Uptown as "the next Lincoln Park."[77] The *Chicago Tribune*, noting that the Lincoln Park area was "so horribly expensive now" and that "the example was set by Old Town more than a decade ago," argued that Uptown was "Bigger than Old Town, New than New Town."[78] "New Town" referred to the vaguely defined area made up of former Old Town and Lincoln Park West residents, aka the "in crowd."[79]

In West Town in 1958, DUR targeted the area for renewal in a plan much like Lincoln Park's and by 1970 city government and business worked to guide gentrification.[80] However, resistance by Puerto Ricans in West Town was more organized. They ran for office and gained political representation by the end of the 1970s, delaying gentrification. To Puerto Ricans in neighborhoods like Uptown, West Town, and Pilsen, Lincoln Park was a lesson: if you are not organized, you are driven out, and, according to John J. Betancur, in those areas gentrification happened at a slower rate.[81]

In the seventies, gentrifiers in cities across the nation worked to turn their neighborhoods into "urban villages."[82] White Chicagoans on the city's North Side had been doing this for almost two decades by that point, and continued on in the 1970s. In 1974 OTTA again went to bat against high-rises, this time against the one known as the Piper's Alley Project along North Avenue from North Park to Wells Street. Between 1972 and 1974, OTTA took the developer to court, filed an appeal after losing, and finally dropped its case when the developer agreed to build only three-story buildings throughout. The association's newsletter proclaimed, "the community prevailed."[83] Speaking at LPCA's 5th Annual Businessmen's Luncheon in 1973, DUR commissioner Lewis Hill noted that he was happy to " meet with friends of long standing to review what we have accomplished working together for a common goal. That goal, or course, was and continues to be the building of a better Lincoln Park . . . a community in which we sought to retain the desirable and distinctive characteristics that Lincoln Park has already possessed in abundance while we found solutions for problems that needed attention."[84]

OTTA also preserved its enclave via historic preservation. From 1967 through 1972, association members worked to place neighborhood buildings on the "permanent list" in the Illinois Department of Conservation and the

Library of Congress.[85] On December 8, 1971, OTTA president Amy Forkert appeared before the board to propose starting a Landmarks Preservation Council.[86] By March, OTTA established its Committee on Historical Preservation.[87] Forkert researched buildings in the neighborhood, held block parties to gather information, and "supervised distribution of questionnaires from the Chicago Historical and Architectural Landmarks organization to Triangle residents." Forkert and others compiled their data and presented it to the Landmarks Commission and the Chicago City Council designated the area a Chicago Landmark in 1977.[88]

Reinvention

In the early 1970s the movement for a more inclusive neighborhood crumbled in the same years that the Black Panther Party began to fall apart, the New Left splintered, and the counterculture both faded away and reinvented itself.[89] However, other residents, some of them new to activism, made their voices heard ushering in an era of transition from one set of goals to others. These activists of various stripes acted less confrontationally than their predecessors.

Cracks in YLO were obvious by February of 1970. Members faced police arrest for even minor infractions. For example, in response to a September 1969 resident complaint, police arrested four youth for disorderly conduct while meeting near the Armitage church.[90] As Jimenez faced possible jail time in 1970 for a mob action charge he received demonstrating against renewal, he attempted to shift power away from him so the organization could stand on its own. Still, the group's own "lack of internal discipline" began to erode its effectiveness. Lords field marshal Cosmo claimed that the group lacked follow-through as so many members were quick to jump on new bandwagons, but failed to turn new ideas into lasting programs, hopping fad to fad. The New York Lords echoed this, citing this inconsistency as the reason they split from the Chicago group.[91] YLO repeatedly tried to redefine itself theoretically as opposed to taking direct action.[92] The FBI had also infiltrated the Lords and authorities often arrested leaders like Jimenez to destabilize it, forcing members to spend time and resources on legal aid. Jimenez went underground for twenty-seven months, appearing in 1972 to serve his jail sentence for theft, which he began by fasting.[93] YLO then switched their focus to health care, but the group finally fizzled.[94] A local priest who claimed that gangs had taken over around his church indicated that on the one hand violence was so bad that people were afraid to leave their homes, but on the other what finally put an end to gang problems was urban renewal, as "the gangs and their parents couldn't afford to live here any longer."[95]

Other activists left as well. Pat Devine moved to California, Dick Vission moved to another area of Chicago.[96] An architect involved in the community argued, "There must have been five to eight years of organizing. They could not maintain the solidarity that was necessary."[97] Paul Sills moved to Wisconsin in 1972.[98] Reed shifted his attention away from urban renewal to health care.[99] Cunningham defended the prisoners who took over Attica prison.[100] He worked both the early criminal trial in the 1970s, and then returned for the civil trial in the early 1990s.[101] NSCM melted away as the churches comprising it cut off funding. After drafting a "series of position papers" reassessing its goals, the group officially disbanded on November 27, 1972.[102]

The Church of the Three Crosses members continued the fight for low-income housing, but many accepted the fact that Lincoln Park was going to be young, affluent, and white, and created new programs for this neighborhood.[103] In 1976, one Mid-North renovator commented, "People coming in now are people with great amounts of money. They're not artists at all. They're very conservative people. They want everything neat and tidy."[104]

The hip presence in Old Town further diminished in the early 1970s. In the summer of 1972, for example, *Seed* informed its readers that "We are finding ourselves in our semi-annual crisis once again—only six people on staff now. . . . We've noticed that we've been drifting away from involvement in the Chicago Community—and a lot of that is due to our people power shortage."[105] Later that year editors wrote, "Hey, we've run into a bit of a problem with our subscriptions. Like, we're broke. . . . We're hurting bad, and we need help."[106] Nonetheless, the paper limped on in the early 1970s, often reprinting news stories from Liberation or Zodiac news services. Now more politically oriented, it covered gay rights, women's rights, and the standoff at Wounded Knee. It continued to include a "Free City Directory" until 1974, when it transitioned to a "Free City/Good Numbers Directory" prior to ending publication later that year.[107]

Yet, as second-wave feminism sprang from the ashes of New Left antiwar groups, local activism in Lincoln Park did not die completely, but took other, less confrontational, forms in the early 1970s. While 1960s style "hip" faded, grassroots activism in the 1970s flourished. The abortion group Jane worked at great risk to aid pregnant women. Jonathan Tuttle continued to minister from a Head Shop in 1970.[108] Old Town's St. Michael's Parish faced lowered enrollment in its school, but fought on by opening it to lower-income and nonwhite students even though, in the words of one teacher, "It's difficult to get people to come to events in Old Town."[109] Meanwhile, a Concerned Puerto Rican Youth Club opened on Armitage Avenue, with eighty-five members tutoring locals for their GEDs. LPCA supported this group, and its director ran unopposed for LPCA's board of directors.[110] In 1971, community activists in the West Side Coalition marched on the Chicago City Council to stop redlining in their neighborhoods. Six hundred initially marched, and when that went unheard, twelve hundred marched on DUR, demanding an investigation. By the year's end, the Department of Housing and Urban Development indicted real estate agents and city and HUD officials for "discriminatory bank practices." The next year the coalition held a national housing conference in Chicago. In attendance were two thousand neighborhood activists from some forty states alongside Mayor Daley himself. Representatives then formed the National People's Action to combat redlining across the country.[111]

And while the Chicago YLO eroded, the fight over renewal brought Cha Cha Jimenez into further public service. In the spring of 1974, he led YLO in a campaign against heroin dealers, even requesting a patrol car be in the area twenty-four hours a day to intimidate them.[112] He ran for 46th ward alderman in 1975 against incumbent Christopher Cohen telling reporters "I was moved nine times by these developers and forced to attend four different elementary schools. Each time I was forced to live in unstable communities filled with drugs, gangs, prostitution and other crimes. I was a victim of the ghetto."[113] Cohen had the support of the 46th Ward Regular Democratic Organization, while the Independent Precinct Organization backed Jimenez.[114] Another Republican candidate rounded out the three-way race. Despite giving up a purple beret for a suit and tie, Jimenez lost, but that Cohen enrolled in a "crash course in Spanish and printed Spanish signs" for his campaign suggests he saw in the former gang leader a real threat to his reelection.[115] Although he lost the election, Jimenez did meet with Illinois State Senator Richard D. Newhouse on his plan to remap the state's congressional districts to better protect Black voters.[116] Carlos

Castro, a Puerto Rican and former leader of a Latino chapter of the Black P. Stone Nation, when himself considering running for alderman of the 26th ward, noted that, "Cha Cha and I have been good friends for a long time. We decided that this is the year of the Latino. We must all work together now to get some Latin elected officials. The younger, second generation Latinos are ready to do it."[117] Additionally, Marison V. Rivera and Judson Jeffries argue that his city council race later assisted Harold Washington's election as Chicago's first Black mayor.[118] The *Chicago Tribune*, using a term all too familiar to Lincoln Park, noted that the 46th ward was a "diverse area that includes the riches of Lake Shore Drive and the poverty of Uptown."[119]

Conclusions

As Lincoln Park residents, between 1948 and 1974, struggled to define their neighborhood, definitions haunt this study. Perhaps this is unsurprising, as it is a history of urban renewal, gentrification, liberalism, the counterculture, police violence, "Long Sixties" activism, the postwar ministry, and the Democratic National Convention, each its own multifaceted subject. Scholars of these topics have offered up useful definitions to explore and clarify them, while others are still in need.

The definitions of urban renewal and gentrification can cause confusion. Both are used to address the processes by which one group of individuals push out another. However, urban renewal is in some ways a more precise term as renewal projects were clearly defined and executed. Additionally, while its start date may be up in the air, Richard Nixon provided a firm end date when he ended renewal in 1973. The term "gentrification" can be traced to 1964. And yet, it took, and takes, various forms and is executed by various individuals over a span of time. Defining the people who renew or gentrify is difficult. They have been portrayed at one end of the spectrum as callous invaders, as innocent idealists at the other, and in other ways at points in between.

In Lincoln Park, the process of gentrification began as early as 1948, when the Old Town Triangle Association formed and united persons who were already rehabilitating homes. After other local organizations came together, the Lincoln Park Conservation Association, a mix of middle- and upper-middle-class white residents with close ties to city hall, formed to carry urban renewal forward. I term their early vision one of cosmetic diversity, but do so with some hesitation in part because it involves adding another word to the list whose definition is difficult: diversity. In the collective eyes of the LPCA in the postwar years, Lincoln Park *was* diverse, despite that, as census and other data clearly point out, it was predominantly white. Their claim was in part relative: compared to other, intensely segregated, parts of Chicago, Lincoln Park did possess a mosaic of individuals. And, in their eyes, ethnic diversity, more precisely European ethnic diversity, was diversity. These establishment liberals did not evaluate diversity in terms of class or race. Systemic issues such as these simply did not factor into their vision. While in the eyes of LPCA founders ethnic diversity was enough, I deem it cosmetic as their goal was, in reality, to preserve and restore the past, and at best refine the present, rather than chart a bold, different future or truly alter the area.

Defining those ministers who pushed for broader inclusion in neighborhood planning also presents challenges. They clearly fall into Mark Wild's term "renewalist," as they were part of this clerical vanguard that wanted to make the Protestant Church more relevant, and wanted to work with non-religious groups to do so. And yet, as we see in the case of persons like Jonathan Tuttle, Lincoln Park ministers embraced the counterculture as well. They were renewalists and hips, liberals and leftists, a unique Chicago clerical vanguard.

Conversely, that Chicago hips allowed a ministerial presence in their vision of the neighborhood adds a twist to the definition of the counterculture. The unique clerical–hip alliance in Chicago also performed the mundane grunt work of meeting with city officials and filing paperwork prior to the 1968 Festival of Life. The Chicago countercultural scene blended business interests, the clergy, and "freaks," and offers us another "diverse" group in this study.

One person's chaotic riot can be another person's planned rebellion, and with this in mind the definitions of violence and confrontation also come into question, and offer insight as to white Chicago liberals' beliefs on protest in the late 1960s. The Chicago Police, after months of carrying out orders to harass hip persons in and around Lincoln Park, committed brutal acts of violence during convention week. And yet, Americans across the nation, and in Chicago, applauded their actions, some indicating they felt officers did not go far enough. In Lincoln Park, white liberals who, prior to the convention and festival, performed reconnaissance for the police sought their protection after. That they sought it from a new coalition of activists, many of them persons of color, is illustrative of white liberal attitudes in the late 1960s. On the one hand, acts of neighborhood violence undoubtedly occurred in the aftermath of the festival and its police violence, from bombings to brutal murders. Yet, when groups like Mid-North asked for police protection, they feared individuals who had publicly committed acts of confrontation. Yes, community meetings were certainly heated in 1969, but jumping up on a stage and seizing a microphone was not bashing someone's skull with a baton. Police violence, later termed a "police riot," received community applause, while community confrontation met with local, state, and federal harassment.

The liberal, white Lincoln Parkers who worked with the city, and the police, force us to consider liberalism's definition, and characteristics, as well. Peniel E. Joseph points out that, "The BPP's high-profile legal battles drew support from a multiracial coalition of liberals, radicals, and civil liberties activists" who formed a "kind of civic defense of the Panthers through high-profile commissions, books, editorials, even cocktail parties."[120] While cocktail parties to back area activists reportedly occurred in Lincoln Park, when those pushing for a more inclusive neighborhood turned to confrontation, they acted just out of the comfort zone of white Lincoln Park liberals who only accepted the *idea* of a more broadly diverse neighborhood. LPCA had embraced the 1968 Alschuler report advocating more low- and moderate-income housing, the CCC, in 1969, resolved that no new demolition should happen until new housing was built, and that same group backed the Poor People's bid for land. However, when those pursuing a more diverse area turned confrontational, those white liberals who were *just* inching their way toward embracing a more diverse neighborhood plan retreated from their baby steps, much like those Americans who claimed to embrace civil rights could not support cries for Black Power. Liberal, white, North Side Chicagoans in the late 1960s and early 1970s (even those critical of Daley and the police after 1968), much like other white liberals across the nation, were only prepared to help the poor and persons of color to a degree, and when the atmosphere, and people, got more confrontational and "radical," they quickly stepped back, revealing their tenuous embrace of diversity and how those intent on preserving the status quo could easily delegitimize those calling for new directions. In assessing the demise of the

Black Panther Party, Joshua E. Bloom and Waldo E. Martin, Jr., emphasize the role allied support plays in "insurgent movements."[121] Takeovers and perceived acts of violence were not about to guarantee the support of LPCA's and CCC's Stephen Shamberg, who repeatedly expressed exasperation at confrontational tactics, while publicly endorsing a stop to demolition and arguing for the building of low- and moderate-income housing. Those who wanted only a cosmetically diverse Lincoln Park could use the behavior of YLO and PPC as a way to ignore the hard issues of race and class. Lincoln Park liberals played a role in the development of postwar Chicago by, through their pursuit of cosmetic diversity, denying the poor and nonwhite a place to live, while at the same time offering a positive image of diversity in the area, a robust nightlife, and a "liberal" attitude, when in reality establishment liberals had one vision and non-establishment liberals another. In the end, liberals on Chicago's North Side, much like across the nation, failed to meaningfully address class and race, and Lincoln Park secured its place in Chicago history by becoming a gentrified enclave.

And yet, as those fighting for broader inclusion lost that battle, they also gained on several fronts, forcing us to think about the definition of "success."[122] Parents whose children benefitted from the Young Lords free breakfast program, and those who found aid at the health clinic, certainly saw improvement. The attorneys at the People's Law Office helped not only Lords and Panthers, but an array of Chicago citizens (in fact, the practice still exists). The coalition of the Concerned Citizens Survival Front, Lincoln Park Town Meeting, North Side Cooperative Ministry, and Poor People's Coalition that became fused to Free City, and the Young Lords was a sustained grassroots movement, one that was intersectional, inclusive, and empowering, and its continued existence in the face of police and FBI harassment was a success in itself. Those fighting development of the tennis court on the site of the People's Park delayed its development. Area leaders such as Dennis Cunningham and Cha Cha Jimenez acted on behalf of others in the courtroom and the ballot box. And some of the same lakefront liberals who did not agree with the tactics of people like Jimenez in time became a part of Harold Washington's coalition.

A national event, the Democratic National Convention, its Festival of Life and its police violence, also had a local impact on the gentrification of Lincoln Park, and occupies a key position in this study but requires redefinition. The protest was devised, albeit loosely, by New York Yips.

Chicagoans then stepped in, and up, to move it forward, redefining it as both a national and local event. Yippies made headlines, but Chicagoans made the news by planning and acting in the protest on their own terms. Chicago 1968 shocked a wide number of people who watched police beat protesters, and within the Movement it further alarmed activists. Locally, however, it changed the atmosphere of a neighborhood and impacted its renewal process.

It would be easy to label Chicago the "Second City" when it came to activism, especially as the Old Town counterculture developed in the shadow of Haight-Ashbury, and as the Young Lords openly patterned themselves on the Black Panthers. However, that label would be misapplied, as the above-mentioned Chicago groups carved out their own unique niches, and because Chicago activism in Lincoln Park was its own distinct blend of peoples and causes. Some Lincoln Parkers advanced their vision of renewal, others resisted; the violence of 1968 changed the atmosphere, and by the early 1970s the neighborhood was an area of robust, revitalized activism, while the curtain closed on renewal.

NOTES

BIBLIOGRAPHY

INDEX

Introduction

1. National Commission on the Causes and Prevention of Violence (hereafter referred to as NCCPV), *Rights in Conflict: The Violent Confrontation of Demonstrators and Police in the Parks and Streets of Chicago During the Week of the Democratic National Convention* (New York: Bantam, 1968), 250–265.

2. Todd Gitlin, *The Sixties: Years of Hope, Days of Rage* (New York: Bantam Books, 1987), 332; David Farber, *Chicago '68* (Chicago: University of Chicago Press, 1988), 199.

3. Gitlin, *The Sixties*, 333; Farber, *Chicago '68*, 200.

4. Frank Kusch, *Battleground Chicago: The Police and the 1968 Democratic National Convention* (Westport, CT: Praeger Press, 2004), 100.

5. NCCPV, *Rights in Conflict*, 263.

6. Gitlin, *The Sixties*, 333; Farber, *Chicago '68*, 201.

7. Amanda I. Seligman makes a convincing case for rejecting the term "riot" in general and instead using more neutral terminology. See her "But Burn—No: The Rest of the Crowd in Three Civil Disorders in 1960s Chicago," *Journal of Urban History* 37, no. 2 (March 2011) 230–255.

8. NCCPV, *Rights in Conflict*, 194.

9. Thomas Buckley, "The Battle of Chicago: From the Yippies' Side," *New York Times*, September 1, 1968, SM28; Sylvan Fox, "Gas Used Again to Quell Protesters," *New York Times*, August 28, 1968, 36.

10. John Schultz, *No One Was Killed: Documentation and Meditation, Convention Week, Chicago—August 1968* (Chicago: Big Table Publishing, 1969), 149–152.

11. NCCPV, *Rights in Conflict*, 195–203.

12. Allan Streyffeler, Lyndon Baines Johnson Library and Museum, Records of the National Committee on the Causes and Prevention of Violence, 1968–1969 (hereafter referred to as LBJ, NCCPV) Box 41, R-241, 5–6; George Knight, LBJ, NCCPV Box 35 OR-252, 7–13; Jonathan Tuttle, LBJ, NCCPV Box 42, R-459, 7–9; Farber, *Chicago '68*, 191–192; David Lewis Stein, *Living the Revolution: The Yippies in Chicago* (Indianapolis: The Bobbs-Merril Company 1969), 102–105.

13. Abe Peck, *Uncovering the Sixties: The Life and Times of the Underground Press* (New York: Citadel Press 1985), 114.

14. See Clayborne Carson, *In Struggle: SNCC and the Black Awakening of the 1960s* (Cambridge: Harvard University Press, 1981); Charles DeBenedetti, *An American Ordeal: The Antiwar Movement of the Vietnam Era* (New York: Syracuse University Press, 1990); Todd Gitlin, *The Sixties*; Kirkpatrick Sale, *SDS* (New York: Random House, 1973); Irwin Unger and Debi Unger, *The Movement: A History of the American Left, 1959–1973* (New York: Dodd, Meade and Company, 1974).

15. Doug Rossinow, *The Politics of Authenticity: Liberalism, Christianity, and the New Left in America* (New York: Columbia University Press, 1998); Paul Lyons, *The People of This Generation: The Rise and Fall of the New Left in Philadelphia* (Philadelphia: University of Philadelphia Press, 2003); Rusty L. Monholon, *This Is America? The Sixties in Lawrence, Kansas* (New York: Palgrave, 2002); Gregg L. Michel, *Struggle for a Better South: The Southern Student Organizing Committee, 1964–1969* (New York: Palgrave Macmillan, 2004); Robert Cohen and David J. Snyder, eds., *Rebellion in Black and White: Southern Student Activism in the 1960s* (Baltimore: John's Hopkins University Press, 2013).

16. David Farber, "New Wave Sixties Historiography," *Reviews in American History* 27 (1999): 298–305; W. J. Rorabaugh, *Berkeley at War: The 1960s* (Oxford: Oxford University Press, 1989), x; Kevin Boyle, "The Times They Aren't A-Changin,'" *Reviews in American History* 29, no. 2 (2001), 304–309; Robbie Lieberman, *Prairie Power: Voices of 1960s Midwestern Student Protest* (Columbia: University of Missouri Press, 2004), 9–11.

17. Larry Bennett, "Rethinking Neighborhoods, Neighborhood Research, and Neighborhood Policy: Lessons from Uptown," *Journal of Urban Affairs* 15, no. 3 (1993), 245, 253; Kenneth Fidel, "End of Diversity: The Long-Term Effects of Gentrification in Lincoln Park," in Ray Hutchinson, ed., *Research in Urban Sociology, A Research Annual: Gentrification and Urban Change*, vol. 2 (Greenwich, CT: JAI Press, 1992), 145–164.

18. Elaine Tyler May coined the term in her *Homeward Bound: American Families in the Cold War Era* (New York: Basic Books, 1988).

19. Quoted in Japonica Brown-Saracino, *The Gentrification Debates: A Reader* (New York: Routledge, 2010), 12.

20. Suleiman Osman, *The Invention of Brownstone Brooklyn: Gentrification and the Search for Authenticity in Postwar New York* (Oxford: Oxford University Press, 2011), 271.

21. Eric Avila and Mark H. Rose, "Race, Culture, and Urban Renewal: An Introduction," *Journal of Urban History*, 35 no. 3 (March 2009), 339.

22. Brown-Saracino, *The Gentrification Debates*, 169.

23. Japonica Brown-Saracino, *A Neighborhood that Never Changes: Gentrification, Social Preservation, and the Search for Authenticity* (Chicago: University of Chicago Press, 2010); Japonica Brown-Saracino, ed., *The Gentrification Debates*; Mary

Pattillo, *Black on the Block: The Politics of Race and Class in the City* (Chicago: University of Chicago Press, 2007); Derek S. Hyra, *The New Urban Renewal: The Economic Transformation of Harlem and Bronzeville* (Chicago: University of Chicago Press, 2008).

24. See Loretta Lees, "A Reappraisal of Gentrification: Towards a 'Geography of Gentrification,'" *Progress in Human Geography*, no. 24 (2000), 392–396; Lees, ed., *The Emancipatory City? Paradoxes and Possibilities* (Thousand Oaks, CA: 2004).

25. David Ley, *The New Middle Class and the Remaking of the Central City* (Oxford: Oxford University Press, 1997).

26. Neil Smith, *The New Urban Frontier: Gentrification and the Revanchist City* (New York: Routledge, 1996).

27. Saracino, *A Neighborhood That Never Changes*, 10.

28. See Samuel Zipp and Michael Carriere, "Introduction: Thinking Through Urban Renewal," *The Journal of Urban History* 39, no. 3 (2012), 359–365; Samuel Zipp, *Manhattan Projects: The Rise and Fall of Urban Renewal in Cold War New York* (Oxford: Oxford University Press, 2010); Jennifer S. Light, *From Warfare to Welfare: Defense Intellectuals and Urban Problems in Cold War America* (Baltimore: Johns Hopkins University Press, 2003); Eric Avila, *Popular Culture in the Age of White Flight: Fear and Fantasy in Suburban Los Angeles* (Berkeley: University of California Press, 2006).

29. Lassiter quoted in Zipp and Carriere, "Introduction," 360; See p. 367 for "visionary and pragmatic."

30. Andrew J. Diamond, *Chicago on the Make: Power and Inequality in a Modern City* (Oakland: University of California Press, 2017), 151.

31. Zipp and Carriere, "Introduction," 361.

32. Avila and Rose, "Race, Culture, and Urban Renewal," 344.

33. Jennifer Hock, "Bulldozers, Busing, and Boycotts: Urban Renewal and the Integrationist Project," *Journal of Urban History* 39, no. 3 (2012), 433–453; Michael Crutcher, *Treme: Race and Place in a New Orleans Neighborhood* (Athens: University Press of Georgia, 2010).

34. Guian M. McKee, "I've Never Dealt with a Government Agency Before: Philadelphia's Somerset Mills Project, the Local State, and the Missed Opportunities of Urban Renewal," *Journal of Urban History* 35, no. 3 (March 2009), 387–409.

35. Jennifer Light, *The Nature of Cities: Ecological Visions and the American Urban Professions, 1920–1960* (Baltimore: Johns Hopkins University Press, 2009).

36. Irene V. Holliman, "From Crackertown to Model City? Renewal and Community Building in Atlanta, 1963–1966," *Journal of Urban History* 35, no. 3 (March 2009), 369–386.

37. See Sharon Zukin, *Loft Living: Culture and Capital in Urban Change* (Baltimore: Johns Hopkins University Press, 1982); Aaron Shkuda, *The Lofts of SoHo:*

Gentrification, Art, and Industry in New York, 1950–1980 (Chicago: University of Chicago Press, 2016); Christopher Mele, *Selling the Lower East Side: Culture, Real Estate and Resistance in New York City* (Minneapolis: University of Minnesota Press, 2000); David Ley, "Artists, Aestheticization, and the Field of Gentrification," *Urban Studies* 40, no. 12 (November 2003), 2527–2544.

38. Carolyn Whitzman, *Suburb, Slum, Urban Village: Transformations in Toronto's Parkdale Neighborhood, 1875–2002* (Vancouver: UBC Press, 2010).

39. Daniel Kay Hertz, *The Battle of Lincoln Park: Urban Renewal and Gentrification in Chicago* (Cleveland, OH: Belt Publishing, 2018), 12.

40. David Freund, *Colored Property: State Policy & White Racial Politics in Suburban America* (Chicago: University of Chicago Press, 2010); Samuel Zipp, "The Roots and Routes of Urban Renewal," *Journal of Urban History* 39, no. 3 (2012), 366–391.

41. Osman, *The Invention of Brownstone Brooklyn*, 154.

42. Abigail Perkiss, *Making Good Neighbors: Civil Rights, Liberalism, and Integration in Postwar Philadelphia* (Ithaca, NY: Cornell University Press, 2014).

43. Arnold Hirsch, *Making the Second Ghetto: Race and Housing in Chicago 1940–1960* (Chicago: University of Chicago Press, 1983), 173–180.

44. Osman, *Brownstone Brooklyn*, 5–6.

45. Brian D. Goldstein, *The Roots of Urban Renaissance: Gentrification and the Struggle Over Harlem* (Cambridge, MA: Harvard University Press, 2017).

46. Brown-Saracino, *The Gentrification Debates*, 64–67.

47. Mark Wild, *Renewal: Liberal Protestants and the American City After World War II* (Chicago: University of Chicago Press, 2019), 36–37.

48. John Hall Fish, *Black Power/White Control: The Struggle of the Woodlawn Organization in Chicago* (Princeton, NJ: Princeton University Press, 1973).

49. Suleiman Osman, "The Decade of the Neighborhood," in Bruce J. Schulman and Julian E. Zelizer, eds., *Rightward Bound: Making America Conservative in the 1970s* (Cambridge, MA: Harvard University Press, 2008), 106–127.

50. Allen J. Matusow, *The Unraveling of America: A History of Liberalism in the 1960s* (New York: Harper and Row, 1984); Jonathan Rieder, *Canarsie: The Jews and Italians of Brooklyn Against Liberalism* (Cambridge: Harvard University Press, 1985); Frederick Siegel, *The Future Once Happened Here* (New York: Free Press, 1997); Jim Sleeper, *The Closest of Strangers: Liberalism and the Politics of Race in New York* (New York: Norton, 1990).

51. Thomas Sugrue, *Origins of the Urban Crisis: Race and Inequality in Postwar Detroit* (Princeton, NJ: Princeton University Press, 1996); Hirsch, *Making the Second Ghetto*; Edward G. Carmines and James A. Stimson, *Issue Evolution: Race and the Transformation of American Politics* (Princeton, NJ: Princeton University

Press, 1989); James R. Ralph, Jr., *Northern Protest: Martin Luther King Jr., Chicago, and the Civil Rights Movement* (Cambridge, MA: Harvard University Press, 1993).

52. In addition to Peck's *Uncovering the Sixties*, see Stuart Henderson, *Making the Scene: Yorkville and Hip Toronto in the 1960s* (Toronto: University of Toronto Press, 2012); Randy Stoecker, *Defending Community: The Struggle for Alternative Redevelopment in Cedar-Riverside* (Philadelphia: Temple University Press, 1994); Osman, *Brownstone Brooklyn.*

53. For Haight-Ashbury, see Alice Echols, *Scars of Sweet Paradise: The Life and Times of Janis Joplin* (New York: Metropolitan Books, 1999) and Charles Perry, *The Haight-Ashbury: A History* (New York: Wenner Books, 2005). For New York, see Mele, *Selling the Lower East Side.* For Los Angeles, see David McBride, "Death City Radicals: The Counterculture in Los Angeles," in David McMillian and Paul Buhle, eds., *The New Left Revisited* (Philadelphia: Temple University Press, 2003), 111–136. More recently, Nicholas G. Meriwether offers a local study of one head shop in "The Counterculture as Local Culture in Columbia, South Carolina," in Robert Cohen and David J. Snyder, eds. *Rebellion in Black and White: Southern Student Activism in the 1960s* (Baltimore: Johns Hopkins University Press, 2013). See also W. J. Rorabaugh, *American Hippies* (Cambridge: Cambridge University Press, 2015); John Anthony Moretta, *The Hippies: A 1960s History* (Jefferson, NC: McFarland and Company, 2017).

54. Damon Bach, *The American Counterculture: A History of Hippies and Cultural Dissidents* (Lawrence: University of Kansas Press, 2020), xviii-xix.

55. David L. Parsons, *Dangerous Grounds: Antiwar Coffeehouses and Military Dissent in the Vietnam Era* (Chapel Hill: University of North Carolina Press, 2017).

56. Farber, *Chicago '68,* 20.

57. Abbie Hoffman, *Soon to Be a Major Motion Picture* (New York: Putnam, 1980), 144–147, 150–152.

58. Abe Peck, "An Open Letter on Yippie," *Seed,* v. 2, n. 11, 23.

59. Sale, *SDS;* Todd Gitlin, *The Sixties;* Charles Kaiser, *1968 in America: Music, Politics, Chaos, Counterculture in the Shaping of a Generation* (New York: Wiedenfield and Nicholson, 1997); DeBenedetti, *An American Ordeal;* Abe Peck, *Uncovering the Sixties;* Jonah Raskin, *For the Hell of It: The Life and Times of Abbie Hoffman* (Berkeley: University of California Press, 1996); Ed Morgan, *The 60s Experience: Hard Lessons About Modern America* (Philadelphia: Temple University Press, 1991); Mark Kurlansky, *1968: The Year that Rocked the World* (New York: Ballantine Books, 2004).

60. See Schultz, *No One Was Killed;* Abbie Hoffman, *Soon to Be a Major Motion Picture;* Norman Mailer, *Miami and the Siege of Chicago: An Informal History of the*

Republican and Democratic Conventions of 1968 (New York: Donald I. Fine, 1968); David Dellinger, *From Yale to Jail: The Life Story of Moral Dissenter* (New York: Pantheon, 1993); Jerry Rubin, *Do It!* (New York: Simon and Schuster, 1970). Bradford Lyttle's more expansive *The Chicago Anti-Vietnam War Movement* (Chicago: Midwest Pacifist Press, 1988); Robert Pierson, *Riots Chicago Style* (New York: Todd and Honeywell, 1984).

61. Farber, *Chicago '68*, and Kusch, *Battleground Chicago*.

62. United States of America vs. David T. Dellinger and Others, No. 69 CR-180 (U.S. Dist. Ct., N. Dist. IL, E. Div., 1969). *Transcript of Proceedings* (New York: Commerce Clearing House, 1970), Chicago, 1970, 13771. Hereafter referred to as U.S. vs. David T. Dellinger and Others.

63. Mike Royko, *Boss: Richard J. Daley of Chicago* (New York: Dutton, 1971), 178.

64. Tom Buckley, "The Battle of Chicago: From the Yippies' Side," *New York Times*, September 15, 1968, SM28.

65. Peck, *Uncovering the Sixties*, 118.

66. Michael W. Flamm sees access to space as central to both demonstrators and Mayor Daley. The former saw the Park as key in a symbolic fight over rights to space, but to the latter it "was a literal place where local citizens—taxpayers or at least residents with a stake in the community—could interact so long as they followed his rules." See his *Law and Order: Street Crime, Civil Unrest, and the Crisis of Liberalism in the 1960s* (New York: Columbia University Press, 2005), 156–157.

67. Allen J. Matusow, *The Unraveling of America*; Sidney Fine, *Violence in the Model City: The Cavanagh Administration, Race Relations, and the Detroit Riot of 1967* (East Lansing: Michigan State University Press, 2007); Gerald Horne's *The Fire This Time: The Watts Uprising and the 1960s* (Charlottesville: University of Virginia Press, 1995); Alyssa Ribeiro, "A Period of Turmoil: Pittsburgh's April 1968 Riots and Their Aftermath," *Journal of Urban History* 39, no. 1 (March 2013), 141–171.

68. Kevin Mumford, *Newark: A History of Race, Rights, and Riots in America* (New York: New York University Press, 2007); Jessica Elfenbein et al., *Baltimore '68: Riots and Rebirth in an American City* (Philadelphia: Temple University Press, 2001); Mandi Isaacs Jackson, *Model City Blues: Urban Space and Organized Resistance in New Haven* (Philadelphia: Temple University Press, 2008).

69. Gitlin, *The Sixties*; William L. O'Neil *Coming Apart: An Informal History of the 1960s* (New York: Quadrangle Books, 1971); Matusow, *The Unraveling of America*; James Miller, *Democracy Is in the Streets: From Port Huron to the Siege of Chicago* (New York: Simon and Schuster, 1987; Maurice Isserman, *If I Had a Hammer: The Death of the Old Left and the Birth of the New Left* (New York: Basic Books, 1989).

70. James Patterson, *The Eve of Destruction: How 1965 Transformed America* (New York: Basic Books, 2012). Kurlansky, *1968*; Kaiser, *1968*.

71. Rob Kirkpatrick, in his *1969: The Year Everything Changed* (New York: Sky-horse Publishing, 2011), makes the case for that year being crucial in culture as well as politics.

72. Rhonda Y. Williams, *Concrete Demands: The Search for Black Power in the 20th Century* (New York: Routledge, 2015), 267.

73. Nikhil Pal Singh, *Black Is a Country: Race and the Unfinished Struggle for Democracy* (Cambridge, MA: Harvard University Press, 2004), 204–205.

74. Hirsch, *Making the Second Ghetto*; Amanda I. Seligman, *Block by Block: Neighborhoods and Public Policy on Chicago's West Side* (Chicago: University of Chicago Press, 2005).

75. Hirsch, *Making the Second Ghetto*, xi.

76. Seligman, *Block by Block*, 5.

1. Diversity and Renewal

1. Bollwahn et al., "The Lincoln Park Community and the Lincoln Park Conservation Association," 8.

2. Prior to World War II the area was commonly known as "North Town." See Commission on Chicago Historical and Architectural Landmarks, Old Town Triangle District, September 1979, 3. While bound by North Avenue, Ogden Avenue, and Clark Street, the lines that defined Old Town were murky to some. For example, as late as 1971, the president of the Old Town Triangle Association complained of the media labeling "Old Town violence" any crime that occurred in the 18th Precinct Boundaries. See James G. Donegan, "Old Town is a Way of Life," *Chicago Tribune*, May 29, 1971, 10.

3. Zipp, "The Roots and Routes of Urban Renewal," 366–391.

4. For an overview of public discourse about cities after the war, see Robert A. Beauregard, *Voices of Decline: The Postwar Fate of U.S. Cities* (Cambridge, MA: Blackwell Publishers, 1993), 109–154.

5. Jon C. Teaford, *The Rough Road to Renaissance: Urban Revitalization in America, 1940–1985* (Baltimore: Johns Hopkins University Press, 1990), 11.

6. Mark I. Gelfand, *A Nation of Cities: The Federal Government and Urban America, 1933–1965* (New York: Oxford University Press, 1975), 148.

7. Beauregard, *Voices of Decline*, 146–152.

8. Samuel Zipp, Manhattan Projects; for Kansas see Kevin Fox Graham, *Race, Real Estate, and Uneven Development: The Kansas City Experience* (Albany: State University of New York Press, 2002); Avila, *Popular Culture in the Age of White Flight*.

9. Carl Condit, *Chicago 1930–1970: Building, Planning and Urban Technology* (Chicago: University of Chicago Press, 1974), 205; John F. Bauman, *Public Housing, Race, and Renewal: Urban Planning in Philadelphia 1920–1974* (Philadelphia: Temple University Press, 1987), 79–82.

10. Roger Biles, "Public Housing and the Postwar Urban Renaissance, 1949–1973," in John F. Bauman, Roger Biles, and Kristin M. Szylvian, *From Tenements to Taylor Homes: In Search of an Urban Housing Policy in 20th Century America* (University Park: Pennsylvania State University Press, 2000), 146; Avila and Rose, "Race, Culture, and Urban Renewal," 338.

11. Light, *The Nature of Cities*, 46, 112, 143.

12. Alexander von Hoffman, "Enter the Housing Industry, Stage Right: A Working Paper on the History of Housing Policy," Joint Center for Housing Studies of Harvard University, February 1, 2008, 8–9, https://www.jchs.harvard.edu/research-areas/working-papers/enter-housing-industry-stage-right-working-paper-history-housing.

13. Freund, *Colored Property*, 8–12.

14. Wendell Pritchett, *Brownsville, Brooklyn: Blacks, Jews, and the Changing Face of the Ghetto* (Chicago: University of Chicago Press, 2002), 139.

15. Lani Guinier, "From Racial Liberation to Racial Literacy," *The Journal of American History* 91, no. 1 (June 2004), 6. Barbara J. Fields, notes that racism was "sufficiently fluid enough" to survive moments of unity against it. See "Ideology and Race in American History" in J. Morgan Kousser and James M. McPherson, eds., *Region, Race, and Reconstruction: Essays in Honor of C. Vann Woodward* (Oxford: Oxford University Press, 1982), 159.

16. Light, *The Nature of Cities*, 74. The rankings, from highest to lowest, were "English, Germans, Scotch, Irish, and Scandinavians best; North Italians; Bohemians or Czechs; Poles; Lithuanians; Greeks; Russian Jews; South Italians Negroes and Mexicans."

17. Seligman, *Block by Block*, 76; Roger Biles, *Richard J. Daley: Politics, Race and the Governing of Chicago* (DeKalb: Northern Illinois University Press, 1995), 50.

18. Robert G. Spinney, *City of Big Shoulders: A History of Chicago* (DeKalb: Northern Illinois University Press, 2000), 217–220.

19. Adam Cohen and Elizabeth Taylor, *American Pharaoh: Mayor Richard J. Daley, His Battle for Chicago, and the Nation* (Boston: Little, Brown, 2000), 174–179.

20. John J. Betancur, "The Politics of Gentrification: The Case of West Town in Chicago," *Urban Affairs Review* 37, no. 6 (July 2002), 785.

21. Cohen and Taylor, *American Pharaoh*, 224–233; Dominic Pacyga, *Chicago: A Biography* (Chicago: University of Chicago Press, 2009), 327, 338; George Rosen, *Decision-Making Chicago-Style: The Genesis of a University of Illinois Campus*

(Urbana: University of Illinois Press, 1980); Thomas Dyja, *The Third Coast: When Chicago Built the American Dream* (New York: Penguin Press, 2013), 368–371.

22. Larry Bennett, *Fragments of Cities: The New American Downtowns and Neighborhoods* (Columbus: Ohio State University Press, 1990), 61; Dominic Pacyga and Ellen Skerrett, *Chicago: City of Neighborhoods, Histories and Tours* (Chicago: Loyola University Press, 1986), 57; Michael Ducey, *Sunday Morning: Aspects of Urban Ritual* (New York: Free Press, 1977), 18; Teaford, *Rough Road to Renaissance*, 118.

23. Malcolm Wise, "Sandburg Village, A Bold New Concept," *Chicago Sun-Times*, October 18, 1962, 52.

24. Condit, *Chicago 1930–1970*, 205–219; Harold M. Mayer and Richard C. Wade, *Chicago: Growth of a Metropolis* (Chicago: University of Chicago Press, 1969), 380–402.

25. Hirsch, *Making the Second Ghetto*, 40–67.

26. Taylor Branch, *At Canaan's Edge: America in the King Years, 1965–68* (New York: Simon and Schuster, 2006), 501–522; Fish, *Black Power/White Control*; Hirsch, *Making the Second Ghetto*; Laura McEnaney, "Nightmares on Elm Street: Demobilizing in Chicago, 1945–1953," *The Journal of American History* 92, no. 4 (2006), 1265–1291; Seligman, *Block by Block*.

27. Biles, *Richard J. Daley*, 10.

28. Biles, *Richard J. Daley*, 10.

29. Arnold Hirsch, "Massive Resistance in the Urban North: Trumbull Park, Chicago, 1953–1966," *The Journal of American History* 82, no. 2 (September 1995), 522–550; Hirsch, *Making the Second Ghetto*, 235; Condit, *Chicago 1930–1970*, 150–151.

30. As one critic of Mayor Daley pointed out, the mayor was "good with buildings, but he is poor with people—and deplorably poor with people who are black." Bill Gleason, *Daley of Chicago* (New York: Simon and Schuster, 1970), 20.

31. Bennett, *Fragments of Cities*, 58–66; Ducey, *Sunday Morning*, 13–22; Amanda Seligman, "Lincoln Park," in James R. Grossman, Ann Durkin Keating, and Janice L. Reiff, eds., *The Encyclopedia of Chicago* (Chicago: University of Chicago Press, 2004), 477–478; Margaret Stockton Warner, *The Renovation of Lincoln Park: An Ecological Study of Neighborhood Change*, PhD Dissertation, Department of Behavioral Sciences, University of Chicago, 1979, 24–36.

32. Jordan Levin, "A History of the Lincoln Park Community from 1824 to 1962," Histories of the LPCA and the Lincoln Park Area, Box 1, Lincoln Park Neighborhood Collection, DePaul University Archives (Hereafter cited as LPNC, DPUA).

33. Church Federation of Greater Chicago, *Lincoln Park and Its Churches*, Church Federation of Greater Chicago, February, 1963, 46.

34. Levin, "A History of the Lincoln Park Community," 24.

35. Church Federation, *Lincoln Park and Its Churches*, 7.

36. Church Federation, *Lincoln Park and Its Churches*, 66, 70.

37. Levin, "A History of the Lincoln Park Community," 77.

38. Church Federation, *Lincoln Park and Its Churches*, 62.

39. Church Federation, *Lincoln Park and Its Churches*, 38–39.

40. Levin, "A History of the Lincoln Park Community," 92.

41. Levin, "A History of the Lincoln Park Community," 60. By 1962, only four movie theaters existed, and most of the bowling alleys and dance halls had closed.

42. Levin, "A History of the Lincoln Park Community,"19–20.

43. Hauser, Philip M. and Evelyn M. Kitagawa, eds., *Local Community Fact Book for Chicago* (Chicago: Chicago Community Inventory, University of Chicago 1950), 34.

44. Church Federation, *Lincoln Park and Its Churches*, 22.

45. William R. Waters, "The Changing Economy of Lincoln Park after World War II to 1980," Lincoln Park Study Group, Box 3, LPNC, DPUA, 1980.

46. Robert Cross, "Big Noise from Lincoln Park," *Chicago Tribune Magazine*, November 1969, 30.

47. Warner, *The Renovation of Lincoln Park*, 87, 31.

48. A. Rod Paolini, *Lincoln Park Conservation Association: The Politics of a Community Organization*, M.A. Thesis, Northwestern University 1970, 5. For Cabrini-Green, see Devereux Bowly, Jr., *The Poorhouse: Subsidized Housing in Chicago* (Carbondale: Southern Illinois University Press, 2012), 31–32, 102–105.

49. Church Federation, *Lincoln Park and Its Churches*, 20, 4, 27.

50. Levin, "A History of the Lincoln Park Community," 73.

51. Church Federation, *Lincoln Park and Its Churches*, 58, 52, 49.

52. Church Federation, *Lincoln Park and Its Churches*, 7, 24, 22.

53. Hauser and Kitigawa, eds., *Local Community Fact Book for Chicago, 1950*, 35.

54. Cohen and Taylor, *American Pharaoh*, 466.

55. Warner, *The Renovation of Lincoln Park*, 87.

56. Richard B. Taub, D. Garth Taylor, and Jan D. Dunham, *Paths of Neighborhood Change: Race and Crime in Urban America* (Chicago: University of Chicago Press, 1984), 103–104.

57. Church Federation, *Lincoln Park and Its Churches*, 28, 31.

58. Levin, "A History of the Lincoln Park Community," 70.

59. Levin, "A History of the Lincoln Park Community," 71.

60. Church Federation, *Lincoln Park and Its Churches*, 29–30.

61. Church Federation, *Lincoln Park and Its Churches*, 54–56.

62. Levin, "A History of the Lincoln Park Community," 80.

63. Levin, "A History of the Lincoln Park Community," 80–81.

64. Church Federation, *Lincoln Park and Its Churches*, 37.

65. Hauser and Kitagawa, *Local Community Fact Book for Chicago, 1950*, 34.

66. Teaford, *Rough Road to Renaissance*, 45–54, 108–121.

67. "400 Councils Sought for Plan Parley," *Chicago Tribune*, September 4, 1958, N4.

68. Light, *The Nature of Cities*, 87–88, 101–127.

69. Light, *The Nature of Cities*, 126–127.

70. George M. Proctor "History and Characteristics of the Lincoln Park Community," Histories of the LPCA and the Lincoln Park Community Box 1, LPNC, DPUA; Seligman, *Block by Block*, 76.

71. Proctor, "History and Characteristics of the Lincoln Park Community," 9.

72. "History of the Founding of the LPCA," Lincoln Park Conservation Association Organizational Files, Board of Directors, Executive Committee, Public Relations, Box 1, LPNC, DPUA. The Urban Community Conservation Act was "specifically designed to prevent the deterioration of residential communities into slums." See Proctor, "History and Characteristics of the Lincoln Park Community," 15.

73. The LPCC was formed in 1954 by members of the OTTA and Mid-North Associations; See Hunter, *Symbolic Communities*, 165; "History and Characteristics of the Lincoln Park Community," Histories of the LPCA and the Lincoln Park Community Box 1, LPNC, DPUA.

74. Proctor, "History and Characteristics of the Lincoln Park Community," 9–10.

75. "History of the Founding of the LPCA," LPNC, DPUA.

76. Light, *The Nature of Cities*, 135–136.

77. Gerald D. Suttles, *The Man-Made City: The Land-Use Confidence Game in Chicago* (Cambridge, MA: Harvard University Press, 1993), 88; The term "defensible space" comes from Oscar Newman's *Defensible Space: Crime Prevention Through Urban Design* (New York: The Macmillan Company, 1972), 3.

78. Taub, Taylor, and Dunham, *Paths of Neighborhood Change*, 121–122.

79. Paolini, *Lincoln Park Conservation Association*, 20–23.

80. Albert Hunter, *Symbolic Communities: The Persistence of and Change of Chicago's Communities* (Chicago: University of Chicago Press, 1974), 160–161.

81. The idea was that "the scope of a conservation program required a separate organization with general direct community support." See Proctor, "History and Characteristics of the Lincoln Park Community," 10. The LPCCC then remained until the LPCA took off, and then the former disbanded and handed its treasury to the latter. See Paul Bollwahn, Wayne Lunder, Cora Meyerson, Craig Munson, Gordon Piper, Robert Taylor, "The Lincoln Park Community and The Lincoln Park Conservation Association: A Study of Poverty, Affluence, and Anomie,"

November 24, 1969. Page 6, footnote 16, DePaul University, Digital Collections, digicol.lib.depaul.edu/cdm/compoundobject/collection/lpnc6/id/1388/rec/1.

82. Warner, *The Renovation of Lincoln Park*, 40.

83. Proctor, "History and Characteristics of the Lincoln Park Community," 11.

84. Howard M. Rieger, *Redeveloping Chicago's Lincoln Park Area*, PhD Dissertation, Department of Government, Southern Illinois University, August 1969, 58.

85. "History of the Neighborhood Plan of Old Town and the Lincoln Park Area," Histories of the LPCA and the Lincoln Park Area, Box 1, LPNC, DPUA. Years later, a Mid-North Association Board member recalled that the LPCA was originally formed by the Old Town Triangle Association and the Mid-North association to "facilitate urban renewal." See March 15, Mid-North Board of Directors Meeting Minutes, Box 1, Board of Directors Meeting Minutes 1972, Mid-North Association Collection, DPUA.

86. *Mid-North News*, v. 1, no. 1, May 26, 1958, Box 1N, Newsletters 1955; 1958–59, Mid-North Association Collection, DPUA.

87. Diamond, *Chicago on the Make*, 137–144. Daniel Kay Hertz places great importance on this relationship in his *The Battle of Lincoln Park*. See pp. 14, 50–51.

88. "City Architect Wants Tougher Building Justice," *Chicago Daily Tribune*, December 31, 1950, W_A2; "Offer 2 Plans for City Hall Repairs Today," *Chicago Daily Tribune* April 15, 1957, 26.

89. "Lincoln Park Area Plans to Fight Blight," *Chicago Daily Tribune*, March 28, 1954, N1.

90. Sarah Jo Peterson, *Planning the Home Front: Building Bombers and Communities at Willow Run* (Chicago: University of Chicago Press, 2019), 77.

91. Trevor Jensen, "John A. Cook," *Chicago Tribune*, October 10, 2008, https://www.chicagotribune.com/news/ct-xpm-2008-10-10-0810090734-story.html. Accessed November 25, 2020.

92. "New Lincoln Park Unit Gets State Charter," *Chicago Daily Tribune*, May 13, 1954, N_A1.

93. Paul Gerhardt, Jr., "Standards of Professional Practice," *Journal of the American Institute of Architects* 9, no. 3 (March 1948), 138.

94. "Unemployables Learn Skills: 3R's Important in J.O.B.S.," *Chicago Tribune*, April 19, 1964, W_A1.

95. Ducey, *Sunday Morning*, 23.

96. Taub, Taylor, and Dunham, *Paths of Neighborhood Change*, 104–105; Ducey, *Sunday Morning*, 23–25.

97. Editorial, *Old Town Triangle Newsletter*, Box 1N, Publications, Newsletters 1960–1964, Old Town Triangle Collection, DPUA.

98. Paolini, *Lincoln Park Conservation Association*, 18–19.

99. Paolini, *Lincoln Park Conservation Association*, 13; By 1967, its annual budget was \$31,000 and it boasted a fifty-person board. See Peter H. Prugh, "Chicago Neighborhood Fights City Hall," *Wall Street Journal*, January 3, 1967, Box 9, Correspondence, Planning Zoning, 1966–1969, Old Town Triangle Association Collection, DPUA.

100. Proctor, "History and Characteristics of the Lincoln Park Community," 11.

101. "History of the Founding of the Lincoln Park Conservation Association," 4; Proctor, "History and Characteristics of Lincoln Park," 13.

102. Proctor, "History and Characteristics of the Lincoln Park Community," 12.

103. William Brashler, "Paddy Bauler's Secret Treasure," *Chicago* 29, no. 2 (1980), 152–159.

104. Richard C. Lindberg, *To Serve and Collect: Chicago Politics and Police Corruption from the Lager Beer Riot to the Summerdale Scandal, 1855–1960* (Carbondale: Southern Illinois University Press, 1998), 240–241.

105. David K. Fremon, *Chicago Politics Ward by Ward* (Bloomington: Indiana University Press, 1988), 284; Ward meetings in the basement, see June Sawyers, "Chicago Politics in the Grand Style of 'Paddy' Bauler," *Chicago Tribune*, September 11, 1988, 19.

106. Cohen and Taylor, *American Pharaoh*, 156.

107. Fremon, *Chicago Politics*, 284; Len O'Connor, *Clout: Mayor Daley and His City* (Chicago: Henry Regnery Company, 1975), 114; Old Town Triangle Association, "Harry Bauler," *Old Town Newsletter*, v. 7 (December 1962), 4.

108. Biles, *Richard J. Daley*, 77.

109. "Lincoln Park Conservation Group Formed," *Chicago Daily Tribune*, April 1, 1956, N6.

110. "Residents Seek Conservation for Lincoln Park," *Chicago Daily Tribune*, June 28, 1956, N1.

111. Proctor, "History and Characteristics of the Lincoln Park Community," 15; "Board Acts Today on Lincoln Park Conservation Plan," *Chicago Daily Tribune*, July 12, 1956, N1; "History of Neighborhood Plan of Old Town and the Lincoln Park Area," LPNC, DPUA; Department of Urban Renewal, "Lincoln Park Project I," Lincoln Park Conservation Association, General Reports Relating to Urban Renewal, Box 85, 2, LPNC, DPUA.

112. "Civic Officials Inspect North Renewal Area: 25 See Problems in Conservation," *Chicago Daily Tribune*, December 2, 1956, N9.

113. Waters, "The Changing Economy of Lincoln Park after World War II to 1980," 15, LPNC, DPUA.

114. Letter from the Ranch Triangle Association to the Community Conservation Board; n.d.; Letter from the Sheffield Neighborhood Association to the Community Conservation Board, April 18, 1961; Suggestions from the

Neighborhood Groups, Lincoln Park Conservation Community Council Box 5, Urban Renewal, Housing, and Zoning, LPNC, DPUA.

115. Suzanne Avery, "Private Funds Start Lincoln Park Renewal," *Chicago Daily Tribune* June 16, 1960, N1.

116. "History of the Founding of the Lincoln Park Conservation Association," 1960, 3.

117. "Lincoln Park Project I," Lincoln Park Conservation Association, Box 85, 3; "Histories of the LPCA and Lincoln Park Area"; "History of the Neighborhood Plan of Old Town and the Lincoln Park Area," LPNC, DPUA.

118. Ducey, *Sunday Morning*, 25. James Dalton asserts that in the early 1960s all CCC members were also LPCA members. When Mayor Daley created the CCC in 1961, the private citizens were to be residents of the area to be renewed. See James J. Dalton, *The Politics of Community Problem-Solving: The Lincoln Park Findings*, advance copy of author's M.A. dissertation, 75–76, LPCA Collection, Box 3, Bound/Catalogued Papers, LPNC, DPUA.

119. "Histories of the LPCA and Lincoln Park Area"; "History of the Neighborhood Plan of Old Town and the Lincoln Park Area," LPNC, DPUA.

120. *Mid-North News*, April 4, 1960, *Mid-North News*, January 9, 1961, *Mid-North News*, March 6, 1961, *Mid-North News*, April 3, 1961, in Box 1N, Publications, Newsletters 1960–1964, Mid-North Association Collection, DPUA.

121. Seligman, *Block by Block*, 53–54.

122. Old Town Triangle letter to the Community Conservation Board, January 31, 1961. Lincoln Park Conservation Community Council (hereafter referred to as LPCCC), Box 5, LPNC, DPUA.

123. Lincoln Central Association letter to the Community Conservation Board, March 28, 1961. LPCCC, Box 5, LPNC, DPUA.

124. Mid-North Association letter to the Community Conservation Board, April 17, 1961. LPCCC, Box 5, LPNC, DPUA.

125. Park West Community Association letter to D. E. Mackelman, April 28, 1961, LPCCC, Box 5, LPNC, DPUA.

126. Mid-North Association letter to the Community Conservation Board, April 17, 1961; Sheffield Neighborhood Association letter to the Community Conservation Board of Chicago, April 18, 1961; Old Town Triangle letter to the Community Conservation Board, January 31, 1961; Lincoln Central Association letter to the Community Conservation Board, March 28, 1961; LPCCC, Box 5, LPNC, DPUA.

127. Lincoln Central Association letter to the Community Conservation Board, March 28, 1961, LPCCC, Box 5, LPNC, DPUA; Mid-North Association letter to the Community Conservation Board, April 17, 1961, LPCCC, Box 5 LPNC, DPUA; Sheffield Neighborhood Association letter to the Community Conservation Board of Chicago, April 18, 1961.

128. Warner, *The Renovation of Lincoln Park*, 43.

129. Mid-North Association, "The Image of Mid-North," Box 3, The Image of Mid-North, Mid-North Association, DPUA.

130. Lincoln Central Association, letter sub-titled "Working Together for a Secure and Stable Family Neighborhood," LPCCC, Box 5, DPUA; Sheffield Neighborhood Association letter to the Community Conservation Board of Chicago, April 18, 1961; Park West Community Association letter to D. E. Mackelman, April 28, 1961, LPCCC, Box 5, LPNC, DPUA.

131. A. J. Liebling, *Chicago: The Second City* (New York: Alfred A. Knopf, 1952), 120–121.

132. Liebling, *Chicago*, 124.

133. Lilia Fernandez, *Brown in the Windy City: Mexicans and Puerto Ricans in Postwar Chicago* (Chicago: University of Chicago Press, 2012), 177.

134. Gabe W. Burton to Mr. Arthur Saltzstein, April 22, 1965, Box 2, Correspondence 1965–1969, Old Town Triangle Association, DPUA.

135. Angel G. Flores-Rodriguez, "The Young Lords, Puerto Rican Liberation, and the Black Freedom Struggle: Interview with Jose 'Cha Cha' Jimenez," *OAH Magazine of History* 26, no. 1 (January 2012), 62.

136. Johanna Fernandez, *The Young Lords: A Radical History* (Chapel Hill: University of North Carolina Press, 2020), 23.

137. Proctor, "History and Characteristics of the Lincoln Park Community," 2.

138. Evelyn M. Kitagawa and Karl E. Taeuben, *Local Community Factbook: Chicago Metropolitan Area 1960* (Chicago: Chicago Community Inventory, University of Chicago 1963, 1967 second printing), 2.

139. Paul Bollwahn et al., "The Lincoln Park Community and the Lincoln Park Conservation Association," 3.

140. Kitagawa and Taeuben, *Local Community Factbook 1960*, 2.

141. Kitagawa and Taeuben, *Local Community Factbook 1960*, 2–3, 28–29, 30–31.

142. Ranch Triangle Association to D. E. Mackelman, n.d.; Mid-North Association letter to the Community Conservation Board, April 17, 1961; Sheffield Neighborhood Association letter to the Community Conservation Board of Chicago, April 18, 1961, LPCCC Box 5, LPNC, DPUA.

143. "OTTA Planning Recommendations," *Old Town Newsletter*, Box 1N, Publications, Newsletters 1960–1964, v. 3, no. 1, January–February 1964, Old Town Triangle Association Collection, DPUA.

144. Box 7, Urban Renewal Opinion Survey, Old Town Triangle Association Collection, DPUA.

145. Box 7, Urban Renewal Opinion Survey, Old Town Triangle Association Collection, DPUA. Respondents were asked only if they thought public housing

"Very Important" (35 percent), "Somewhat Important" (16 percent), "Not Desirable" (31 percent), with 18 percent not voting.

146. Letter from D. E. Mackelman to David Landis, June 20, 1961, Box 9, Correspondence and Planning, Zoning 1961–62, Old Town Triangle Association Collection, DPUA.

147. "Old Town's Newest—28 Story Apartment Building," *Old Town Newsletter* v. 2, no. 5 (November–December 1963), Box 1N, Publications, Newsletters, 1960–1964, Old Town Triangle Association Collection, DPUA.

148. "More About Housing and Zoning," *Old Town Newsletter,* May 1966 (no volume, number), Box 1N, Publications, Newsletters, 1960–1964, Old Town Triangle Association Collection, DPUA.

149. Editorial, *Old Town Newsletter,* v. 1, no. 4, September 1962, Box 1N, Newsletters 1960–1964, Old Town Triangle Association Collection, DPUA.

150. *Old Town Newsletter,* December 1965 (no number or volume), Box 1N, Publications, Newsletters, 1965–1969, Old Town Triangle Association Collection, DPUA.

151. Monhollon, *This Is America?,* 46–47, 52–53.

152. Lisa McGirr, *Suburban Warriors: The Origins of the New American Right* (Princeton, NJ: Princeton University Press, 2001), 184–185.

153. Sugrue, *The Origins of the Urban Crisis,* 227.

154. Flamm, *Law and Order,* 32–33.

155. Peter H. Rossi and Robert A. Dentler, *The Politics of Urban Renewal: The Chicago Findings* (Westport, CT: Greenwood Press, 1961), 50.

156. Julia Abrahamson, *A Neighborhood Finds Itself* (New York: Biblo and Tannen, 1971), 14–20, 277–278

157. Bettie B. Sarchet, *Block Groups and Community Change: An Evaluation of the Block Program of the Hyde Park-Kenwood Community Conference* (Chicago: University of Chicago Human Dynamics Laboratory, 1955), 35.

158. Mid-North Association Minutes of Meeting of Board of Directors, Monday, April 4, 1966, Box 1, Board of Directors Minutes 1966, Mid-North Association, DPUA.

159. Roger Biles, *Richard J. Daley,* 39, 63, 81, 136.

160. Alan Brinkley, *The End of Reform: New Deal Liberalism in Recession and War* (New York: Vintage Books, 1995), 165–170; Ruth Feldstein, *Motherhood in Black and White: Race and Sex in American Liberalism, 1930–1965* (Ithaca, NY: Cornell University Press, 200), 73–75.

161. Matusow, *Unraveling of America,* 32–33.

162. Cheryl Greenberg, "Liberal NIMBY: American Jews and Civil Rights," *Journal of Urban History* 38, no. 3 (March 22, 2012), 458.

163. Preston H. Smith II, *Racial Democracy and the Black Metropolis: Housing Policy in Postwar Chicago* (Minneapolis: University of Minnesota Press, 2012).

164. Minutes of Meeting of Members of Mid-North Association, Monday, March 9, 1964, Box 1, Board of Directors Meeting Minutes, 1964, Mid-North Association Collection, DPUA.

165. Mid-North Association Minutes of Meeting of Board of Directors, Monday, April 4, 1966, Box 1, Board of Directors Meeting Minutes, Mid-North Association Collection, DPUA.

166. Warner, *The Renovation of Lincoln Park*, 53.

167. "Lincoln Park Renewal Gets Federal O.K.," *Chicago Daily Tribune*, January 23, 1962, 14.

168. "Lincoln Park Renewal Plan Spurs Building," *Chicago Daily Tribune*, October 3, 1962, 16; "Lincoln Park Renewal Plan Draws Funds," *Chicago Daily Tribune*, October 11, 1962, N6.

169. "Lincoln Park Renewal Unit Spurs Action," *Chicago Daily Tribune*, February 17, 1963, N6.

170. "Lincoln Park Area Survey Has Started," *Chicago Daily Tribune*, September 22, 1963, N5.

171. Thomas Buck, "U.S. Approves Lincoln Park Renewal Fund," *Chicago Daily Tribune*, February 15, 1963, B15.

172. Lincoln Park Project I, LPCA Box 85, 3–4, LPNC, DPUA; Robert Hawkins, "Lincoln Park Area Plan Told," *Chicago Tribune*, February 23, 1964, N2.

173. Editorial, *Old Town Newsletter*, v. 2, no. 3 (April 1963), Box 1N, Publications, Newsletters 1960–1964, Old Town Triangle Collection, DPUA.

174. Lincoln Park Project I, LPCA Box 85, 3–5, LPNC, DPUA.

175. Lincoln Park Project I, 1, 2, 3, 4, 6, 9–10, LPCA Box 85, LPNC, DPUA.

176. Lincoln Central Association letter to the Community Conservation Board, March 28, 1961, LPCCC Box 5, LPNC, DPUA.

177. Lincoln Park Project I, 9–10, LPCA Box 85, DPUA.

2. Inclusion and Renewal

1. For this vanguard see Wild, *Renewal*, 65–117.

2. Mark Wild, "Liberal Protestants and Urban Renewal," *Religion and American Culture: A Journal of Interpretation* 25, no. 1 (Winter 2015), 112–114, 122. For urban renewal and clergy of color, see page 123.

3. Sydney Ahlstrom, *A Religious History of the American People* (New Haven, CT: Yale University Press, 2004), 1082–1083.

4. James Hudut-Beumler, *Looking for God in the Suburbs: The Religion of the American Dream and its Critics, 1945–1965* (New Brunswick, NJ: Rutgers University Press, 1994), 177.

5. Hudut-Beumler, *Looking for God*, 185–188; Patrick Allitt, *Religion in America Since 1945: A History* (New York: Columbia University Press, 2003), 72–80.

6. Robert Wuthnow, *After Heaven: American Spirituality Since the 1950s* (Berkeley: University of California Press, 1998), 73; Mark Silk, *Spiritual Politics: Religion and America Since World War II* (New York: Simon and Schuster, 1988), 133–134.

7. Hudut-Beumler, *Looking for God*, 186.

8. Hudnut-Beumler, *Looking for God*, 131–133.

9. Syndney E. Ahlstrom, "The Radical Turn in Theology and Ethics: Why It occurred in the 1960s," *The Annals of the American Academy of Political and Social Science* 387 (January 1970), 6.

10. James T. Laney, "The New Morality and the Religious Communities," *The Annals of the American Academy of Political and Social Science* 387 (January 1970), 14–21.

11. Hudnut-Beumler, *Looking for God*, 176.

12. James F. Findlay, Jr., *Church People in the Struggle: The National Council of Churches and the Black Freedom Movement, 1950–1970* (Oxford: Oxford University Press, 1993), 58.

13. Hudnut-Beumler, *Looking for God*, 198–199.

14. Jill K. Gill, *Embattled Ecumenism: The National Council of Churches, The Vietnam War, and the Trials of the Protestant Left* (DeKalb: Northern Illinois University Press, 2001), 6.

15. Richard Henry Luecke, "Protestant Clergy: New Forms of Ministry, New Forms of Training," in Richard D. Lambert, ed., *The Annals of the American Academy of Political and Social Science* 387 (January 1970), 88.

16. Luecke, "Protestant Clergy," 90–92.

17. Ducey, *Sunday Morning*, 39.

18. "An Answer to Irrelevance," Concern, July–August 1965, 1, University of Illinois at Chicago, North Side Cooperative Ministry Collection (hereafter cited as UIC, NSCM) Folder 140.

19. 1962 Report and Fact Sheet, LPCA Box 80, 3, LPNC, DPUA. See also Ducey, *Sunday Morning*, 49–52.

20. Preamble to the Constitution of the North Side Cooperative Ministry, LPCA Box 80, LPNC, DPUA.

21. "The Christian Remnant," Correspondence, 1962–71, LPCA Box 80, LPNC, DPUA.

22. Janette T. Harrington, "North Side Chicago: The Troops Go into Action," *Presbyterian Life*, September 1, 1965, UIC, NSCM Folder 140.

23. *NSCM Newsletter,* September 1962, LPCA Box 80, LPNC, DPUA.

24. Preamble to the Constitution of the North Side Cooperative Ministry from the 1962 Report and Fact Sheet, LPCA Box 80, LPNC, DPUA. That the organization would examine itself annually is supported by Church of the Three Crosses flyer, UIC, NSCM Folder 59.

25. Minutes 1962–1971, NSCM, no date, LPCA Box 80, LPNC, DPUA.

26. *NSCM Newsletter,* February 1963, LPCA Box 80, LPNC, DPUA. Present at early meetings were members of the following churches: Christ Church (Presbyterian), Christian Fellowship Methodist, Diversey Parkway E.U.B., Grace Lutheran Church, Lakeview Methodist, Lake View Presbyterian, Olivet Presbyterian, Second E.U.B. Church, Seminary Avenue Federated, Trinity Lutheran, Wellington Avenue Congregational, Wesley Methodist. See Minutes of the North Side Cooperative Ministry, 1963, LPCA Box 80, LPNC, DPUA. By 1969, the group boasted twenty-five churches as members. See North Side Cooperative Ministry, Agenda for Mission 1969, LPCA Box 80, LPNC, DPUA; Janette T. Harrington, "North Side Chicago: The Troops Go into Action," *Presbyterian Life,* UIC, NSCM Folder 140.

27. Harrington, "North Side Chicago," 1, 6.

28. Summary on David Doering, UIC, NSCM Folder 146.

29. Harrington, "North Side Chicago," 1.

30. Wild, *Renewal,* 91, 150.

31. Dave Doering, "An Answer to Irrelevance," Concern July–August 1965, 1 UIC, NSCM Folder 140. Dave Doering, "The Motion of the Church," *The City Church,* May–June 1964, UIC, NSCM Folder 140.

32. David Doering, "The Vision and History of the North Side Cooperative Ministry, 1962–1972," UIC NSCM Folder 526.

33. *NSCM Newsletter,* October 1962, LPCA Box 80, LPNC, DPUA.

34. Doering, "The Motion of the Church," 12.

35. Doering, "An Answer to Irrelevance," 1.

36. Doering, "The Motion of the Church," 12.

37. Annual Report of Co-Ordinator, LPCA Box 80, LPNC, DPUA.

38. *NSCM Newsletter,* June 6, 1965, 1, LPCA Box 80, LPNC, DPUA. For the estimate of twenty thousand young adults on the North Side, see also Janette T. Harrington, "North Side Chicago: The Troops Go into Action," *Presbyterian Life,* UIC, NSCM Folder 140.

39. Ethel Vrana, Committee on Young Adults, "Coffee House NSCM," November 11, 1962, LPCA Box 80, LPNC, DPUA.

40. North Side Cooperative Ministry, "News and Notes," no date, 2, LPCA Box 80, LPNC DPUA.

41. Official Announcements from the North Side Cooperative Ministry, November 1963, LPCA Box 80, LPNC, DPUA.

42. Doering, "The Motion of the Church," 12.

43. North Side Cooperative Ministry, "News and Notes," February 1, 1964, LPCA Box 80, LPNC, DPUA.

44. NSCM Special Ministries Report, LPCA Box 80, LPNC, DPUA.

45. Letter Dated January 30, 1968, UIC, NSCM Folder 124.

46. *NSCM Special Ministries Report,* LPCA Box 80, LPNC, DPUA.

47. *NSCM Newsletter,* September 1962, LPCA Box 80, LPNC, DPUA.

48. *NSCM Newsletter,* November 1962, LPCA Box 80, LPNC, DPUA.

49. *NSCM Newsletter,* February 1963, DPUA LPCA Box 80.

50. North Side Cooperative Ministry, "News and Notes," February 1963, 3, LPCA Box 80, LPNC, DPUA.

51. North Side Cooperative Ministry Housing Task Force Real Estate Proposal UIC, NSCM Folder 204.

52. North Side Cooperative Ministry Housing Task Force Real Estate Proposal UIC, NSCM Folder 204.

53. David Doering to William Friedlander, September 10, 1962, NSCM Correspondence, LPCA Box 80, LPNC, DPUA.

54. William Friedlander to David Doering, September 14, 1962, NSCM Correspondence, LPCA Box 80, LPNC, DPUA.

55. William Friedlander to Lorne Walsh, October 14, 1965, LPCA Box 80, LPNC, DPUA.

56. William Friedlander to David Doering, June 2, 1966, LPCA Box 80, LPNC, DPUA.

57. Board of Directors Minutes, February 8, 1962, LPCA Box 2, LPNC, DPUA.

58. Common Diaconate, LPCA Box 80, LPNC, DPUA.

59. Minutes to NSCM Clergy Staff Meeting, July 25, 1968, UIC, NSCM Folder 89.

60. *Special Civil Rights Newsletter,* LPCA Box 80, 1, LPNC, DPUA.

61. North Side Cooperative Ministry, "News and Notes," September 1966, LPCA Box 80, LPNC, DPUA.

62. *Special Civil Rights Newsletter,* LPCA Box 80, LPNC, DPUA.

63. North Side Cooperative Ministry Housing Task Force Real Estate Proposal UIC, NSCM Folder 204.

64. *Special Civil Rights Newsletter,* LPCA Box 80, LPNC, DPUA.

65. *Special Civil Rights Newsletter,* LPCA Box 80, LPNC, DPUA.

66. *NSCM Special Ministries Report,* 2, LPCA Box 80, LPNC, DPUA.

67. Letter from Dave Doering to Phillip Hampson, May 31, 1967, UIC, NSCM Folder 202.

68. Marty Jezer, *Abbie Hoffman: American Rebel* (New Brunswick, NJ: Rutgers University Press, 1993), 128. Hoffman later criticized himself for this.

69. Letter from The Quiet Answer to the North Side Cooperative Ministry, May 10, 1968, Letter from the Quiet Answer to the North Side Cooperative Ministry, June 20, 1968 UIC, NSCM Folder 59.

70. DeBendetti, *American Ordeal*, 142.

71. David Doering, "The North Side Cooperative Ministry and Viet Nam," UIC, NSCM Folder 90.

72. David Doering, "The North Side Cooperative Ministry and Viet Nam," UIC, NSCM Folder 90.

73. See announcement dated August 9, 1968, UIC, NSCM Folder 73.

74. NSCM Common Council UIC, NSCM Folder 89.

75. Paolini, *Lincoln Park Conservation Association*, 66–67, 38–39.

76. Dalton, *The Politics of Community Problem Solving*, 77; Peter H. Prugh, "Chicago Neighborhood Fights City Hall," *Wall Street Journal*, January 3, 1967, Box 9, Correspondence, Planning Zoning, 1966–1969, Old Town Triangle Association Collection, DPUA.

77. Rieger, *Redeveloping Chicago's Lincoln Park*, 87–88; See also Ducey, *Sunday Morning*, 26.

78. Dalton, *Politics of Community Problem-Solving*, 77; Peter H. Prugh, "Chicago Neighborhood Fights City Hall," *Wall Street Journal*, January 3, 1967, Box 9, Correspondence, Planning Zoning, 1966–1969, Old Town Triangle Association Collection, DPUA.

79. "History of Concerned Citizens of Lincoln Park from October 1966 to February 1968," UIC, NSCM Folder 106.

80. Letter from the Concerned Citizens of Lincoln Park to the Department of Urban Renewal and the Lincoln Park Conservation Association, October 4, 1966, LPCA Box 79, LPNC, DPUA.

81. Letter from the Concerned Citizens of Lincoln Park to The Department of Urban Renewal and the Lincoln Park Conservation Association, October 4, 1966, LPCA Box 79, LPNC, DPUA.

82. Morgan, *The 60s Experience*, xx-xi; Branch, *At Canaan's Edge*, 501–559.

83. Dalton, *The Politics of Community Problem Solving*, 51; David Doering, *The Vision and History of the North Side Cooperative Ministry, 1962–1972*, NSCM UIC Folder 526.

84. Rieger, *Redeveloping Chicago's Lincoln Park Area*, 89–90; "History of Concerned Citizens of Lincoln Park from October 1966 to February 1968," UIC, NSCM Folder 106.

85. "Concerned Citizens of Lincoln Park," LPCA Box 79, LPNC, DPUA.

86. "Concerned Citizens of Lincoln Park," LPCA Box 79, LPNC, DPUA.

87. "History of Concerned Citizens of Lincoln Park from October, 1966 to February 1968," UIC, NSCM Folder, 106.

88. *Lincoln Park Economist*, January 19, 1967, LPCA Box 79, LPNC, DPUA.

89. Roy Larson, "Minister with a Catholic View Takes on the Inner City," *Chicago Sun-Times*, Saturday, January 2, 1971, LPCA Box 79, LPNC, DPUA.

90. Board of Directors Minutes, February 14, 1963, and March 11, 1965, LPCA Box 2, LPNC, DPUA.

91. Board of Directors Minutes, 1965, LPCA Box 2, LPNC, DPUA.

92. Ducey, *Sunday Morning*, 26.

93. Mid-North Association, Minutes of Meeting of Board of Directors, Monday, May 1, 1967, Box 1, Board of Directors Meeting Minutes, 1967, Mid-North Association, DPUA.

94. Larry Dutenhaver to LPCA Members in Attendance at the Annual Meeting, n.d., LPCA Box 79, LPNC, DPUA.

95. "A Letter Sent to a Part of the LPCA Membership," n.d., LPCA Box 79, LPNC, DPUA.

96. Francis Grady and Doug Bruckner to "All Signers of the Proxy Letter," January 31 1967, LPCA Box 79, LPNC, DPUA.

97. *Lincoln Park Economist*, January 19, 1967. LPCA, Box 79, LPNC, DPUA.

98. Grady and Bruckner, "All Signers," LPCA Box 79, LPNC, DPUA.

99. Concerned Citizens of Lincoln Park, "Lincoln Park: Renewal or Replacement?" April 6, 1967, Position Paper presented to the Lincoln Park Community, LPCA Box 79, LPNC, DPUA. According to Howard Rieger, parts of this appeared in the *Chicago Tribune*, as well. See *Redeveloping Chicago's Lincoln Park Area*, 90–91.

100. Concerned Citizens of Lincoln Park, "Lincoln Park: Renewal or Replacement?" April 6, 1967, Position Paper presented to the Lincoln Park Community, LPCA Box 79, LPNC, DPUA.

101. "A Study of Family Units in the Southwest Section of the Lincoln Park Area. The Rents Which Families Can Afford," LPCA Box 79, LPNC, DPUA.

102. Concerned Citizens of Lincoln Park, "Report and Recommendations from Research and Education Committee," June 22, 1967, LPCA Box 79, LPNC, DPUA.

103. History of Concerned Citizens of Lincoln Park from October 1966 to February 1968 UIC, NSCM Folder 106; Dalton, *The Politics of Community Problem-Solving*, 78.

104. Hunter, *Symbolic Communities*, 158.

105. Devine is listed as a new Mid-North Association member in the group's April 1968 newsletter. See *Mid-North News*, April 1968, Box 1N, Newsletters 1968, Mid-North Association Collection, DPUA.

106. Patricia Devine-Reed, interview by José Jiménez, February 10, 2012, transcript, Grand Valley State University Special Collections and University Archives,

"The Young Lords in Lincoln Park," http://gvsu.cdmhost.com/cdm/singleitem /collection/p16015c0116/id/11/rec/47

107. Pat Devine to Members of Concerned Citizens and representatives of other Lincoln Park Organizations, December 7, 1967, LPCA Box 79, LPNC, DPUA.

108. Church of the Three Crosses flyer, UIC, NSCM Folder 59; Ducey, *Sunday Morning*, 59–62; announcement dated October 13, 1966, UIC, NSCM Folder 59.

109. Bylaws of the Church of the Three Crosses, UIC, NSCM Folder 59.

110. Unsigned letter to Larry Dutenhaver, n.d., UIC, NSCM Folder 89; United States of America vs. David T. Dellinger, 13746.

111. Unsigned letter to Larry Dutenhaver, n.d., UIC, NSCM Folder 89.

112. *Handclasp*, December 1966, UIC, NSCM Folder 59.

113. *Handclasp*, October 1967, UIC, NSCM.

114. North Side Cooperative Ministry Common Council Minutes, July 25, 1968, UIC, NSCM Folder 90. For Reed's affiliation, see Ducey, *Sunday Morning*, 26.

115. *Handclasp*, October 1967, UIC, NSCM.

116. NSCM Common Council UIC, NSCM Folder 89.

3. The Counterculture

1. Peter H. Prugh, "Chicago Neighborhood Fights City Hall," *Wall Street Journal*, January 3, 1967, Box 9, Correspondence, Planning Zoning, 1966–1969, Old Town Triangle Association Collection, DPUA.

2. Kitagawa and Taeuber, *Local Community Factbook 1960*, 29.

3. Shirley Baugher, *Our Old Town: A History of the Neighborhood* (Chicago: Old Town Triangle Association, 2001), 3.

4. Warner, *The Renovation of Lincoln Park*, 35.

5. Norma Lee Browning, "Old Town: It's an Artists' Colony, a Garden Spot, a Friendly Village in the Heart of Bustling Chicago," *Chicago Daily Tribune*, December 1, 1957, G10.

6. David Grazian, *Blue Chicago: The Search for Authenticity in Urban Blues Clubs* (Chicago: University of Chicago Press, 2003), 167–168.

7. Warner, *The Renovation of Lincoln Park*, 46.

8. Grazian, *Blue Chicago*, 168.

9. "Madness in Defense of Sanity," *Seed*, v. 1, no. 8, September 22–October 12, 1967, 5. A Note on *Seed*: Issues at times offered dates of publication, volume, and author articles, other times not.

10. Alex Small, "New Bustle on Wells Street Is a Puzzler," *Chicago Tribune*, September 29, 1963, NW1.

11. Donna Gill, "Chicago's Old Town Tourist Attraction," *Chicago Tribune*, December 3, 1967, 10.

12. See Miranda J. Martinez, *Power at the Roots: Gentrification, Community Gardens, and Puerto Ricans of the Lower East Side* (Lanham, MD: Lexington Books, 2010), 8, 18; Richard Florida, *The Rise of the Creative Class . . . and How It's Transforming Work, Leisure, Community and Everyday Life* (New York: Basic Books, 2002), 190–211.

13. Smith, *The New Urban Frontier*, 18–20, 198–200.

14. Quoted in Baugher, *Our Old Town*, 119.

15. John Handley, "'Square' Is Idea Man on Wells Street," *Chicago Tribune*, April 19, 1964, NW1.

16. Donna Gill, "Old Town: Gold Rush in a Cabbage Patch," *Chicago Tribune*, December 4, 1967, A1.

17. Donna Gill, "Store Owners in Old Town Are Smiling," *Chicago Tribune*, December 6, 1967, C26; "Old Town Swings Back to Life," *Business Week*, August 1967, 81.

18. Old Town Triangle Association, Box 9, Urban Renewal, Correspondence and Memos, Planning and Zoning, 1961–62, Old Town Triangle Collection, DPUA.

19. "Sept. 19th Triangle Meeting Rocked Old Town," *Old Town Newsletter*, v. 2, no. 4 (October 1963), Box 1N, Old Town Newsletters 1960–64, Old Town Triangle Collection, DPUA.

20. "Sept. 19th Triangle Meeting."

21. Sheila Wolfe, "Wells Street Natives Long for Old Time Peace; Tourists Turn Once Sedate Area into 'Madhouse,'" *Chicago Tribune*, May 29, 1966, B8.

22. *Old Town Newsletter*, July–August 1965 (no volume or number), Box 1N, Publications, Old Town Triangle Association Collection, DPUA.

23. Baugher, *Our Old Town*, 120.

24. Donna Gill, "Old Town Living, Pros and Cons," *Chicago Tribune*, December 5, 1967, B14.

25. Sheila Wolfe, "Wells Street Natives Long for Old Time Peace; Tourists Turn Once Sedate Area into 'Madhouse,'" *Chicago Tribune*, May 29, 1966, B8. The Beef and Bourbon was south of North Avenue.

26. Quoted in Baugher, *Our Old Town*, 120.

27. Janet L. Abu-Lughod, *From Urban Village to East Village: The Battle for New York's Lower East Side* (Oxford: Basil Blackwood, 1994); Mele, *Selling the Lower East Side*; Clayton Patterson, ed., *Resistance: A Radical Social and Political History of the Lower East Side* (New York: Seven Stories Press, 2007).

28. Paulina Olsen, *Portland in the 1960s: Stories from the Counterculture* (Charleston and London: History Press, 2012).

29. Stoecker, *Defending Community*.

30. "The City: No Squares on the Square," *Time*, May 18, 1962, LXXIX, no. 20, 79–80; Thomas Crone, *Gaslight Square: An Oral History* (St. Louis, MO: William and Joseph Press, 2004).

31. McBride, "Death City Radicals," 110–136.

32. Henderson, *Making the Scene*.

33. Herb Lyon, "Tower Ticker," *Chicago Tribune*, July 7, 1966, 20; Mary Merryfield, "Rebellion, Boredom Affect Teen Dress," *Chicago Tribune*, December 8, 1966, D1; Robert Cross, "The Immortals: LSD and the Hippie Life in Chicago," *Chicago Tribune*, August 20, 1967, J20; Terry Galanoy, "Kids in Trouble," *Chicago Tribune*, January 14, 1968, G26.

34. For a discussion over the definition of "counterculture," see David Farber, "Building the Counterculture, Creating Right Livelihoods: The Counterculture at Work," *The Sixties: A Journal of History, Politics and Culture* 6, no. 1 (2013), 1–4. For narratives that place the coasts as the original sites of the counterculture, see Gitlin, *The Sixties*, 206–214, 222–241; Matusow, *Unraveling*, 296–302, Terry H. Anderson, *The Movement and The Sixties: Protest in America from Greensboro to Wounded Knee* (New York: Oxford University Press, 1995), 170–176.

35. Bach, *American Counterculture*, 129.

36. Warner, *Redeveloping Chicago's Lincoln Park Area*, 46–47, 121.

37. Donna Gill, "Old Town Living: Pros and Cons," *Chicago Tribune*, December 5, 1967, B14.

38. "April 3 Date for Electric Theater," *Lincoln Park Booster*, February 28, 1968, 13.

39. Roger Lewis, *Outlaws of America: The Underground Press and Its Context* (Middlesex, England: Penguin Books, 1972), 24–25; Michael L. Johnson, *The New Journalism: The Underground Press, the Artists of Nonfiction, and Changes in the Established Media* (Lawrence: University of Kansas Press, 1971), 5–6.

40. Peck, *Uncovering the Sixties*, 89.

41. Laurence Leamer, *The Paper Revolutionaries: The Rise of the Underground Press* (New York: Simon and Schuster, 1972), 78.

42. Robert J. Glessing, *The Underground Press in America* (Bloomington: Indiana Press, 1970), 25.

43. Leamer, *Paper Revolutionaries*, 75.

44. Warner, *Redeveloping Chicago's Lincoln Park Area*, 127.

45. Peck, *Uncovering the Sixties*, 89.

46. Joshua Clark Davis, "The Business of Getting High: Head Shops, Countercultural Capitalism, and the Marijuana Legalization Movement," *The Sixties: A Journal of History, Politics and Culture* 8, no. 1 (2015), 27–39.

47. Nicholas G. Meriwether, "The Counterculture as Local Culture in Columbia, South Carolina," in Cohen and Snyder, eds., *Rebellion in Black and White*, 218–234.

48. Joshua Clark Davis, *From Head Shops to Whole Foods: The Rise and Fall of Activist Entrepreneurs* (New York: Columbia University Press, 2017).

49. James Lato, LBJ, NCCPV Box 41, R-337, 1.

50. Perry, *The Haight-Ashbury*, xviii, 6; Echols, *Scars of Sweet Paradise*, 97.

51. Perry, *The Haight-Ashbury*, 73, 86, 98, 193; Echols, *Scars of Sweet Paradise*, 96; Peter Coyote, *Sleeping Where I Fall: A Chronicle* (Washington, DC: Counterpoint, 1998), 80, 89; Rorabaugh, *American Hippies*, 62.

52. Miller, *Democracy*, 124–144; Coyote, *Sleeping Where I Fall*, 75; Echols, *Scars of Sweet Paradise*, 156.

53. "Tribes Assemble on North Avenue Beach," *Seed*, v. 1, no. 3, May 1967, 2.

54. Barbara Amazaki, "Former Church Echoes with Sounds of Theater," *Chicago Tribune*, September 17, 1967, L4.

55. Echols, *Scars*, 98.

56. Bach, *American Counterculture*, 93–95.

57. Emmett Grogan, *Ringolevio: A Life Played for Keeps* (New York: Citadel Underground, 1990), 246.

58. Perry, *The Haight-Asbury*, 110, 274–275; Coyote, *Sleeping Where I Fall*, 95–96; Grogan, *Ringolevio*, 416, 440–43.

59. Bach, *American Counterculture*, 67. For an examination of "free" see Rorabaugh, *American Hippies*, 141–144. Joshua Clark Davis refers to "Free Spaces" as "hubs of movement culture." See *From Head Shops to Whole Foods*, 21.

60. "Diggers," *Seed*, v. 1, no. 2, April 1967, 6.

61. "Diggers Started," *Seed*, v. 1, no. 3, May 1967, 15.

62. "Message Scrawled on Wall of Barbara's Bookstore by Diggers Passing Through," *Seed*, v. 1, no. 5, July, 1967, 16.

63. "Free Store," *Seed*, v. 2, no. 1, January 1968, 3.

64. Tim Hodgdon notes the Oracle reference in his *Manhood in the Age of Aquarius: Masculinity in Two Countercultural Communities, 1965–83* (New York: Columbia University Press, 2008), 7; See also Richard Kempton, *Provo: Amsterdam's Anarchist Revolt* (New York: Autonomedia, 2007); Rorabaugh, *American Hippies*, 138, 156.

65. "Provo," "Free Store," *Seed*, v. 1, no. 9, October 14–November 31, 1967, 4.

66. "Switchboard," *Seed*, v. 2, no. 1, January 1968, 3.

67. Editorial, *Seed*, v. 1, no. 13, Jan 5–25 1968, 3.

68. Editorial, *Seed*, v. 1, no. 5, July 21–August 5, 1967, 3.

69. "An Open Letter to the Hippy [sic.] Community of Chicago," *Seed*, v. 1, no. 3, May 1967, 2.

70. Larry Reynolds, "Feedback," *Seed*, v. 1, no. 10, 1967, 18.

71. Editorial, *Seed*, v. 1, no. 6, August 11–25, 1967, 2. Another reader, while praising the magazine, criticized its "frenetic" nature and claimed it was "lacking in peace and tranquility." See Editorials, *Seed*, v. 1, no. 9, October 14–November 3, 1967, 18.

72. "Free Store: Fucked Up or Forward?" *Seed*, v. 1, no. 12, 2.

73. Thomas Frank, *The Conquest of Cool: Business Culture, Counterculture, and the Rise of Hip Consumerism* (Chicago: University of Chicago Press, 1998). Of San Francisco rock musicians, Alice Echols notes that, "None of the bands—not even the Dead, whose scraggly, scowling keyboardist, Pigpen, was always scaring off record companies—was opposed to making money." See her *Shaky Ground: The 60s and its Aftershocks* (New York: Columbia University Press, 2001), 39.

74. Farber, "Building the Counterculture, Creating Right Livelihoods: The Counterculture at Work," *The Sixties: A Journal of History, Politics, and Culture* 6, no. 1 (2013), 1–24.

75. Norma Lee Browning, "Wild Cheetah Club Leaps to the West," *Chicago Tribune*, April 6, 1967, C9.

76. "The Electric Theater," *Seed*, v. 2, no. 1, 4.

77. "Hippies Find Business Not All That Bad," *Chicago Tribune*, September 10, 1967, A14.

78. Donna Gill, "Store Owners in Old Town Are Smiling: New High Rises to Bring in Money," *Chicago Tribune*, December 5, 1967, B14.

79. Evelyn Livingstone, "The 'With It' Look from Wells Street," *Chicago Tribune*, July 26, 1966, A1.

80. McBride, "Death City Radicals," 110–136.

81. Donna Gill, "Keeping Area Green Problem in Old Town," *Chicago Tribune*, December 7, 1967, D8.

82. Robert Lynsky interview by the Chicago Study Team Investigation, National Commission on the Causes and Prevention of Violence, Lyndon Baines Johnson Library and Archive (hereafter cited as LBJ, NCCPV) Box 42, R-502, 2.

83. *Lincoln Park Press*, v. 1, no. 4, 1968, 3. Lincoln Park Newspapers, LPNC, DPUA.

84. "150 Police Raid Women for Peace," *Seed*, v. 1, no. 1, April 1967, 1.

85. "Free Wells Street Liberate Old Town," *Seed*, v. 1, no. 1, April 1967, 7.

86. "Summary of the Events at Promontory Point on July 4, 1967," *Seed*, v. 1, no. 5, July 1967, 3, 6.

87. Mark Podolner, "Dear Seed," *Seed*, v. 1, no. 5, July 1967, 3.

88. *Seed*, v. 1, no. 5, September 22–October 12, 1967, 7.

89. "Why It Didn't Happen Here: Cops Harass to Prevent Riots," *Seed*, v. 1, no. 9, October 14–November 31, 1967, 3.

90. "6 Arrested in Old Town Narcotic Raid," *Chicago Tribune*, August 30, 1967, B8.

91. Robert Cross, "The Immortals: LSD and the Hippie Life in Chicago," *Chicago Tribune*, August 20, 1967, 48.

92. Farber, *Chicago '68*, 3–16; Raskin, *For the Hell of It*, 128–131; Jezer, *Abbie Hoffman*, 123–128; Stein, *Living the Revolution*, 6; Paul Krassner, *Confessions of a Raving, Unconfined Nut* (New York: Simon and Schuster, 1993) 156–157; Milton Viorst, *Fire in the Streets: America in the 1960s* (New York: Simon and Schuster, 1979), 443–444.

93. Sanders, LBJ, NCCPV Box 42, R-548, 1. He also claims that Rubin set up committees as early as December 1967. Brad Fox corroborates the UN assertion in LBJ, NCCPV Box 42, R-549, 1. MOBE activist Richard M. Pfeffer also claims to have first heard something in December of 1967, LBJ, NCCPV Box 42, R-600, 1.

94. Farber, *Chicago '68*, 3–5; Jonah Raskin claims Hoffman was planning as early as November. See *For the Hell of It*, 125.

95. U.S. vs. Dave Dellinger and Others, 12633; Carol Kramer, "Eastern Yippies Plan for Chicago," *Chicago Tribune*, March 20, 1968, B2.

96. Farber, *Chicago '68*, 3–27; Matusow, *Unraveling of America*, 412–413; Michael William Doyle, "Staging the Revolution: Guerilla Theater as Countercultural Practice 1965–1968," in Peter Braunstein and Michael J. Doyle, eds., *Imagine Nation: The American Counterculture of the 1960s and 70s* (New York: Routledge, 2001), 85–91.

97. For hippies, see Miller, *Democracy*, 134.

98. James Shiflett, LBJ, NCCPV Box 40, R-022.

99. Raskin, *For the Hell of It*, 129–131; Farber, *Chicago '68*, 14–20.

100. David Doering, NCCPV LBJ, Box 41, R-258. He also comments that the groups themselves were separate from each other; Peck 105. Activist Fred Halstead, who called the Lake Villa conference "pretty much a waste of time" also indicated that attendance was by invitation only. See his *Out Now! A Participant's Account of the American Movement Against the Vietnam War* (New York: Monad Press, 1978), 384–385.

101. J. Anthony Lukas, "Dissenters Focusing on Chicago," *New York Times*, August 18, 1968, 1.

102. From January through March the two promoted the group and the festival through alternative press articles, held meetings, and opened an office at 32 Union Square along with members Paul Krassner, Keith Lampe, and Ed Sanders. See Farber, *Chicago '68*, 16–27, for more. Rubin was away, but Abbie Hoffman did put in periodic appearances that summer. Steven Treeman recalled that in April, or early May, Hoffman returned briefly to Chicago to appear on John Madigan's

At Random television program. He also called the Park District, and made no progress before leaving the next day. Abe Peck, LBJ, NCCPV Box 41, R-231, 2.

103. Abe Peck, LBJ, NCCPV Box 41, R-231, 1; The Yips also released a leaflet that month announcing Chicago. See Keith Lampe, LBJ, NCCPV Box 42, R-494.

104. Peck, *Uncovering the Sixties*, 100–101. In Peck's Walker interview he says he and Rubin met in the *Seed* offices, LBJ, NCCPV, Rights in Conflict, Box 41, R-231; Viorst, *Fire in the Streets*, 444.

105. Peck, *Uncovering the Sixties*, 48–50, 73–74, 89.

106. "Yippie," "The Seed's First Bust (All True)," "Freedom from the Press Department," *Seed*, v. 2, no. 1, January or February 1968, 2; Peck, *Uncovering the Sixties*, 89.

107. Farber, *Chicago '68*, 36; Abe Peck, LBJ, NCCPV Box 41, R-231; Tuttle, LBJ, NCCPV Box 41, R-314; U.S. vs. Dave Dellinger and Others, 12656–12659.

108. Farber, *Chicago '68*, 37.

109. Otto Liljenstople, LBJ, NCCPV Box 42 R-422, 8.

110. Abe Peck, LBJ, NCCPV Box 41, R-231; David Stahl, LBJ, NCCPV Box 41-R-308, 1–2; Farber, *Chicago '68*, 36–37.

111. "Princess Rainwater," Abe Peck, LBJ, NCCPV Box 41, R-231, 2; "Helen Running Water" is mentioned in Farber, *Chicago '68*, 36–37; U.S. vs. David T. Dellinger and Others, 505, 12659–12665.

112. Brad Fox, LBJ, NCCPV Box 42 R-549, 7–8. Yippie press secretary Keith Lampe claimed his only connections were with the underground press. See LBJ, NCCPV Box 42, R-494, 2.

113. Gitlin, *The Sixties*, 235.

114. Farber, *Chicago '68*, 20–21.

115. Raskin, *For the Hell of It*, 143.

116. Matusow, *Unraveling of America*, 413,

117. Kusch, *Battleground Chicago*, 48.

118. Biles, *Richard J. Daley*, 140.

119. Donna Gill, "Keeping Area Green Problem in Old Town," *Chicago Tribune*, December 7, 1967, D8.

120. Flamm, *Law and Order*, 156–157.

121. Cohen and Taylor, *American Pharaoh*, 466.

122. Royko, *Boss*, 181; J. Anthony Lukas, NCCPV LBJ, Box 46, SOR-013, 1; Lewis Chester, Godfrey Hodgson, and Bruce Page, *An American Melodrama: The Presidential Campaign of 1968* (New York: Viking Press, 1969), 521.

123. Kusch, *Battleground Chicago*, 50. For more on police attitudes see pp. 49–52.

124. Photo Caption, *Seed*, v. 2, no. 4, March 15–29, 1968, 2–3, and v. 2, no. 5 (n.d.), 3. For harassment of Bay Area hips see Miller, *Democracy*, 145–148.

125. Abe Peck and Stephen Treeman, LBJ, NCCPV Box 41, R-231. As for their own press, Brad Fox claimed the Yips only put out one paper, which they promptly dropped due to lack of funds, NCCPV, 68; Brad Fox, LBJ, NCCPV Box 42, R-549; David Stahl, LBJ, NCCPV Box 41, R-308.

126. Gleason, *Daley of Chicago*, 75–76.

127. Biles, *Richard J. Daley*, 143–146.

128. David Doering, NCCPV LBJ, Box 41, R-258.

129. Emerging Peoples Summer Task Force Agenda April 2, 1968, 2 UIC, NSCM Folder 90.

130. NSCM Common Council Meeting, April 25, 1968, UIC, NSCM Folder 89.

131. *Lincoln Park Press*, v. 1, no. 4, 1968, 1–3, Lincoln Park Newspapers, LPNC, DPUA.

132. "Community Needs to Meet the Urban Crisis," LPCA Box 80, LPNC, DPUA.

133. Lyttle, *Chicago Anti-Vietnam War Movement*, 100.

134. Joseph L. Sander, "A Study in Law and Order," *Nation*, May 20, 1968, 655–657.

135. Sparling et al., *Dissent and Disorder: A Report to the Citizens of Chicago on the April 27 Peace Parade* (Chicago: April 27th Investigating Committee, 1968), 10–20.

136. Frank Donner, *Protectors of Privilege: Red Squads and Police Repression in Urban America* (Berkeley: University of California Press, 1990), 106–107.

137. Lyttle, *Chicago Anti-Vietnam War Movement*, 100–103. See also Farber, *Chicago '68*, 82–83, 94–96; Chester, Hodgson, and Page, An American Melodrama, 518; Sparling et al., *Dissent and Disorder*, 31–33.

138. Lyttle, *Chicago Anti-Vietnam War Movement*, 100–105.

139. Doyle, in Doyle and Braunstein, *Imagine Nation*, 80–85.

140. Gitlin, *The Sixties*; Matusow, *The Unraveling of America*.

141. John Tuttle, LBJ, NCCPV Box 41, R-314, 1; Carl Burnette, "The Free City Survival Committee Is Alive and Well in Chicago," *Liberation News Service*, June 7, 1968, 3–4.

142. Abe Peck, LBJ, NCCPV Box 41, R-231, 3.

143. Letter from Abe Peck to David Stahl, n.d., LBJ, NCCPV Box 41, R-308, attachment.

144. *Seed*, v. 2, no. 9, 2.

145. Burnett, "The Free City Survival Committee," 4.

146. "Vanguard Ministry," *Seed*, v. 1, no. 8, September 22–October 12, 1967, 15.

147. Timothy Miller, *The Hippies and American Values* (Knoxville: University of Tennessee Press, 1991), 105–108; On the rejection of money by the Diggers see Bradford D. Martin, *The Theater is in the Streets: Politics and Performance in Sixties America* (Amherst and Boston: University of Massachusetts Press, 2004), 87–89,

104–106. For Digger ideas about freedom, a critique of Hoffman and Rubin, and details regarding Free Stores see Coyote, *Sleeping Where I Fall*, 68–71, 89–91.

148. Miller, *The Hippies and American Values*, 97.

149. Stein, *Living the Revolution*, 66.

150. NSCM Common Council Meeting Minutes July 25, 1968, UIC NSCM Folder 90.

151. Report on the Events from February—September in Regard to NSCM Convention Mobilization, UIC NSCM Folder 90.

152. Report of the Events from February.

153. Ministry to the Emerging Peoples: Yippie/Hippie Community, UIC, NSCM Folder 304.

154. Report of the Events from February–September in Regard to NSCM Convention Mobilization, UIC, NSCM Folder 90.

155. Ministry to the Emerging Peoples: Yippie/Hippie Community, UIC, NSCM Folder 304. Quote is excerpted from the *Approach Newspaper*, same folder.

156. Jonathan Tuttle, "Gentlemen," *Seed*, v. 1, no. 12, 16.

157. Jon Tuttle, "The New Evangelism," UIC, NSCM Folder 248.

158. Larry Dutenhaver, LBJ, NCCPV Box 41, R-240, 1.

159. Report of the Events from February–September in Regard to NSCM Convention Mobilization, UIC, NSCM Folder 90.

160. Miller, *The Hippies and American Values*, 88.

161. David Stahl, LBJ, NCCPV Box 41-R-308, 1; U.S. vs. David T. Dellinger and Others, 609; Burnette, "Free City Survival Committee Is Alive and Well," 4.

162. David Doering, NCCPV LBJ, Box 41, R-258, 4.

163. David Stahl, LBJ, NCCPV Box 41-R-308, 1.

164. Letter from the Free City Survival Committee to Mayor Daley, LBJ, NCCPV Box 41, R-308, attachment.

165. Rohrbaugh, *Berkeley at War*, 147.

166. Olsen, *Portland in the 1960s*, 17.

167. McBride, "Death City Radicals," 118, 127–128.

168. Anderson, *The Movement*, 218; Farber, *Chicago '68*, 44–45.

169. Arthur Marwick, *The Sixties: Cultural Revolution in Britain, France, Italy and the United States, c. 1958–c.1974* (Oxford: Oxford University Press, 1998) 584–675; Martin Klimke and Jochim Scharloth, eds., *1968 in Europe: A History of Protest and Activism, 1956–1977* (New York: Palgrave Macmillan, 2008); *The American Historical Review* 114, no. 1, February 2009, 42–135, and 114, no. 2, (April 2009), 329–404; On the Sixties in Northern Ireland, see *The Sixties: A Journal of History, Politics, and Culture* 2, no. 2 (2009).

170. Al Rosenfeld, "Up Front," *Seed*, v. 2, no. 6, 2.

171. Reginald Walker, "Mace in the Face," *Seed*, v. 2, no. 6, 21.

172. David Stahl, LBJ, NCCPV Box 41 R-308, 4.

173. Untitled Document, LBJ, NCCPV Box 41, R-308, attachment.

174. Abe Peck, "An Open Letter to Mayor Richard J. Daley," *Seed*, v. 2, no. 7, 2.

175. Al Rosenfeld, "Up Front," *Seed*, v. 2, no. 7, 3.

176. Abe Peck, LBJ, NCCPV Box 41, R-231, 3–4; Joseph Ettinger, LBJ, NCCPV Box 42, R-484, 1–2.

177. U.S. vs. Dave Dellinger and Others, 12675–12677.

178. U.S. vs. Dave Dellinger and Others, 12680–12681; Peck, *Uncovering the Sixties*, 107; Donna Gill, "Hippies Find Mother Who Rejects Gift," *Chicago Tribune*, May 13, 1968, 7; "Apple Pie and Mother's Day Parade," *Seed*, v. 2, no. 8, 5.

179. Abe Peck and Rudy Schwartz, "Breakthrough Part One," *Seed*, v. 2, no. 9, June 1968, 18.

180. "Free City Is Selling Out," *Seed*, v. 2, no. 9, June 1968, 8.

181. Abe Peck, LBJ, NCCPV Box 41, R-231; Joseph Ettinger, NCCPV Box 42, R-484, 23–24.

182. "Electric Theater Raided," *Lincoln Park Booster*, May 30, 1968, 1; "Police Pull Electric Theater Plug; Nab 29," *Chicago Tribune*, May 21, 1968, C7.

183. Abe Peck, LBJ, NCCPV Box 41, R-231, 4; Abe Peck, LBJ, NCCPV Box 43, R-819, 2; Jonathan Tuttle, LBJ, NCCPV Box 41, R-314, 1 (Tuttle incorrectly names the month as March); Farber, *Chicago '68*, 42.

184. Farber, *Chicago '68*, 41.

185. William Granger, "Cops Keep Up Drive to Clear Wells Street," *Chicago Tribune*, May 27, 1968, 26.

186. Farber, Chicago '68, 41–43; U.S. vs. Dave Dellinger and Others, 12683.

187. Letter from the Free City Survival Committee to David Stahl, n.d., LBJ, NCCPV Box 41, R-308, attachment.

188. Abe Peck, LBJ, NCCPV Box 41, R-231, 2.

189. "Police Ignore Hippie 'Bust-In' in Old Town," *Chicago Tribune*, June 2, 1968, 24.

190. Abe Peck, LBJ, NCCPV Box 41, R-231, 5–6; Jonathan Tuttle, LBJ, NCCPV Box 41 R-314.

4. "Wear Some Armor in Your Hair"

1. "Plan Commission OKs 5 Sites," *Lincoln Park Booster*, January 31, 1968, 1.

2. *Lincoln Park Conservation Association Newsletter*, 1, LPCA Box 1N, LPNC, DPUA, Newsletters 1968.

3. *Lincoln Park Conservation Association Newsletter*, 1. LPCA Box 1N, LPNC, DPUA, Newsletters 1968; *Lincoln Park Booster*, January 10, 1968, 4.

4. No exact date is given on the document, but it is realistic to suggest that this appeared in the weeks before January 31. Chicago Conservation, Urban Renewal and LPCA, Box 2, LPNC, DPUA.

5. Chicago Conservation, Urban Renewal and LPCA, Box 2, LPNC, DPUA.

6. *Lincoln Park Press*, v. 1, no. 2, 1968, 1, Lincoln Park Newspapers, LPNC, DPUA.

7. The *Lincoln Park Booster* reported that the city in 1967 ordered 123 buildings demolished in Lincoln Park and Lake View. See *Lincoln Park Booster*, February 28, 1968, 11.

8. *Lincoln Park Press*, v. 1 no. 2, 2, 1968, Lincoln Park Newspapers, LPNC, DPUA.

9. *Lincoln Park Press*, v. 1, no. 3, 1968, 1, 3, Lincoln Park Newspapers, LPNC, DPUA.

10. "Clergy Launch Plan for Housing, Peace," *Lincoln Park Booster*, February 14, 1968, 9.

11. Board of Directors minutes, January 29, 1968, LPCA Box 3, LPNC, DPUA.

12. Board of Directors Minutes, June 1968, LPCA Box 3, LPNC, DPUA.

13. North Side Cooperative Ministry Open Hearing: Testimony, Planning Documents, Suggestions UIC, NSCM Folder 89.

14. Proposal to the North Side Cooperative Ministry from Concerned Citizens of Lincoln Park, UIC, NSCM Folder 89.

15. John H. Alschuler, "Housing in Lincoln Park, A summary of statement to the North Side Co-operative Ministry, June 8, 1968," Box 13, Housing Committee Correspondence, Mid-North Association, DPUA.

16. From a newsletter marked "Probably July 1968" in pencil. *Lincoln Park Conservation Association Newsletter*, 1, LPCA Box 1N, LPNC, DPUA; "Statement from Roland D. Whitman, President, Lincoln Park Conservation Association," UIC, NSCM Folder 89.

17. Board of Directors Minutes, June 26, 1968, LPCA Box 3, LPNC, DPUA.

18. *Lincoln Park Conservation Association Newsletter*, February 1968. LPCA Box 1N, LPNC, DPUA.

19. *Lincoln Park Conservation Association Newsletter*, March 1968. LPCA Box 1N, LPNC, DPUA.

20. *Lincoln Park Conservation Association Newsletter*, March 1968, 1. LPCA Box 1N, LPNC, DPUA; Dalton, Politics of Community Problem Solving, 82; Lincoln Park Conservation Association Board of Directors Minutes, June 26, 1968, LPCA Box 3, LPNC, DPUA; Barbara Amazaki, "Housing Study Completed," *Chicago Tribune*, June 16, 1968, Box 9, Correspondence, Planning Zoning, 1966–1969, Old Town Triangle Association Collection, DPUA; Lincoln Park Conservation Association, Sub-Committee on Housing Recommendations for Land

Disposition, May 29, 1968, Box 13, Recommendations for Land Disposition, Mid-North Association Collection, DPUA.

21. Abe Peck, LBJ, NCCPV Box 41, R-231, 5. George Sells also claims Stahl missed half the meetings, in LBJ, NCCPV Box 41, R-314, 1–2.

22. *Seed*, v. 2. no. 9 (n.d.—seems July 1968), 8, 10, 18.

23. Abe Peck, LBJ, NCCPV Box 43, R-819, 1; David Stahl, LBJ, NCCPV Box 41, R-308, 2; Farber, *Chicago '68*, 43–44, 47–49; U.S. vs. Dave Dellinger and Others, 12678.

24. Letter from the Free City Survival Committee to the Commissioner of the Chicago Parks District, 15 July 1968, LBJ, NCCPV Box 41, R-308, attachment.

25. Abe Peck, LBJ, NCCPV Box 41, R-231, 8–9.

26. Letter from the Free City Survival Committee to the Commissioner of the Chicago Parks District, n.d., LBJ, NCCPV Box 41, R-308, attachment.

27. J. Anthony Lukas, "Dissenters Focusing on Chicago," *New York Times*, August 18, 1968, 1.

28. Report on the Events from February—September in Regard to NSCM Convention Mobilization UIC NSCM Folder 90. See also Dave Doehring, LBJ, NCCPV Box 41, R-258, 2.

29. Report on the Events from February—September in Regard to NSCM Convention Mobilization UIC NSCM Folder 90. For Coalition for an Open Convention see Farber, 100–101, 110.

30. Report on the Events from February—September in Regard to NSCM Convention Mobilization UIC NSCM Folder 90; Dave Doehring, LBJ, NCCPV Box 41, R-258, 1.

31. Report on the Events from February.

32. Brad Fox, LBJ, NCCPV Box 42, R-549, 10. Jeff A. Barker contends that Sills's theater was, technically, called "The Theater," and only became "The Free Theater" after the Convention. See Jeff A. Barker, *Paul Sills' Life in the Theater: The First Half Century (1927–1979)*, M.A. Thesis, Department of Theater Arts, Northern Illinois University, May 1981, 138.

33. Barker, *Paul Sills' Life in the Theater*, 2, 5–7; Chris Jones, "Father of Improv Comedy," *Chicago Tribune*, June 3, 2008, 1, 14.

34. Barker, *Paul Sills' Life in the Theater*, 118–120.

35. Barker, *Paul Sills' Life in the Theater*, 122.

36. U.S. vs. David T. Dellinger and others, 13647, 13651; Stein, *Living the Revolution*, 59, 69; Barker, *Paul Sills' Life in the Theater*, 130.

37. "History and Characteristics of the Lincoln Park Community," Histories of the LPCA and the Lincoln Park Community Box 1, LPNC, DPUA, 7.

38. Basil Kane to Amy Forkert, LBJ, NCCPV Box 8, A-242.

39. Richard Hoerger to Whom it may Concern, August 3, 1968; Unsigned letter, 2 August 1968, LBJ, NCCPV Box 8, A-242.

40. David L. Watt to Mrs. Maurice Forkert, 24 July 1968, LBJ, NCCPV Box 8, A-242.

41. Flyer "Love Needs Care," LBJ, NCCPV Box 8, A-242.

42. O. M. Forkert, Untitled document, September 19, 1968, LBJ, NCCPV Box 8, A-242.

43. Special Committee on Neighborhood Problems, LBJ, NCCPV Box 8, A-242.

44. O. M. Forkert, Confidential letter to Clarence Braasch, August 7, 1968, LBJ, NCCPV Box 8, A-242.

45. O. M. Forkert, Confidential letter to Sidney Smith, August 7, 1968, LBJ, NCCPV Box 8, A-242.

46. O.M. Forkert, Untitled document, September 19, 1968, LBJ, NCCPV Box 8, A-242.

47. Memo to from Ralph Markum to Sidney Smith, August 12, 1968, LBJ, NCCPV Box 8, A-242.

48. Memorandum from James R. Jung to Sidney Smith, August 15, 1968, LBJ, NCCPV Box 8, A-242.

49. Thomas Lyons, LBJ, NCCPV Box 43, R-723, 3.

50. Donner, *Protectors of Privilege*, 117.

51. Jezer, *Abbie Hoffman*, 150; Pierson, *Riots*, 82–92.

52. MOBE largely kept to itself and handed Lincoln Park to Yippie. Sylvia Kushner, LBJ, NCCPV Box 42 R-489, 1–2. MOBE marshal Richard M. Pfeffer asserted that "Yippie . . . was in charge of Lincoln Park" and that while in the park himself he "did not see any Mobilization leadership." See LBJ, NCCPV Box 42, R-600, 10–12. The MOBE did not see things in terms of Lincoln Park or Chicago, but in terms of independent, entrepreneurial "Movement Centers," thus reducing their street-level presence outside of free-floating "Marshals." See LBJ, NCCPV Box 8, A-270, 278, 286, Box 43 R-633 for more. William Chayes asserted that MOBE flyer distribution was weak during convention week. See LBJ, NCCPV Box 43, R-633, 16.

53. Jonah Raskin also places him in Chicago only at the beginning of August. See *For the Hell of It*, 143–149; Hoffman, *Soon to Be a Major Motion Picture*, 150. YIP press secretary Keith Lampe only came into Chicago on the eighteenth. See LBJ, NCCPV Box 42, R-494, 4.

54. Viorst, *Fire in the Streets*, 451.

55. U.S. vs. David T. Dellinger and others, 12741.

56. Jeffrey Haas, *The Assassination of Fred Hampton: How the FBI and the Chicago Police Murdered a Black Panther* (Chicago: Lawrence Hill Books, 2010), 36.

57. Jerry Rubin, *Growing Up at Thirty-Seven* (New York: M. Evans and Company, 1976), 82; Farber, *Chicago '68*, 17–19; Raskin, *For the Hell of It*, 156–157.

58. *Seed*, v. 2, no. 11, August 9, 1968, 2, 23.

59. Abe Peck, "An Open Letter on Yippie," *Seed*, v. 2, no. 11, 23.

60. Farber, *Chicago '68*, 48.

61. Abe Peck, LBJ, NCCPV Box 41, R-231, 8.

62. Abe Peck LBJ, NCCPV Box 41, R-231, 9; Jonathan Tuttle, LBJ, NCCPV Box 41, R-314, 2; Jonathan Tuttle, LBJ, NCCPV Box 42, R-459, 2.

63. U.S. vs. David T. Dellinger and others, 12716–12718.

64. Robert Lynsky, LBJ, NCCPV Box 42, R-502, 1.

65. Abe Peck, LBJ, NCCPV Box 41, R-231, 9; Farber 49–51; Peck, *Uncovering the Sixties*, 108–113.

66. U.S. vs. David T. Dellinger and others, 12718–12727; Farber, *Chicago '68*, 50–51; Peck, *Uncovering the Sixties*, 110.

67. Farber, *Chicago '68*, 54, 110, 112; U.S. vs. David T. Dellinger and others, 12747–12748; NCCPV, 59; Cohen and Taylor, *American Pharaoh*, 467–468; Peck, *Uncovering the Sixties*, 110; Viorst, *Fire in the Streets*, 449.

68. NCCPV, *Rights in Conflict*, 91; Farber, *Chicago '68*, 52.

69. Hoffman, *Soon to be a Major Motion Picture*, 144–145; Matusow, *Unraveling of America*, 413.

70. Robert Lynsky, LBJ, NCCPV Box 42, R-502, 2.

71. NCCPV, *Rights in Conflict*, 31.

72. Larry Dutenhaver, LBJ, NCCPV Box 41, R-240, 2.

73. Stein, *Living the Revolution*, 39.

74. Larry Dutenhaver, LBJ, NCCPV Box 41 R-240, 2. The Chicago Peace Council's Sylvia Kushner estimated that some fifteen churches provided sleeping room for the convention, that her group kept a file of persons willing to offer housing, and that some "several thousand" persons, "at least" were housed by the churches and the Chicago Peace Council, an umbrella group of many anti-war groups. Sylvia Kushner LBJ, NCCPV Box 42, R-489, 3.

75. Dave Doehring, LBJ, NCCPV Box 41, R-258, 5; David Doering, *The Vision and History of the North Side Cooperative Ministry, 1962–1972*, NSCM, UIC Folder 526.

76. Dave Doehring, LBJ, NCCPV Box 41, R-258, 2; John Doe #1 and #2, LBJ, NCCPV Box 42 R-407, 1.

77. Dave Doering, LBJ, NCCPV Box 41, R-258, 2.

78. "North Side Cooperative Ministry Convention Mobilization," LPCA Box 79, LPNC, DPUA.

79. LBJ, NCCPV Box 8, A-242, LBJ, NCCPV Box 8 A-260, 261, 264, 268, 269, 281, Box 7 M-650. The McCarthy people also dispersed flyers. See LBJ, NCCPV Box 7, A-172.

80. Dave Doering, LBJ, NCCPV Box 41, R-258, 4.

81. Patricia Devine-Reed, interview by José Jiménez, February 10, 2012, transcript. Grand Valley State University Special Collections and University Archives, "The Young Lords in Lincoln Park," http://gvsu.cdmhost.com/cdm/singleitem /collection/p16015c0116/id/11/rec/47

82. Memo from Jay Ridinger to Roland Whitman, August 16, 1968, LPCA Box 79, LPNC, DPUA.

83. Board of Directors Minutes, August 21, 1968, LPCA Box 3, LPNC, DPUA.

84. Telegram from the LPCA to David Stahl, Ray Simon, Thomas Barry, James Conlisk, Richard Daley, 3:20 P.M., August 22, 1968, LPCA Box 79, LPNC, DPUA.

85. "Hippie Killed by Policemen in Old Town," Chicago Tribune, August 23, 1968, C14; Stein, Living the Revolution, 37; Lyttle, The Chicago Anti-Vietnam War Movement, 108; Farber, Chicago '68, 165–167.

86. Stein, Living the Revolution, 42–43; Jezer, Abbie Hoffman, 152–153.

87. "Army Troops, Guardsmen Move into Chicago Areas," Washington Post, Times Herald, August 24, 1968, A4.

88. Matusow, The Unraveling of America, 416.

89. Anderson, The Movement, 217–219, 223; Miller, Democracy, 295–297.

90. Nicholas von Hoffman, "Chicago, Chicago...," Washington Post, Times Herald, August 25, 1968, A1.

91. Blacks interviewed by the Walker team indicated that the Black community wanted little or nothing to do with the DNC. See Arthur Brozier, LBJ, NCCPV Box 43, R-807; Reverend Calvin Morris, LBJ, NCCPV Box 43, R-808; Cecil Butler, LBJ, NCCPV Box 43, R-765; Douglas Parks, LBJ, NCCPV Box 43, R-793; Edith Coleman, LBJ, NCCPV Box 43, R-720. While the protest surrounding the convention was largely a white one, gangs and those who worked with them reported that Puerto Rican youths drove through the area, but did not participate, and that three Puerto Rican youths scuffled with hippies, but retreated when outnumbered. See Special Report of Chuck Cooper on the Potential Involvement of Youth Gangs and Youth Gangs and Youth Groups as Victims or Perpetrators of Violence, LBJ, NCCPV Box 8, A-322.

92. Calvin Lockridge, LBJ, NCCPV Box 42, R-526, 3.

93. Cohen and Taylor, American Pharaoh, 472; Matusow, Unraveling of America, 418; Lyttle, The Chicago Anti-Vietnam War Movement, 108; Dennis Cunningham, LBJ, NCCPV Box 41, R-234, 10.

94. Raskin, For the Hell of It, 166; Schultz, No One Was Killed, 78, 86; Gitlin, The Sixties, 328; NCCPV, Rights in Conflict, 148, 150, 154, 156; Miller, Democracy, 299; Mary Teetor, LBJ, NCCPV Box 43, R-789, 9; Paul Sills, LBJ, NCCPV Box 42, R-021, 3–4, 6; Chester et al., An American Melodrama, 523.

95. Stein, Living the Revolution, 49.

96. Schultz, *No One Was Killed*, 77; Viorst, *Fire in the Streets*, 450.

97. Robert Lynsky, LBJ, NCCPV Box 42, R-502, 4.

98. Schultz, *No One Was Killed*, 15.

99. Sarah Switzer, *Love, Blood, Sweat, and Gas: Print Media and the 1968 Democratic Convention*, Unpublished M.A. Thesis, University of Montana, 2001, 64, 86.

100. "North Side Cooperative Ministry Convention Mobilization 'Help Centers,'" LPCA Box 79, LPNC, DPUA; Address List, LBJ, NCCPV Box 8, A-242; List of Movement Centers, LBJ, NCCPV Box 7, M-650.

101. David Doering, LBJ NCCPV, Box 41, R-258, 6.

102. Peck, *Uncovering the Sixties*, 112.

103. *Seed*, v. 2, no. 12.

104. Lyttle, *Chicago Anti-Vietnam War Movement*, 108; Nicholas von Hoffman, "Yippies Trot Out Candidate—A Pig," *Washington Post, Times Herald*, August 24, 1968, A5; Farber, *Chicago '68*, 167.

105. Dennis Cunningham, LBJ, NCCPV Box 41, R-234, 1–2.

106. Dave Doehring, LBJ, NCCPV Box 41, R-258, 2.

107. U.S. vs. David T. Dellinger and others, 13659.

108. Jack Hoffman and Daniel Simon, *Run, Run, Run: The Lives of Abbie Hoffman* (New York: G. P. Putnam's Sons, 1994), 99; Dennis Cunningham, LBJ, NCCPV Box 41, R-234, 2.

109. Lieberman, *Prairie Power*, 16.

110. Krassner, *Confessions*, 161–162.

111. Peck, *Uncovering the Sixties*, 114.

112. Dennis Cunningham, LBJ, NCCPV Box 41, R-234, 5.

113. Info about crash pads circulated throughout the event. Stein, *Living the Revolution*, 60; Dennis Cunningham, LBJ, NCCPV Box 41, R-234, 2–4. For Hoffman and Rubin's writings encouraging people not to fight for the park, see Jezer, *Abbie Hoffman*, 157–158; Nancy Zaroulis and Gerald Sullivan, *Who Spoke Up?: American Protest Against the War in Vietnam, 1963–1975* (New York: Doubleday, 1984), 184; Viorst, *Fire in the Streets*, 452; Mailer, *Miami and the Siege of Chicago*, 145. Jack Hoffman and Daniel Simon assert that Abbie wanted to stay in the park Saturday, but was outvoted by "more moderate" Yips. See Hoffman and Simon, *Run, Run, Run*, 99.

114. Chester et al., *An American Melodrama*, 521.

115. Lyttle, *Chicago Anti-Vietnam War Movement*, 108; Matusow, *Unraveling of America*, 415.

116. Jezer, *Abbie Hoffman*, 157–159; "Yippies Face Police, Beat Fast Retreat," *Chicago Tribune*, August 25, 1968, 8.

117. Schultz, *No One Was Killed*, 79, 81.

118. Paul Sills, LBJ, NCCPV, Box 40, R-021, 1.

119. Farber, *Chicago '68*, 178; James V. Lato, LBJ, NCCPV Box 41, R-337, 7–8; Abe Peck, LBJ, NCCPV Box 41, R-347, 1–2.

120. "Police Repel Jeering Mob of Peaceniks," *Chicago Tribune*, August 26, 1968, 1.

121. Terrence Dorsey, LBJ, NCCPV Box 33, OR-014, 3.

122. Paul Sills, LBJ, NCCPV Box 40, R-021, 4; Abe Peck, LBJ, NCCPV Box 41, R-347, 2.

123. Robert Cross, "Who Took the Yip from the Yippies?" *Chicago Tribune*, August 28, 1968, B2.

124. *Lincoln Park Press*, August 26, 1968, UIC NSCM Folder 325.

125. George Knight, LBJ, NCCPV Box 35, OR-252, 1; Sylvia Kushner, LBJ, NCCPV Box 42, R-489.

126. Paul Sills, LBJ, NCCPV Box 40, R-021, 5.

127. Schultz, *No One Was Killed*, 116–117; George Knight, LBJ, NCCPV Box 35, OR-252, 2; Allan Streyffeler, LBJ, NCCPV, Box 41, R-241, 1; Jonathan Tuttle, LBJ, NCCPV, Box 42, R-459, 6.

128. U.S. vs. David T. Dellinger and Others, 13750, 13765.

129. Allan Streyffeler, LBJ, NCCPV Box 41, R-241, 1.

130. Schultz, *No One Was Killed*, 124.

131. Dennis Cunningham, LBJ, NCCPV Box 41, R-234, 12.

132. Robert Lynsky, LBJ, NCCPV Box 42, R-502, 5.

133. Sylvan Fox, "300 Police Use Tear Gas to Breach Young Militants' Barricade in Chicago Park," *New York Times*, August 27, 1968, 29.

134. Jezer, *Abbie Hoffman*, 162.

135. Dennis Cunningham, LBJ, NCCPV Box 41, R-234, 12–13; Allan Streyffeler, LBJ, NCCPV, Box 41, R-241, 3; Viorst, *Fire in the Streets*, 454–455.

136. Schultz, *No One Was Killed*, 116–117; George Knight, LBJ, NCCPV Box 35, OR 252, 2; Allan Streyffeler Interview, NCCPV, LJ Box 41, R-241, 5–7; Jonathan Tuttle, NCCPV LBJ, Box 42, R-459, 6.

137. Schultz, *No One Was Killed*, 138; Biles, *Richard J. Daley*, 156.

138. Larry Dutenhaver, "Notes on Lincoln Park Experience During the Week of the Democratic Convention," NCCPV LBJ, Box 43, R-782; U.S. vs. David T. Dellinger and Others, 13750, 13765.

139. Schultz, *No One Was Killed*, 115.

140. Robert C. Maynard, "Police, Protesters Clash in an Atmosphere of Hatred," *Washington Post, Times Herald*, August 27, 1968, A6; "Hundreds of Protesters Block Traffic in Chicago," *New York Times*, August 26, 1968, 25.

141. Dennis Cunningham, LBJ, NCCPV Box 41, R-234, 14–15; Paul Sills, NCCP, LBJ Box 40, R-021, 6.

142. George Knight, LBJ, NCCPV Box 35, OR 252, 5.

143. Schultz, *No One Was Killed*, 116–117; George Knight, LBJ, NCCPV Box 35, OR 252, 2; Allan Streyffeler, NCCPV, LJ Box 41, R-241, 5–6; Jonathan Tuttle, NCCPV LBJ, Box 42, R-459, 6–7.

144. Anderson, *The Movement*, 222; U.S. vs. David T. Dellinger and Others, 13768.

145. Some hips avoided hotels on principle, as a hotel "ruins his [yippy's] sense of community with other Yippies." Jonathan Tuttle, LBJ, NCCPV Box 42, R-459, 5–6.

146. Bradford Lyttle, LBJ, NCCPV Box 45, S-153, 2.

147. Paul Sills, LBJ, NCCPV Box 40, R-021, 6; Barker, Paul Sills, 137.

148. Kusch, *Battleground Chicago*, 85.

149. George Knight recalled "there were Methodists, Presbyterians, United Church of Christ, Lutherans, Covenant, Roman Catholics, Episcopalians mingled together arm in arm, working on the different tasks." See LBJ, NCCPV Box 35, OR-252, 21.

150. George Knight, LBJ, NCCPV Box 35, OR 252, 8; James Shiflett, LBJ, NCCPV Box 40, R-022, 12; Ducey, *Sunday Morning*, 165.

151. Dennis Cunningham, LBJ, NCCPV Box 41-R234, 15–16; Paul Sills, NCCP, LBJ Box 40, R-021, 6–8; Robert Lynsky, LBJ, NCCPV Box 42, R-502, 11.

152. Jezer, *Abbie Hoffman*, 164.

153. John O'Brien, "Parents Seek Lost Children Among Hippies," *Chicago Tribune*, August 28, 1968, B9.

154. Paul Sills, LBJ, NCCPV Box 40 R-021, 8.

155. Allan Streyffeler, LBJ NCCPV, Box 41, R-241, 3.

156. Schultz, *No One Was Killed*, 135–136; Paul Sills, LBJ, NCCPV Box 40 R-021, 7.

157. Dennis Cunningham, LBJ, NCCPV Box 41, R-234, 16; Allan Streyffeler, LBJ, NCCPV, Box 41, R-241, 3–4.

158. Cunningham, LBJ, NCCPV Box 41-R234, 15–16; Paul Sills, LBJ, NCCPV Box 40, R-021, 8; Robert Lynsky, LBJ, NCCPV Box 42, R-502, 11; Report on the Events from February–September in Regard to NSCM Convention Mobilization UIC NSCM Folder 90.

159. James Shiflett, LBJ, NCCPV Box 40, R-022, 12.

160. Mary Teetor, "Notes from a Participant Observant," NCCPV LBJ, Box 43, R-789, 6.

161. Jerry Goethe, NCCPV LBJ, Box 43, R-782, 10.

162. Schultz, *No One Was Killed*, 157.

163. Dennis Cunningham, LBJ, NCCPV Box 41-R234, 15–16; Paul Sills, LBJ, NCCPV Box 40 R-021, 8.

164. Jeffrey Sweet, *Something Wonderful Right Away: An Oral History of the Second City and the Compass Players* (New York: Proscenium, 2003), 23.

165. Jerry Goethe, NCCPV LBJ, Box 43, R-782, 6; Tuttle, LBJ, NCCPV Box 42, R-459, 10.

166. Tom Arkwright, LBJ, NCCPV Box 43, R-663, 2.

167. Jonathan Tuttle, LBJ, NCCPV Box 41, R-314, 5.

168. Allen Ginsberg, LBJ, NCCPV Box 34, OR-132, 5; Stein, *Living the Revolution*, 102.

169. Paul Sills, LBJ, NCCPV Box 40, R-021, 8.

170. Schultz, *No One Was Killed*, 149–151. Dave Doering claimed that the worship service was designed to ease tensions, and that the idea for it came from a similar approach that had worked at Berkeley. See Dave Doehring, LBJ, NCCPV Box 41, R-258, 5.

171. One small barricade was assembled, but it failed to draw attention away from the cross. Schultz, *No One Was Killed*, 149–151.

172. Allan Streyffeler, LBJ, NCCPV, Box 41, R-241, 5; Zaroulis and Sullivan, *Who Spoke Up?*, 188.

173. Allan Streyffeler, LBJ, NCCPV, Box 41, R-241, 6.

174. Sylvan Fox, "Gas Again Used to Quell Protest," *New York Times*, August 28, 1968, 36.

175. Allen Ginsberg, LBJ, NCCPV Box 34, OR-132, 5.

176. Jonathan Tuttle, LBJ, NCCPV Box 41, R-314, 5; Jonathan Tuttle, LBJ, NCCPV Box 42, R-459, 8.

177. Larry Dutenhaver, "Notes on Lincoln Park Experience During the Week of the Democratic Convention," LBJ, NCCPV, Box 43, R-782; U.S. vs. David T. Dellinger and Others, 13778.

178. Michael O'Sullivan, LBJ, NCCPV Box 42, R-435, 9.

179. Jonathan Tuttle, LBJ, NCCPV Box 41, R-314, 5.

180. Richard M. Pfefer, LBJ, NCCPV Box 42, R-600, 8.

181. Jonathan Tuttle, LBJ, NCCPV Box 41, R-314, 6.

182. Farber, *Chicago '68*, 194; Raskin, *For the Hell of It*, 167.

183. Dennis Cunningham, LBJ, NCCPV Box 41, R234, 16, 18: Paul Sills, LBJ, NCCPV Box 40 R-021, 9.

184. Allan Streyffeler, NCCPV, LJ Box 41, R-241, 6.

185. Report on the Events from February–September in Regard to NSCM Convention Mobilization UIC NSCM Folder 90; George Knight, LBJ, NCCPV Box 35, OR 252, 14–18.

186. Matusow, *Unraveling of America*, 420; Farber, *Chicago '68*, 201–203; Zaroulis and Sullivan, *Who Spoke Up?*, 193–197.

187. Dennis Cunningham, LBJ, NCCPV Box 41-R234, 16, 18; Interview with Paul Sills, LBJ, NCCPV Box 40 R-021, 9.

188. Jonathan Tuttle, LBJ, NCCPV Box 42, R-459, 9.

189. Stein, *Living the Revolution*, 130–131.

190. Jezer, *Abbie Hoffman*, 171; Farber, *Chicago '68*, 204, Zaroulis and Sullivan, *Who Spoke Up?*, 196.

191. Farber, *Chicago '68*, 204–205; Zaroulis and Sullivan, *Who Spoke Up?*, 196–197.

192. Jezer, *Abbie Hoffman*, 171.

193. Farber, *Chicago '68*, 205.

194. Zaroulis and Sullivan, *Who Spoke Up?*, 199.

195. Report on the Events from February—September in Regard to NSCM Convention Mobilization UIC NSCM Folder 90.

196. Stein, *Living the Revolution*, 130–131, 141.

197. Viorst, *Fire in the Streets*, 460–461; NCCPV, *Rights in Conflict*, 351–358.

198. George Knight, LBJ, NCCPV Box 35, OR 252, 18–23. He wrote "Thank God for the battle of Lincoln Park."

199. Jerry Goethe, LBJ, NCCPV Box 43, R-782, 6.

200. William C. Henzlik, "Battle of Chicago: Clergy Group Among Billy Clubs, Flying Bottles," *Christian Advocate*, 28, UIC NSCM Folder 90.

201. *Lincoln Park Press* folder, UIC NSCM Folder 325.

202. Anderson, *The Movement*, 224.

203. Abe Peck, LBJ, NCCPV Box 41, R-347, 2.

5. 1969

Epigraph: "Wells Street: The Convention Aftermath," *Seed*, v. 3, no. 2, 10.

1. Seligman, *Block by Block*, 220.

2. Robert Cross, "Big Noise from Lincoln Park," *Chicago Tribune Magazine*, November 1969, 28.

3. Rieger, *Redeveloping Chicago's Lincoln Park Area*, 212–216.

4. William Chayes, LBJ, NCCPV Box 43, R-633, 11–12.

5. Letter from Concerned Citizens of Lincoln Park, UIC NSCM Folder 106.

6. Rieger, Redeveloping Chicago's Lincoln Park Area, 208, 76.

7. Hirsch, *Making the Second Ghetto*, 238.

8. Biles, "Public Housing," in Bauman et al., *From Tenements to the Taylor Homes*, 148–150.

9. Gleason, *Daley of Chicago*, 98.

10. Mollenkopf, *The Contested City*, 180.

11. Mollenkopf, *The Contested City*, 184–195.

12. Mary Merryfield, "Chicago's Runaway Hippies," *Chicago Tribune*, October 6, 1968, F1. For the Haight, see Anderson, *The Movement*, 170–176; Peck, *Uncovering the Sixties*, 51–52; Morgan, *The 60s Experience*, 184.

13. Laura Kaplan, *The Story of Jane: The Legendary Underground Feminist Abortion Service* (Chicago: University of Chicago Press, 1995), 67.

14. Merryfield, "Chicago's Runaway Hippies," F1.

15. "Wells Street," *Seed*, v. 3, no. 2, 10. Members of the Vietnam Veterans Against the War felt "depressed and powerless" in the wake of Chicago and lost members. See Andrew E. Hunt, *The Turning: A History of Vietnam Veterans Against the War* (New York: New York University Press, 1999), 30.

16. "4 Face Charge of Obscenity in Newspaper," *Chicago Tribune*, January 19, 1969, A10.

17. "18 Arrested in Dope Raid on Hippie Store," *Chicago Tribune*, February 18, 1969, 2; "Doc Gandolf," *Seed*, v. 4, no. 12, 30; "Sauron Visits Gandalf," *Seed*, v. 3, no. 8, 6.

18. Carolyn C. Barrett to Sgt. William Harrington, February 25, 1969, Box 4, Community Police Council, Correspondence, Mid-North Association, DPUA.

19. "Community" section, *Seed*, v. 3, no. 8, 18.

20. Kaplan, *Story of Jane*, 135.

21. "Alternate Society," *Seed*, v. 3, no. 8, 5.

22. "Alternate Society," *Seed*, v. 3, no. 8, 16–17, 19, 21.

23. "Harassment of Young Lords Continues," "Young Patriots Fight Model Cities," "Radical Jesus Winning," *Seed*, v. 3, no. 8, 18.

24. "The Post-Competitive, Comparative Game of a Free City," *The Digger Papers*, August of 1968, http://www.diggers.org/digpaps68/postcomp.html.

25. Mary Merryfield, "Chicago's Runaway Hippies," *Chicago Tribune*, October 6, 1968, F1.

26. "Alice's Place for Hippies Is Told to Move," *Chicago Tribune*, August 14, 1969, B24.

27. "Alice's Restaurant She's Closed," *Seed*, v. 4, no. 6, 12.

28. Racism Education Committee, June 6, 1968, UIC NSCM Folder 304.

29. "A Look at White Racism and the Future," UIC NSCM Folder 304.

30. Dave Doering, "Needed: A New Vision of the Kingdom. Some Grass-Roots Reactions to COCU," *Christian Century* 87, February 25, 1970, 239–240.

31. David Doering, "The Mission of the Church: A Position Paper Relating to Issues, Needs, Target Groups and Target Structures." UIC, NSCM Folder 279.

32. Doering, "The Mission of the Church," 3–5.

33. "Lincoln Park Town Meeting Watches Police," *Lincoln Park Booster,* November 13, 1968, 1, 8.

34. Warner, *The Renovation of Lincoln Park,* 53–54.

35. Schultz, *No One Was Killed,* 136; Barker, *Paul Sills' Life in the Theater,* 138–144.

36. Terry Sebela, "Town Meeting and Police Brutality," *Seed,* v. 3, n. 4, 6.

37. "Cops Get Harassment," Lincoln Park Booster, February 16, 1969, 1.

38. "Cop on the Beat Is Back," *Lincoln Park Booster,* February 26, 1969, 1.

39. Schultz, *No One Was Killed,* 136–137.

40. Lincoln Park Town Meeting News, August 9, 1969, LPCA Box 79, LPNC, DPUA.

41. Bach, *American Counterculture,* xvii; Rorabaugh, *American Hippies,* 83.

42. Lincoln Park Town Meeting News, August 9, 1969, LPCA Box 79, LPNC, DPUA; Tera Agyepong, "In the Belly of the Beast: Black Policemen Combat Police Brutality in Chicago, 1968–1983," *The Journal of African American History* 98, no. 2 (Spring 2013), 257.

43. Schultz, *No One Was Killed,* 286–288.

44. "The LPCA Needs You," *Lincoln Park Booster,* April 20, 1969.

45. "Survival Front," *Lincoln Park Booster,* March 30, 1969.

46. Concerned Citizens Survival Front of Lincoln Park, UIC NSCM Folder 106.

47. Bollwahn et al., "The Lincoln Park Community," footnote 32, 13, https://digicol.lib.depaul.edu/digital/collection/lpnc6/id/1388/rec/1.

48. Neighborhood Program of Concerned Citizens Survival Front of Lincoln Park, UIC NSCM Folder 106.

49. "Survival Front: How One Community Group Views Its Role," *Lincoln Park Booster,* March 30, 1969, 2.

50. Concerned Citizens Survival Front of Lincoln Park Proposed By Laws, UIC NSCM Folder 106.

51. Fernandez, *Brown in the Windy City,* 179.

52. Peter H. Prugh, "Chicago Neighborhood Fights City Hall," *Wall Street Journal,* January 3, 1967, Box 9, Correspondence, Planning Zoning, 1966–1969, Old Town Triangle Association Collection, DPUA.

53. Felix Padilla, *Puerto Rican Chicago* (Notre Dame, IN: University of Notre Dame Press, 1987), 120, 56.

54. Ana Y. Ramos-Zaya, *National Performances: The Politics of Class, Race, and Space in Puerto Rican Chicago* (Chicago: University of Chicago Press, 2003), 46.

55. Padilla, *Puerto Rican Chicago,* 58.

56. Ramos-Zayas, *National Performances,* 50, 47–48.

57. *Mid-North News,* February 1966, Box 1N, Newsletters 1960–1964, Mid-North Association Collection, DPUA.

58. Report of Activities of Fieldworker Brian Aldrich (September 1962–May 1963), Box 13, Correspondence, Sheffield Neighborhood Collection, DPUA.

59. Andrew J. Diamond, *Mean Streets: Chicago Youths and the Everyday Struggle for Empowerment in the Multiracial City, 1908–1969* (Berkeley: University of California Press, 2009), 168–170.

60. James Gilbert, *A Cycle of Outrage: America's Reaction to the Juvenile Delinquent in the 1950s* (New York: Oxford University Press, 1986), 143–195.

61. Fernandez, *Brown in the Windy City*, 181.

62. The nickname referred to his ability to dance. See Rodolpho Gonzales, *Tierra y libertad: Two interviews with Corky Gonzales and Cha Cha Jimenez*, pamphlet, Special Collections, Deering Library, Northwestern University, 11.

63. Jeffrey O. G. Ogbar, "Puerto Rico en mi corazon: The Young Lords, Black Power, and Puerto Rican Nationalism in the U.S. 1966–1972," *CENTRO Journal* 18, no. 1 (Spring 2006), Ogbar, 154; Judson Jeffries, "From Gang-Bangers to Urban Revolutionaries: The Young Lords of Chicago," *Journal of the Illinois State Historical Society* (Autumn 2003), 289–291. The group at one point claimed to have one thousand members, but refused to publicly disclose how many were really in the organization. See Jeffries, "From Gang-Bangers," 292. Angel G. Flores-Rodriguez, "The Young Lords, Puerto Rican Liberation, and the Black Freedom Struggle: Interview with Jose 'Cha Cha' Jimenez," *OAH Magazine of History* 26, no. 1 (January 2012), 62; Fernandez, *The Young Lords*, 36–38. For the Black Panther Party's transition to a political organization see Donna Murch, *Living for the City: Migration, Education and the Rise of the Black Panther Party of Oakland, California* (Chapel Hill: University of North Carolina Press, 2010).

64. Karen A. Secrist, "Occupy Lincoln Park: The Militant Drama of the Young Lords Organization," *Journal of African American Studies* 23 (2019), 389–404, 394. For Jimenez's relationship with Hampton see Judson L. Jeffries, "An Interview with Jose 'Cha Cha' Jimenez: Leader of the Young Lords Organization," *Journal of African American Studies* 22 (2018), 270.

65. Ogbar, "Puerto Rico en mi corazon," 155–156; Flores-Rodriguez, "The Young Lords," 63; Rodolpho Gonzales, *Tierra y libertad: Two interviews with Corky Gonzales and Cha Cha Jimenez*, pamphlet, Special Collections, Deering Library, Northwestern University, 12; Interview with Omar Lopez by Miguel Morales, Lincoln Park Project: An Oral History of the Young Lords Organization, February 10, 1995, DPUA, 6.

66. Jeffries, "From Gang Bangers," 292.

67. "Why a Y.L.O. Newspaper?," *Y.L.O.* 1, no. 1, 1, DePaul University Young Lords Newspaper Collection, https://digicol.lib.depaul.edu/digital/collection/younglords/id/12/rec/6.

68. *Y.L.O.* 1, no. 1, 9, DePaul University Young Lords Newspaper Collection, https://digicol.lib.depaul.edu/digital/collection/younglords/id/8/rec/6. For use of "the people" by the New York Young Lords see Darrel Enck-Wanzer, "Decolonizing Imaginaries: Rethinking 'the People' in the Young Lords Church Offensive," *Quarterly Journal of Speech* 98, no. 1 (February 2012), 1–23.

69. Ogbar, "Puerto Rico en mi Corazon," 155.

70. Gina M. Perez, *The Near Northwest Side Story: Migration, Displacement, and Puerto Rican Families* (Berkeley: University of California Press, 2004), 84; See also Jose Jimenez Interview and Biography, Interview 1, Grand Valley State University, Special Collections and University Archives, Young Lords in Lincoln Park Interviews, https://digitalcollections.library.gvsu.edu/document/24559.

71. Michael Robert Gonzales, *Ruffians and Revolutionaries: The Development of the Young Lords Organization in Chicago*, Master's Thesis, University of Wisconsin-Milwaukee, May 2015, 110.

72. Gang Research.net, "Cha Cha Jimenez: The Origins of Puerto Rican Gangs in Chicago, Excerpted from an Interview by Ralph Cintron and Erika Rodriguez, June 2002," http://gangsresearch.net/ChicagoGangs/younglords/chacha.htm (accessed September 16, 2019). Jimenez also refers to his visit to the Democratic National Convention protests as a "field trip." See also Secrist, "Occupy Lincoln Park," 443–444, for a similar account also provided by Jimenez. See also Jose Jimenez Interview and Biography, Interview 1, Grand Valley State University, Special Collections and University Archives, Young Lords in Lincoln Park Interviews, https://digitalcollections.library.gvsu.edu/document/24559.

73. Diamond, *Mean Streets*, 297.

74. Frank Browning, "From Rumble to Revolution: The Young Lords," *Ramparts*, October 1970, 19–25. Poor People's Coalition—Correspondence, LPCA Box 81, LPNC, DPUA; Ogbar, "Puerto Rico en mi corazon," 154–156.

75. Jeffrey O. G. Ogbar, "Brown Power to Brown People: Radical Ethnic Nationalism, the Black Panthers, and Latino Radicalism, 1967–1973," in Jama Lazerow and Yohuru Williams, eds., *In Search of the Black Panther Party: New Perspectives on a Revolutionary Movement* (Durham, NC: Duke University Press, 2006), 268.

76. Diamond, *Mean Streets*, 305–306; Amy Sonnie and James Tracy, *Hillbilly Nationalists, Urban Race Rebels, and Black Power: Community Organizing in Radical Times* (New York: Melville House, 2001), 66–67; Jakobi Williams, *From the Bullet to the Ballot: The Illinois Chapter of the Black Panther Party and Racial Coalition Politics in Chicago* (Chapel Hill: University of North Carolina Press, 2013), 127–131. Jimenez later asserted that he, Hampton, and Preacherman were the leaders of the Coalition. See Judson L. Jeffries, "Interview with Jose 'Cha Cha' Jimenez," 22, 272.

77. Williams, *From the Ballot to the Bullet*, 130, 132.

78. Ramos-Zayas, *National Performances*, 53–54.

79. Padilla, *Puerto Rican Chicago*, 121.

80. Singh, *Black Is a Country*, 196–200.

81. Jeffries, "From Gang Bangers," 291.

82. Fred, UIC NSCM Folder 34; Extent of Subversion in the "New Left," Testimony of Hugh Patrick Feely and Harry F. Port, Jr. Hearings Before the Subcommittee to Investigate the Administration of the Internal Security Act and Other Internal Security Laws of the Committee of the Judiciary, United States Senate, Ninety-First Congress, Second Session, Part 7, August 3, 1970, 1054 (hereafter cited as SISS Hearings) LPCA Box 81, LPNC, DPUA; Rodolpho Gonzales, *Tierra y libertad: two interviews with Corky Gonzales and Cha Cha Jimenez*, pamphlet, Special Collections, Deering Library, Northwestern University, 14.

83. "Gang Leader Denies a Mob Action Charge," *Chicago Tribune*, June 21, 1969, W2.

84. Fred, UIC NSCM Folder 34.

85. "4 Young Lords Free on Bond," *Chicago Tribune*, September 5, 1969, 15. Interestingly, they still had the day care center there.

86. Haas, *Assassination of Fred Hampton*, 45–54.

87. Haas, *Assassination of Fred Hampton*, 56. See also Dennis Cunningham, interviewed by Cha Cha Jimenez, Grand Valley State, Digital Collections, Young Lords in Lincoln Park Interviews, https://digitalcollections.library.gvsu.edu/document /24635.

88. Haas, *Assassination of Fred Hampton*, 57.

89. Dick Vission, "Manuel Ramos, Young Lords Organization," *Seed*, v. 3, no. 11, 3–5.

90. Browning, "From Rumble to Revolution," 20.

91. Fernandez, *Brown in the Windy City*, 188.

92. "YLO Told Probe Being Conducted," *Lincoln Park Booster*, May 29, 1969; "Power to the People," *Seed*, v. 3, no. 12, 5.

93. Dick Vission, "Manuel Ramos, Young Lords Organization," *Seed*, v. 3, no. 11, 3–5.

94. Al Rosenfeld, "Ramos Inquest," *Seed*, v. 3, no. 13, 5, 8.

95. "Clergy Form Group Against 'Cop Violence,'" *Lincoln Park Booster*, May 18, 1969.

96. "Protest for the Poor," *Lincoln Park Booster*, May 4, 1969; "Power to the People," *Seed*, v. 3, no. 12, 5, 18; Y.L.O., 1, no 2 (May 1969), 4, https://digicol.lib .depaul.edu/digital/collection/younglords/id/16/rec/7

97. Ronald Koziol, "Parley Fails: Gang Holds Seminary Unit," *Chicago Tribune*, May 16, 1969, 17.

98. Carolyn Shojai, "Business Men are Told About Seminary Sit-It," *Chicago Tribune*, June 1, 1969, N5.

99. "Young Lords Demand Church for Rent or Sale," *Lincoln Park Booster*, June 15, 1969; Padilla, 120; Mike Abrahams, "All Power to the Children," *Seed*, v. 4, no. 1, 4; NA, "Gang Members Begin Sit-In at N. Side Church, *Chicago Tribune*, June 12, 1969, B22.

100. NA, "Young Lords Still Holding N. Side Church," *Chicago Tribune*, June 14, 1969, N4.

101. Frank Browning, "From Rumble to Revolution: The Young Lords," *Ramparts*, October 1970, 20, DPUA LPCA Box 81, Poor People's Coalition—Correspondence; Padilla, *Puerto Rican Chicago*, 121.

102. Interview with Omar Lopez by Miguel Morales, Lincoln Park Project: An Oral History of the Young Lords Organization, February 10, 1995, DPUA, 11.

103. "All Power to the Children," *Seed*, v. 4, no. 1, 4.

104. Martha M. Arguello, "We Joined Others Who Were Poor: The Young Lords, the Black Freedom Struggle, and the 'Original' Rainbow Coalition," *Journal of African American Studies* 23 (2019), 443, 446–447.

105. Concerned Citizens of Lincoln Park, LPCCC Box 3, LPNC, DPUA.

106. Carolyn Shojai, "Threats, Shouts at Lincoln Park Council Meeting," *Chicago Tribune*, May 25, 1969, N5.

107. "Police Arrest YLO Head," *Lincoln Park Booster*, June 8, 1969.

108. Diane Taylor, Confrontation at LPCCC—sequence of events, LPCA News, LPCCC Box 3, LPNC, DPUA; Carolyn Shojai, "Gangs Disrupt Lincoln Park Unit's Meeting," *Chicago Tribune*, July 30, 1969, B12.

109. Diane Taylor, Confrontation at LPCCC—sequence of events, LPCA News, LPCCC Box 3, LPNC, DPUA.

110. Diane Taylor, Confrontation at LPCCC—sequence of events, LPCA News, LPCCC Box 3, LPNC, DPUA.

111. "Melee in Lincoln Park—It Might've Been Avoided," *Lincoln Park Booster*, August 3, 1969; Carolyn Shojai, "Gangs Disrupt Lincoln Park Unit's Meeting," *Chicago Tribune*, July 30, 1969, B12; *Lincoln Park Press*, v. 1, no. 4, 1968, 1–3, Lincoln Park Newspapers, LPNC, DPUA; "Last Tuesday Night," *Seed*, v. 4, no. 3, 5; "Open Meetings in Peril," *Chicago Daily News*, Thursday, July 31, 1969, 6.

112. Dalton, *The Politics of Community Problem-Solving*, 85, LPCA Box 3, LPNC DPUA.

113. "Wires Demand Brown Ouster," *Lincoln Park Booster*, August 3, 1969.

114. Merle Kaminsky, "Court Case of 4 Men Indicted for LP Mob Action Continued," *Lerner Booster*, March 1, 1970, Box 15, Various Newspaper Articles, Sheffield Neighborhood Association, DPUA.

115. "Double Standard Won't Work in Dealing with LP Violence," *Lerner Booster*, October 12, 1969; James Dalton claims that Peter Bauer and Stephen Shamberg pressed for the indictments of Brown and the others. Dalton, *The Politics*

of Community Problem-Solving, 86, LPCA Box 3, LPNC DPUA; "LPCCC's Mayer Resigns," *Lincoln Park Booster,* November 1, 1969, 1; "6 indicted in beating and threat to TV men," *Chicago Today,* October 13, 1969, Box 15, Various Newspaper Articles, Sheffield Neighborhood Association, DPUA; "LP Men Face Charges of Mob Action October 27," *Lerner Booster,* October 22, 1969, Box 15, Various Newspaper Articles, Sheffield Neighborhood Association, DPUA.

116. "Disrupter Given 5 Years' Probation," Lerner Newspapers, LPCCC Box 3, LPNC, DPUA.

117. "LPCC's Mayer Resigns," *Lincoln Park Booster,* November 1, 1969.

118. "Disrupter," *Lincoln Park Booster,* April 1970, 8.

119. *Seed,* v. 3, no. 13, 2.

120. "Lincoln Park Unit Considers Charges Against Disrupters," *Chicago Tribune,* July 31, 1969, N12.

121. Dalton, *The Politics of Community Problem-Solving,* 87; SISS Hearings, 1057, LPCA Box 81, LPNC DPUA.

122. Michael Hirsley, "More 'Renewal' for Lincoln Park," *Chicago Today,* September 12, 1969, Box 1, Correspondence 1969, Sheffield Neighborhood Collection, DPUA.

123. Bollwahn et al., "The Lincoln Park Community," 9.

124. Letter from members of the community to Lyle Mayer, August 4, 1969, LPCCC Box 3, LPNC, DPUA.

125. Lyle Mayer to Raymond F. Simon, August 13, 1969, LPCCC Box 3, LPNC, DPUA.

126. Dalton, *The Politics of Community Problem-Solving,* 3, 83.

127. Poor and Working Demands to the Conservation Community Council, LPCA Box 80, LPNC, DPUA. Members of the CCSF had, in January of 1969, asked that the DUR turn Augustana Hospital's facilities into a "poor people's clinic." See *Mid-North Association Newsletter,* April 1969, Box 1N, Newsletters 1969, Mid-North Neighborhood Association Collection, DPUA.

128. Miller, *Democracy,* 155–166; Bach, *American Counterculture,* 160–161.

129. "People's Tot Lot," *Lincoln Park Booster,* June 22, 1969.

130. "Comancheros, Residents Work to Build and Keep 'People's Park,'" *Lincoln Park Booster,* August 17, 1969.

131. Dalton, *The Politics of Community Problem-Solving,* 85 LPCA Box 3, LPNC DPUA; "Roaches," *Seed,* v. 4, no. 10, 9.

132. "O.K. Harford Housing Bid," *Chicago Tribune,* June 14, 1970, N9; "Poor Screwed Again," *Seed,* v. 4, no. 13, 2.

133. The newsletter of the Mid-North Association reported that approximately sixty different statements were read at the meeting, and a "majority" of them favored Hartford's bid, not the Poor People's Coalition. See Mid-North

Association, February 1, 1970, Box 1N, Newsletters 1970, Mid-North Neighborhood Association Collection, DPUA.

134. Dalton, *The Politics of Community Problem-Solving*, 90, LPCA Box 3, LPNC DPUA; "Poor Screwed Again," *Seed*, v. 4, no. 13, 2; Paolini, *Lincoln Park Conservation Association*, 73–77.

135. Thomas Buck, "Renewal Hearing Disrupted," *Chicago Tribune*, February 12, 1970, 1.

136. Thomas Buck, "7 Hit Lincoln Park Renewal Plan," *Chicago Tribune*, February 10, 1969, 9; "Seven LPCCC Members to Quit if Housing Suggestion Not Followed," *North-Center Booster*, February 11, 1970.

137. "Board Resignations Put Off," *North-Central Booster*, February 18, 1969.

138. "O.K. Hartford Housing Bid," *Chicago Tribune*, June 14, 1970, N9.

139. "Hartford Bid on Larrabee Wins Approval," *North-Central Booster*, June 1970.

140. Dalton, *Politics of Community Problem Solving*, 95, LPCA Box 3, LPNC DPUA.

141. John Indian, "Bum Trip at Acid Rescue," *Seed*, v. 4, no. 3, 5 (July–August 1969); "Comin' Down," *Seed*, v. 4, no. 4, 6.

142. Warner, *The Renovation of Lincoln Park*, 54.

143. "Some Notes in the Form of a Narrative Toward a Reconstruction of the Political History of Lincoln Park, 1853–1971," Box 1, Folder 9, Lincoln Park Study Group, DPUA, 72.

144. "Lincoln Park Fire Bombs," *Seed*, v. 4, no. 6, 18; Dalton, Politics of Community Problem Solving, 87; LPCA Box 3, LPNC DPUA; SISS Hearings, 1057, LPCA Box 81, LPNC, DPUA.

145. "Arson Probed at Offices of Two Aldermen," *Chicago Sun Times*, September 16, 1969, Box 1, Correspondence 1969, Sheffield Neighborhood Collection, DPUA.

146. "Church Raps McCutcheon, Defends Gang," *Chicago Tribune*, September 23, 1969, A26.

147. "City Helps Clean 'People's Park,'" *Lincoln Park Booster*, October 12, 1969.

148. "Civic Leader Finds Bomb in His Mailbox," *Chicago Tribune*, May 29, 1969, 18.

149. "Press Release After 6 P.M., Monday, September 15, 1969," Box 1, Board of Directors Meeting Minutes 1969, Mid-North Association Collection, DPUA.

150. "Minister and Wife Are Slain in Chicago," *New York Times*, September 30, 1969, 26.

151. John O'Brien, "N. Side Cleric, Wife, Slain: Couple Found Stabbed in Their Home: Minister Aided Street Gangs," *Chicago Tribune*, September 30, 1969, 1; Richard Philbrick, "Friends Recall Slain Cleric as 'Great Guy,'" *Chicago Tribune*, September 30, 1969, 2; John O'Brien, "Clews [sic.] Fading in Murder of Cleric, Wife," *Chicago Tribune*, October 1, 1969, 6.

152. SISS Hearings, 1058, LPCA Box 81, LPNC, DPUA. The *Chicago Tribune* estimated that two thousand people attended a memorial processional that began at the People's Park. See Robert Svejcara, "Their People Honor Slain Pastor, Wife," *Chicago Tribune*, October 2, 1969, B19.

153. Dalton, *The Politics of Community Problem-Solving*, 88, LPNC DPUA Box 3; Gitlin, *The Sixties*, 393–395; Matusow, *Unraveling of America*, 341–342; Ayers, *Fugitive Days*, 166–177.

154. Jeremy Varon, *Bringing the War Home: The Weather Underground, The Red Army Faction, and Revolutionary Violence in the Sixties and Seventies* (Berkely: University of California Press, 2004), 78, 82.

155. SISS Hearings, 1083–1084, LPCA Box 81, LPNC, DPUA.

156. Susan Stern, *With the Weathermen: The Personal Journal of a Revolutionary Woman* (New York: Doubleday, 1975), 136, 145.

157. Varon, *Bringing the War Home*, 82–83; Cathy Wilkerson, *Flying Close to the Sun: My Life and Times as a Weatherman* (New York: Seven Stories Press, 2007), 302, footnote on p. 418.

158. Varon, *Bringing the War Home*, 84.

159. Wilkerson, *Flying Too Close to the Sun*, 298, 317.

160. Minutes of the Board of Directors, Mid-North Association, September 17, 1969, Box 1, Board of Directors Meeting Minutes, Mid-North Association, DPUA.

161. Mark J. Arlen, *An American Verdict* (New York: Doubleday and Company, 1973), 102–103, 166–168.

162. Diamond, *Chicago on the Make*, 218.

163. For eyewitness accounts of the shooting see Bud Schultz and Ruth Schultz, *The Price of Dissent: Testimonies to Political Repression in America* (Berkeley: University of California Press, 2001), 225–227, 232–235; Peck, *Uncovering the Sixties*, 223–225. For more recent overviews see Bloom and Martin Jr., *Black Against Empire*, 226–246, and Williams, *From the Bullet to the Ballot*, 167–190.

164. Haas, *Assassination of Fred Hampton*, 89, 92. People's Law Office attorney Flint Taylor recalls a team from that office covertly transporting evidence "to the attic of a north side church for safekeeping." See his *The Torture Machine: Racism and Violence in Chicago* (Chicago: Haymarket Press, 2019), 3.

165. Anderson, *The Movement*, 327; Nelson Blackstock, *COINTELPRO: The FBI's Secret War on Political Freedom* (New York: Monad Press, 1977), 16; Ward Churchill and Jim Vander Wall, *Agents of Repression: The FBI's Secret Wars Against the Black Panther Party and the American Indian Movement* (Boston: South End Press, 1988), 68–73; Ward Churchill and Jim Vander Wall, *The COINTELPRO Papers: Documents from the FBI's Secret Wars Against Domestic Dissent* (Boston: South End Press, 1990), 139–142.

166. Haas, *The Assassination of Fred Hampton*, 108.

167. Ranch Triangle Conservation Association to Edward V. Hanrahan, December 30, 1969, Box 2, Correspondence 1960–1969, Mid-North Association, DPUA.

6. Confrontation and Gentrification

1. Bollwahn, et al., "The Lincoln Park Community," 9.

2. Dalton, *The Politics of Community Problem-Solving*, 82, LPCA Box 3, LPNC DPUA; Carolyn Shojai, "Threats, Shouts at Lincoln Park Council Meeting," *Chicago Tribune*, May 25, 1969, N5.

3. Isserman and Kazin, *America Divided*; Thomas Burns Edsall and Mary D. Edsall, *Chain Reaction: The Impact of Race, Rights, and Taxes on American Politics* (New York: W. W. Norton, 1992); William Berman, *America's Right Turn: From Nixon to Bush (The American Moment)* (Baltimore: Johns Hopkins University Press, 1994); Rieder, *Canarsie*; Jim Sleeper, *The Closest of Strangers: Liberalism and the Politics of Race in New York* (New York: W. W. Norton and Company, 1990); Dan T. Carter, *Politics of Rage: George Wallace, the Origins of the New Conservatism, and the Transformation of American Politics* (New York: Simon and Schuster, 1995).

4. Anderson, *The Movement*, 225–226.

5. Flamm, *Law and Order*, 159.

6. "Business Men Support Cops in Riot Action," *Chicago Tribune*, November 16, 1968, C19.

7. Rudolph Unger, "Police Leader Hails Men in Convention," *Chicago Tribune*, June 7, 1969, S_A18.

8. The *Wall Street Journal* announced that the LPCA "is against any high-rise public housing." Peter H. Prugh, "Chicago Neighborhood Fights City Hall," *Wall Street Journal*, January 3, 1967, Box 9, Correspondence, Planning Zoning, 1966–1969, Old Town Triangle Association Collection, DPUA.

9. "Staying on Top of Renewal," *Lincoln Park Booster*, March 13, 1969, 8.

10. "LPCCC Appointees Draw Renewed Complaints," *Lincoln Park Booster*, March 23, 1969, 1.

11. "Group in Lincoln Park to Finish Study on Housing," *Chicago Tribune*, June 1969, N10.

12. Frederic Soll and Jack Houston, "Taxes, Rents, Renewal Loosen Lincoln Park Loyalty," *Chicago Tribune*, May 23, 1971, WA3.

13. "LPCA Bids for Members, Funds," *Old Town Newsletter*, January 1972, Box 1N, Newsletters, 1970–74, Old Town Triangle Association Collection, DPUA.

14. *Special Secret Report*, LPCCC Box 3, LPNC, DPUA.

15. Letter from Ivan Fuldaer to Lewis Hill, n.d. (attached handout dated June 14, 1969), Box 12, Correspondence with Commissioner Lewis Hill, Department of Urban Renewal, Mid-North Association, DPUA.

16. Carolyn Shojai, "Lincoln Park Council Disruptions Hit," *Chicago Tribune*, June 22, 1969, N3.

17. Stephen Shamberg to LPCA Members, June 3, 1969, LPCCC Box 3, LPNC, DPUA.

18. "Disruption Attempt Blasted," *Lincoln Park Booster*, June 8, 1969; "LPCA Presidents Says Complaints Don't Justify Disruptive Tactics," *Lincoln Park Booster*, June 15, 1969.

19. Stephen Shamberg to LPCA Members, June 3, 1969, LPCCC Box 3, LPNC, DPUA.

20. "LPCA President Responds to LPCCC Meeting," *LPCA News*, 3. LPCCC Box 3, LPNC, DPUA.

21. "Lincoln Park Unit Considers Charges Against Disrupters," *Chicago Tribune*, July 31, 1969, N12.

22. "Lincoln Park Community: Council Chairman Calls Housing Biggest Need," *Chicago Tribune*, December 14, 1969, N8.

23. Mamie B. Govean to George Barr McCutcheon, August 25, 1969; Mamie B. Govean to Emmett Dedmon, August 22, 1969, LPCCC Box 3, LPNC, DPUA.

24. Untitled Letter, no author, LPCCC Box 3, LPNC, DPUA.

25. Frederick Trost, "Disorder in LP: What It Means," n.d., LPCCC Box 3, LPNC, DPUA.

26. "Dear Mr. Shawnower," August 21, 1969, Box 1, Correspondence 1969, Sheffield Neighborhood Collection, DPUA.

27. Mrs. O. M. Forkert, President Old Town Triangle Association to Commissioner Lewis W. Hill, September 6, 1969, Box 12, Correspondence with Commissioner Lewis Hill, Department of Urban Renewal, Mid-North Association, DPUA.

28. *Mid-North Association Newsletter*, May 1969, Box 1N, Newsletters 1969, Mid-North Neighborhood Collection, DPUA.

29. Mid-North Association letter from Carolyn C. Barrett, LPCCC Box 3, LPNC, DPUA; *Mid-North Association Newsletter*, August 4, 1969, Box 1N Newsletters 1969, Mid-North Neighborhood Collection, DPUA; Dear Chief Lynsky, After Midnight, Tuesday 29, Box 4, Community Police Council Correspondence, Mid-North Association, DPUA.

30. Letter from Carolyn C. Barret to C. E. Braasch, August 18, 1969, Box 4, Community Safety Committee, Community Police Council Correspondence, 1965–1976, Mid-North Collection, DPUA.

31. Peter A. Bauer, Letter to Mid-North Association members, August 4, 1969, LPCCC Box 3, LPNC, DPUA; "Lincoln Park Terrorism," *Lerner Booster*, September 24, 1969, Box 1, Correspondence 1969, Sheffield Neighborhood Collection, DPUA.

32. "Lincoln Park Scene Focused on Police," *Lincoln Park Booster*, September 14, 1969.

33. Minutes of Board of Directors, Mid-North Association, August 14, 1969, Box 1, Board of Directors Meeting Minutes, 1969, Mid-North Association Collection, DPUA.

34. Mid-North Association to Commander O. E. Braasch, September 3, 1969, Box 2, Correspondence 1960–1969, Mid-North Association, DPUA. About one hundred members came to that meeting, where they viewed a film called *Let's Work Together* with Deputy Chief Lynsky, who discussed gangs and youth. See Carolyn C. Barrett to Robert J. Lynsky, September 11, 1969, Box 2, Correspondence 1960–1969, Mid-North Association, DPUA.

35. "To Whom it May Concern," September 1969, Box 2, Correspondence 1960–1969. Mid-North Association, DPUA.

36. Ranch Triangle Conservation Association to Mrs. Elizabeth McLean, April 22, 1971, Box 4, Planning Committee Correspondence 1970–1979, Ranch Triangle Conservation Association, DPUA.

37. Dalton, *The Politics of Community Problem-Solving*, 88, LPCA Box 3, LPNC, DPUA.

38. "Young Lord Terror in Lincoln Park Told," *Chicago Tribune*, December 8, 1969, 1.

39. "Candidates to LPCA Challenged," *North-Center Booster*, January 21, 1970.

40. Ducey, *Sunday Morning*, 53; Donner, *Protectors of Privilege*, 150.

41. SISS Hearings, 1052–1062, LPCA Box 81, LPNC DPUA.

42. Russell Freeburg, "Church 'Influence' on New Left Told," *Chicago Tribune*, December 30, 1970, 6; SISS Hearings, 1068–1086, LPCA Box 81, LPNC DPUA.

43. "North Side Ministry Admits Some Aid Went to Street Gangs," *Chicago Tribune*, January 1, 1971, 8.

44. Roy Larson, "Minister with a Catholic View Takes on the Inner City," *Chicago Sun Times*, Saturday, January 2, 1971, LPCA Box 15, LPNC, DPUA; Ducey, *Sunday Morning*, 53–54.

45. Glen Elsasser, "2 Chicagoans Give Look at Life in the New Left," *Chicago Tribune*, August 20, 1970, B5.

46. "SISS Mischief," *Christian Century*, 88, March 24, 1971, 365–366. For whatever reason, the magazine also claimed that the LPCA's urban renewal plan "runs contrary even to the Daley establishment's urban renewal program."

47. Bobbie Wells, Secretary North Side Cooperative Ministry to the Board of Directors, Lincoln Park Conservation Association, December 31, 1970, Box 2, Correspondence 1970–1979, Mid-North Association Collection, DPUA. By January of 1971 Mid-North was concerned about groups like NSCM, but rather than testify before Congress merely agreed to withhold support from such groups, and send a letter to churches informing them of the harm gangs they supported did to the neighborhood. See Mid-North Safety Committee, January 6, 1971, and February 3, 1971, Box 4, Community Safety Committee Meeting Minutes, 1971–1995, Mid-North Association, DPUA.

48. David Doering, *The Vision and History of the North Side Cooperative Ministry, 1962–1972*, NSCM UIC, Folder 526.

49. Patricia Krizmis, "Residents of Old Town Fringe Feel Fear," *Chicago Tribune*, May 13, 1971, 7.

50. SISS Hearings, 1095, LPCA Box 81, LPNC, DPUA.

51. "Dear Friend and Neighbor," Letter from 18th District Community Service Sergeant William J. Harrington and District Commander John R. O'Shea; "Dear Member," Letter from C. E. Braasch, September 4, 1969, Box 4, Community Safety Committee Correspondence, 1971–1995, DPUA.

52. Larry Glass to John O'Shea, January 12, 1971, Box 2, Correspondence 1970–1979, Mid-North Association, DPUA.

53. Mid-North Community Safety Committee Meeting, March 3, 1971, Box 4, Community Safety Committee Correspondence, 1971–1995, DPUA.

54. Donner, *Protectors of Privilege*, 137–138.

55. Diamond, *Chicago on the Make*, 213.

56. Churchill and Vander Wall, the *COINTELPRO Papers*, 138–139, 208–211.

57. "LP Men Face Charges of Mob Action October 27," *Lerner Booster*, October 22, 1969, Box 15, Various Newspaper Articles, Sheffield Neighborhood Association, DPUA.

58. Interview with Omar Lopez by Miguel Morales, Lincoln Park Project: An Oral History of the Young Lords Organization, February 17, 1995, DPUA, 7.

59. Interview with Angie Adorno Navedo by Mary Martinez, Young Lords Oral History Project, January 27, 1995, DPUA, 22.

60. Warner, *The Renovation of Lincoln Park*, 117–119.

61. Warner, *The Renovation of Lincoln Park*, 131, 134.

62. Oral History Transcript: Bruce Longdecker, Box 1, Lincoln Park Community Research Initiative, DPUA, 6.

63. 43rd Ward Citizens Committee, *Serendipity City: A Selective Guide to the Best in Shopping, Dining, Entertaining, and Existing in the Lincoln Park Neighborhood*, vol. 2 (Chicago: Swallow Press, 1972), 9–13, 17–27, 39–53, 101–109.

64. *Chicago Fact Book Consortium, Local Community Fact Book: Chicago Metropolitan Area, 1980* (Chicago: Chicago Review Press, 1984), 19–20.

65. Larry Bennett, *Neighborhood Politics: Chicago and Sheffield* (New York: Garland Publishing, 1997), 64.

66. Terri Schultz, "Construction Brings Hope of New Life for Old Town," *Chicago Tribune,* October 10, 1971, SCL3.

67. Donna Gill, "Store Owners in Old Town are Smiling," *Chicago Tribune,* December 6, 1967, C26.

68. Joy Darrow, "High Rise Plan Stirs Debate on Old Town Philosophy," *Chicago Tribune,* April 18, 1968, N1.

69. Stanley Ziemba, "Old Town Wins High-Rise Battle," *Chicago Tribune,* April 24, 1974, 9.

70. "Old Warehouse is Focal Point of Apartment, Shopping Complex," *Chicago Tribune,* January 21, 1973, W_A1.

71. "New High Rise Has 10 Models," *Chicago Tribune,* May 12, 1973, N_A19.

72. "High-Rise Design Shaping Up How People Want to Live," *Chicago Tribune,* June 9, 1973, N24.

73. "New Inside, Old Outside: Parkway Hotel Gutted for Condos," *Chicago Tribune,* June 10, 1973, S_A1.

74. "Residents Buying at 2400 Lakeview," *Chicago Tribune,* November 4, 1973, N_A11; NA, "First 2400 Lakeview Condos on View Today," *Chicago Tribune,* March 2, 1974, N_B13.

75. Warner, *The Renovation of Lincoln Park,* 57.

76. Larry Bennett, *Neighborhood Politics: Chicago and Sheffield* (New York: Garland Publishing, 1997), 76–86; Ruth Moore, "Uptown Area Gets Full-Scale Plan for Urban Renewal," *Chicago Sun-Times,* May 17, 1962, 32.

77. Bennett, "Rethinking Neighborhoods," 245, 253.

78. Robert Cross, "Uptown's Future: Are the Swingers at the Gates?," *Chicago Tribune,* September 29, 1974, H20.

79. Donald Yabus, "'Hottest' Place Around: In Crowd Discovers Lincoln Park West," *Chicago Tribune,* May 3, 1973, N_A1.

80. Betancur, "The Politics of Gentrification," 785–786, 806–808.

81. John J. Betancur, "Gentrification and Community Fabric in Chicago," *Urban Studies* 48, no. 2 (February 2011), 390, 397.

82. Osman, "The Decade of the Neighborhood," 108–127.

83. "Major Victory in Fight Against High-Rises. Piper's Alley Project Sharply Scaled Down," *Old Town Newsletter,* October–November 1973, Box 1N, Newsletters 1970–1974, Old Town Triangle Association Collection, DPUA.

84. "Remarks by Lewis W. Hill, May 31, 1973," Box 2, Correspondence and Memos, 1970–1979, Mid-North Association Collection, DPUA.

85. Baugher, *Our Old Town*, 136.

86. *Old Town Newsletter*, v. 5, no. 1, January 1972, Box 1N, Publications, Old Town Triangle Association Collection, DPUA.

87. *Old Town Newsletter*, v. 5, no. 2, March 1972, Box 1N, Publications, Old Town Triangle Association Collection, DPUA. Amy Forkert was OTTA President in 1969, and Maurice in 1976 and 1977. See Bauer, *Our Old* Town, 140–141, and "Otto Maurice Forkert," *Chicago Sun-Times*, May 14, 1991, 59.

88. Baugher, *Our Old Town*, 46–47.

89. Damon Bach argues the counterculture underwent five phases: its origins (1945–65), "inchoate years" (1965–66), "flowering" 1967–1970, "apogee" (early 1970s), then "decline" beginning in 1972. See *The American Counterculture*, xxiii.

90. "4 Young Lords Free on Bond," *Chicago Tribune*, September 5, 1969, 15.

91. Frank Browning, "From Rumble to Revolution: The Young Lords," *Ramparts* 9 (1970–1971), 19–25; Poor People's Coalition—Correspondence LPCA Box 81, LPNC DPUA; "6 Young Lords Seized in Rock Tossing Melee," *Chicago Tribune*, April 29, 1970, 2.

92. Jeffries, "From Gang-Bangers," 298–300; Flores-Rodriguez, "The Young Lords, Puerto Rican Liberation," 64; Interview with Omar Lopez by Miguel Morales, Lincoln Park Project: An Oral History of the Young Lords Organization, February 10, 1995, DPUA, 19.

93. Clarence Page, "Young Lords Leader Surrenders to Police," *Chicago Tribune*, December 7, 1972; "Young Lords Chief Vows Fast," *Chicago Tribune*, December 8, 1972, A14.

94. Dalton, *The Politics of Community Problem-Solving*, 91.

95. Baugher, *Our Old Town*, 108–109.

96. Dalton, *The Politics of Community Problem-Solving*, 91; Ducey, *Sunday Morning*, 169; SISS Hearings, 1068, LPCA Box 81, LPNC, DPUA.

97. Warner, *The Renovation of Lincoln Park*, 115.

98. Barker, *Paul Sills' Life in the Theater*, 143.

99. Dalton, *The Politics of Community Problem-Solving*, 91.

100. Haas, *Assassination of Fred Hampton*, 155, 161–62, 202.

101. Heather Ann Thompson, *Blood in the Water: The Attica Prison Uprising of 1971 and Its Legacy* (New York: Pantheon Books, 2016), 322–323, 467.

102. David Doering, *The Vision and History of the North Side Cooperative Ministry, 1962–1972*, NSCM UIC, Folder 526; Mary Ann Bamberger, North Side Cooperative Ministry Collection Introduction and Index, UIC NSCM.

103. Ducey, *Sunday Morning*, 169.

104. Warner, *The Renovation of Lincoln Park*, 130–131.

105. *Seed*, v. 8, no. 9, 3, 1972.

106. *Seed*, v. 9, no. 1, October 18–Nov 1, 1972, 2. *Independent Voices: An Open Access Collection of an Alternative Press*, https://voices.revealdigital.org/?a=d&d =BHGFDEC19721018.1.2&e=———en-20-1—txt-txIN—————1.

107. "Free City/Good Numbers," *Seed*, v. 9, no. 10, February 8, 1974, 2. *Independent Voices: An Open Access Collection of an Alternative Press*, https://voices .revealdigital.org/?a=d&d=BHGFDEC19740208.1.2&e=———en-20-1—txt -txIN—————1. For *Seed's* end, see June Sawyers, "The Seed: Giving a Voice to the Flower Children," *Chicago Tribune*, August 31, 1986. https://www .chicagotribune.com/news/ct-xpm-1986-08-31-8603050198-story.html. Patrick Sisson, "Nymphs, Pigs, and Mayor Daley for Thanksgiving: The Radical Art of Chicago Seed," *Chicago Reader*, July 29, 2014, https://www.chicagoreader.com /Bleader/archives/2014/07/29/nymphs-pigs-and-mayor-daley-for-thanksgiving-the -radical-art-of-chicago-seed.

108. Mary Merryfield, "God Is Alive—But Is the Church?" *Chicago Tribune*, January 7, 1970, B1.

109. Terri Schultz, "'Jiving' Parish Hangs On," *Chicago Tribune*, April 18, 1971, NA3.

110. Wayne Dunham, "Youths Set Goals to Improve Lincoln Park Area," *Chicago Tribune*, January 4, 1970, N_A3.

111. Anderson, *The Movement*, 387–388.

112. The *Chicago Tribune* originally reported that Jimenez downplayed the problem. See David Satter, "Community Demands Action: City Street Corner Becomes Open-Air Drug Market," *Chicago Tribune*, March 31, 1974, 41. Jimenez denied this, and noted his request for the squad car. See Steven Pratt, "Latin Gang Tells Fight Against Drugs," *Chicago Tribune*, April 2, 1974, A7.

113. David Young, "Jimenez Runs for Alderman," *Chicago Tribune*, June 21, 1974, A1.

114. "Cohen Wins Support of Regular Dems," *Chicago Tribune*, December 1, 1974, 4; NA, "46th Ward IPO Backs Jimenez," *Chicago Tribune*, January 7, 1975, A5.

115. Robert Davis, "'Ideal Immigrants'" Join Mainstream, *Chicago Tribune*, May 5, 1975, 10.

116. "Newhouse Plans to Introduce an Alternative Remap," *Chicago Tribune*, April 24, 1975, A1.

117. Clarence Page, "Carlos Castro: Latin to Watch," *Chicago Tribune*, June 30, 1974, 33.

118. Marisol V. Rivera and Judson Jeffries, "From Radicalism to Representation: Jose 'Cha Cha' Jimenez's Journey into Electoral Politics," *Journal of African American Studies* 23 (2019), 299–319.

119. Frank Zahour, "Diverse Candidates Run in 46th Ward," *Chicago Tribune*, February 20, 1975, A1.

120. Peniel E. Joseph, *Waiting 'Til the Midnight Hour: A Narrative History of Black Power in America* (New York: Henry Holt and Company, 2006), 248.

121. Bloom and Martin, *Black Against Empire*, 397–398.

122. Karen Secrest is just one historian who urges us to avoid "unproductive debates regarding the political efficacy of social movements." See "Occupy Lincoln Park," 392.

BIBLIOGRAPHY

Archival Sources

DePaul University Archives and Special Collections: Lincoln Park Neighborhood
Collection (including Records of the Lincoln Park Conservation Association).
Lincoln Park Community Research Initiative.
Lincoln Park Study Group.
Lyndon Baines Johnson Library, Austin, TX: Findings of the Walker Report,
Chicago Study Team to the National Commission on the Causes and Preven-
tion of Violence.
Mid-North Association Collection.
Old Town Triangle Association Collection.
Park West Neighborhood Association Collection.
RANCH Triangle Association Collection.
Sheffield Neighborhood Association Collection.
University of Illinois at Chicago: North Side Cooperative Ministry Collection.

Published Primary Sources

Ayers, Bill. *Fugitive Days: A Memoir.* Boston: Beacon Press, 2001.
Coyote, Peter. *Sleeping Where I Fall: A Chronicle.* New York: Counterpoint, 1998.
Dellinger, David. *From Yale to Jail: The Life Story of a Moral Dissenter.* New York:
Pantheon, 1993.
Grogan, Emmett. *Ringolevio: A Life Played for Keeps.* New York: Citadel Under-
ground, 1990.
Halstead, Fred. *Out Now!: A Participant's Account of the American Movement
Against the Vietnam War.* New York: Monad Press, 1978.
Hoffman, Abbie. *Soon to Be a Major Motion Picture.* New York: G. P. Putnam's
Sons, 1980.
Krassner, Paul. *Confessions of a Raving, Unconfined Nut.* New York: Simon and
Schuster, 1993.
Mailer, Norman. *Miami and the Siege of Chicago: An Informal History of the
Republican and Democratic Conventions of 1968.* New York: World Publishing
Company, 1968.

Pierson, Robert. *Riots, Chicago Style*. New York: Todd and Honeywell, 1984.

Rubin, Jerry. *Growing Up at Thirty-Seven*. New York: M. Evans and Company, 1976.

Schultz, John. *No One Was Killed: Documentation and Meditation: Convention Week, Chicago—August 1968*. Chicago: Big Table, 1969.

Stein, David Lewis. *Living the Revolution: The Yippies in Chicago*. Indianapolis: Bobbs-Merrill Company, 1969.

Stern, Susan. *With the Weathermen: The Personal Journal of a Revolutionary Woman*. New York: Doubleday, 1975.

United States v. David Dellinger and Others, Transcript of proceedings, United States District Court, Northern District of Illinois, Eastern Division.

Wilkerson, Cathy. *Flying Close to the Sun: My Life and Times as a Weatherman*. New York: Seven Stories Press, 2007.

Newspapers and Magazines

Chicago Sun-Times, Chicago Tribune, Christian Century, Liberation News Service, Lincoln Park Booster, Nation, New York Times, North-Central Booster, Ramparts, Seed, Y.L.O.

Unpublished Dissertations and Theses

Barker, Jeff A. *Paul Sills' Life in the Theater: The First Half Century (1927–1979)*. M.A. Thesis, Department of Theater Arts, Northern Illinois University, May 1981.

Dalton, James J. *The Politics of Community Problem-Solving: The Lincoln Park Findings*. Advance Copy of the author's M.A. Dissertation, Bound and Catalogued Papers, Lincoln Park Neighborhood Collection, DePaul University.

Flanery, James. *Chicago Newspapers' Coverage of the City's Major Civil Disorders of 1968*. M.A. Thesis, Northwestern Illinois University, 1971.

Gonzales, Michael Robert. *Ruffians and Revolutionaries: The Development of the Young Lords Organization in Chicago*. M.A. Thesis, University of Wisconsin-Milwaukee, May 2015.

Love, Sarah Switzer. *Blood, Sweat, and Gas: Print Media and the 1968 Democratic Convention*. M.A. Thesis, University of Montana, 2001.

Paolini, A. Rod. *Lincoln Park Conservation Association: The Politics of a Community Organization*. M.A. Thesis, Northwestern University, May 1970.

Rieger, Howard M. *Redeveloping Chicago's Lincoln Park Area*. PhD Dissertation, Department of Government, Southern Illinois University, August 1969.

Warner, Margaret Stockton. *The Renovation of Lincoln Park: An Ecological Study of Neighborhood Change*. PhD Dissertation, Department of Behavioral Sciences, University of Chicago, 1979.

Internet Sources

DePaul University Library Digital Collections, https://digicol.lib.depaul.edu/.

Gang Research.net, "Cha Cha Jimenez: The Origins of Puerto Rican Gangs in Chicago, Excerpted from an interview by Ralph Cintron and Erika Rodriguez, June 2002," http://gangsresearch.net/ChicagoGangs/younglords/chacha.htm

Grand Valley State University Special Collections and University Archives, "The Young Lords in Lincoln Park," https://www.gvsu.edu/library/specialcollections/young-lords-in-lincoln-park-22.htm

Independent Voices: An Open Access Collection of an Alternative Press, *Seed* Collection," https://www.jstor.org/site/reveal-digital/independent-voices/?searchkey=1702585357238

Published Secondary Sources

Abrahamson, Julia. *A Neighborhood Finds Itself*. New York: Biblo and Tannen, 1971.

Abu-Lughod, Janet L. *From Urban Village to East Village: The Battle for New York's Lower East Side*. Oxford: Basil Blackwood, 1994.

Agyepong, Tera. "In the Belly of the Beast: Black Policemen Combat Police Brutality in Chicago, 1968–1983." *The Journal of African American History* 1, no. 2 (Spring 2013), 253–276.

Ahlstrom, Sydney. *A Religious History of the American People*. New Haven, CT: Yale University Press, 2004.

Allitt, Patrick. *Religion in America Since 1945: A History*. New York: Columbia University Press, 2003.

American Civil Liberties Union. *Dissent and Disorder: A Report to the Citizens of Chicago on the April 27 Investigating Commission*. Chicago: American Civil Liberties Union, 1968.

Anderson, Terry H. *The Movement and the Sixties: Protest in America from Greensboro to Wounded Knee*. New York: Oxford University Press, 1995.

Arguello, Martha M. "We Joined Others Who Were Poor: The Young Lords, the Black Freedom. Struggle, and the 'Original' Rainbow Coalition." *Journal of African American Studies* 23 (2019), 435–454.

Arlen, Mark J. *An American Verdict*. New York: Doubleday and Company, 1973.

Avila, Eric. *Popular Culture in the Age of White Flight: Fear and Fantasy in Suburban Los Angeles* (Berkeley: University of California Press, 2006).

Avila, Eric, and Mark. H. Rose, "Race, Culture, and Urban Renewal: An Introduction." *Journal of Urban History* 35, no. 3 (March 2009).

Bach, Damon. *The American Counterculture: A History of Hippies and Cultural Dissidents.* Lawrence: University of Kansas Press, 2020.

Baugher, Shirley. *Our Old Town: A History of the Neighborhood.* Chicago: Old Town Triangle Association, 2001.

Bauman, John F. *Public Housing, Race, and Renewal: Urban Planning in Philadelphia 1920–1974.* Philadelphia: Temple University Press, 1987.

Bauman, John F., Roger Biles, and Kristin M. Szylvian. *From Tenements to the Taylor Homes: In Search of an Urban Housing Policy in 20th Century America.* University Park: Penn University State Press, 2000.

Beauregard, Robert A. *Voices of Decline: The Postwar Fate of U.S. Cities.* Cambridge, MA: Blackwell Publishers, 1993.

Bennett, Larry. *Fragments of Cities: The New American Downtowns and Neighborhoods.* Columbus: Ohio State University Press, 1990.

———. *Neighborhood Politics: Chicago and Sheffield.* New York: Garland Publishing, 1997.

———. "Rethinking Neighborhoods, Neighborhood Research, and Neighborhood Policy: Lessons from Uptown." *Journal of Urban Affairs* 15, no. 3 (1993).

Berman, William. *America's Right Turn: From Nixon to Bush (The American Moment).* Baltimore: Johns Hopkins University Press, 1994.

Betancur, John J. "Gentrification and Community Fabric in Chicago." *Urban Studies* 48, no. 2 (February 2011).

———. "The Politics of Gentrification: The Case of West Town in Chicago." *Urban Affairs Review* 37, no. 6 (July 2002).

Biles, Roger. *Richard J. Daley: Politics, Race, and the Governing of Chicago.* DeKalb: Northern Illinois University Press, 1995.

Blackstock, Nelson. *COINTELPRO: The FBI's Secret War on Political Freedom.* New York: Monad Press, 1975.

Bloom, Joshua, and Waldo E. Martin Jr. *Black Against Empire: The History and Politics of the Black Panther Party.* Berkeley: University of California Press, 2013.

Bowly, Devereux Jr. *The Poorhouse: Subsidized Housing in Chicago.* Carbondale: Southern Illinois University Press, 2012.

Branch, Taylor. *At Canann's Edge: America in the King Years, 1965–68.* New York: Simon and Schuster, 2010.

Braunstein, Peter, and Michael William Doyle, eds. *Imagine Nation: The American Counterculture of the 1960s and 70s.* New York: Routledge, 2001.

Brinkley, Alan. *The End of Reform: New Deal Liberalism in Recession and War.* New York: Vantage Books, 1995.

Brown-Saracino, Japonica. *A Neighborhood that Never Changes: Gentrification, Social Preservation, and the Search for Authenticity.* Chicago: University of Chicago Press, 2010.

———, ed. *The Gentrification Debates: A Reader.* New York: Routledge, 2010.

Carmines, Edward G., and James A. Stimson. *Issue Evolution: Race and the Transformation of American Politics.* Princeton, NJ: Princeton University Press, 1989.

Carson, Clayborne. *In Struggle: SNCC and the Black Awakening of the 1960s.* Cambridge, MA: Harvard University Press, 1981.

Carter, Dan T. *Politics of Rage: George Wallace, the Origins of the New Conservatism, and the Transformation of American Politics.* New York: Simon and Schuster, 1995.

Chester, Lewis, Godfrey Hodgson, and Bruce Page. *An American Melodrama: The Presidential Campaign of 1968.* New York: Viking Press, 1969.

Chicago Citizens Commission to Study the Disorders of the Convention Week. *Dissent in a Free Society,* 1969.

Chicago Department of Law. *The Strategy of Confrontation: Chicago and the Democratic National Convention,* 1968.

Chicago Fact Book Consortium. *Local Community Fact Book Chicago Metropolitan Area Based on the 1970 and 1980 Censuses.* Chicago: University of Chicago, 1984.

Churchill, Ward, and Jim Vander Wall. *Agents of Repression: The FBI's Secret Wars Against the Black Panther Party and the American Indian Movement.* Boston: South End Press, 1988.

———. *The COINTELPRO Papers: Documents from FBI's Secret War Against Dissidents in the United States.* Boston: South End Press, 1990.

Cohen, Adam, and Elizabeth Taylor. *American Pharaoh: Mayor Richard J. Daley, His Battle for Chicago, and the Nation.* Boston: Little, Brown, 2000.

Cohen, Robert, and David J. Snyder, eds., *Rebellion in Black and White: Southern Student Activism in the 1960s.* Baltimore: Johns Hopkins University Press, 2013.

Condit, Carl. *Chicago 1930–1970: Building, Planning, and Urban Technology.* Chicago: University of Chicago Press, 1974.

Crutcher, Michael. *Treme: Race and Place in a New Orleans Neighborhood.* Athens: University Press of Georgia, 2010.

Davis, Joshua Clark. *From Head Shops to Whole Foods: The Rise and Fall of Activist Entrepreneurs.* New York: Columbia University Press, 2017.

———. "The Business of Getting High: Head Shops, Countercultural Capitalism, and the Marijuana Legalization Movement." *The Sixties: A Journal of History, Politics, and Culture* 8, no. 1 (2015), 27–39.

DeBennedetti, Charles. *An American Ordeal: The Antiwar Movement of the Vietnam Era*. New York: Syracuse University Press, 1990.

Diamond, Andrew J. *Chicago on the Make: Power and Inequality in a Modern City* Oakland: University of California Press, 2017.

———. *Mean Streets: Chicago Youths and the Everyday Struggle for Empowerment in the Multiracial City, 1908–1969*. Berkeley: University of California Press, 2009.

Donner, Frank. *Protectors of Privilege: Red Squads and Police Repression in Urban America*. Berkeley: University of California Press, 1990.

Ducey, Michael H. *Sunday Morning: Aspects of Urban Ritual*. New York: Free Press, 1977.

Echols, Alice. *Scars of Sweet Paradise: The Life and Times of Janis Joplin*. New York: Metropolitan Books, 1999.

———. *Shaky Ground: The 60s and its Aftershocks*. New York: Columbia University Press, 2001.

Edsall, Thomas Burns, and Mary D. Edsall. *Chain Reaction: The Impact of Race, Rights, and Taxes on American Politics*. New York: W. W. Norton, 1992.

Elfenbein, Jessica, Thomas L. Hollowak, and Elizabeth M. Nix, eds. *Baltimore '68: Riots and Rebirth in an American City*. Philadelphia: Temple University Press, 2011.

Enck-Wanzer, Darrel. "Decolonizing Imaginaries: Rethinking 'the People' in the Young Lords Church Offensive." *Quarterly Journal of Speech* 98, no. 1 (February 2012), 1–23.

Farber, David. "Building the Counterculture, Creating Right Livelihoods: The Counterculture at Work." *The Sixties: A Journal of History, Politics and Culture* 6, no. 1 (2013), 1–24.

———. *Chicago '68*. Chicago: University of Chicago Press, 1988.

Feldstein, Ruth. *Motherhood in Black and White: Race and Sex in American Liberalism, 1930–1965*. Ithaca, NY: Cornell University Press, 2000.

Fernandez, Johanna. *The Young Lords: A Radical History*. Chapel Hill: University of North Carolina Press, 2020.

Fernandez, Lilia. *Brown in the Windy City: Mexicans and Puerto Ricans in Postwar Chicago*. Chicago: University of Chicago Press, 2012.

Findlay, James F. *Church People in the Struggle: The National Council of Churches and the Black Freedom Movement, 1950–1970*. Oxford: Oxford University Press, 1993.

Fine, Sidney. *Violence in the Model City: The Cavanaugh Administration, Race Relations, and the Detroit Riot of 1967*. Ann Arbor: University of Michigan Press, 1989.

Fish, John H. *Black Power/White Control: The Struggle of the Woodlawn Organization in Chicago*. Princeton, NJ: Princeton University Press, 1973.

Flamm, Michael F. *Law and Order: Street Crime, Civil Unrest, and the Crisis of Liberalism in the 1960s*. New York: Columbia University Press, 2005.

Flores-Rodriguez, Angel G. "The Young Lords, Puerto Rican Liberation, and the Black Freedom Struggle: Interview with Jose 'Cha Cha' Jimenez." *OAH Magazine of History* 26, no. 1 (January 2012).

Florida, Richard. *The Rise of the Creative Class . . . and How It's Transforming Work, Leisure, Community and Everyday Life*. New York: Basic Books, 2002.

Frank, Thomas. *The Conquest of Cool: Business Culture, Counterculture, and the Rise of Hip Consumerism*. Chicago: University of Chicago Press, 1998.

Fremon, David K. *Chicago Politics Ward by Ward*. Bloomington: Indiana University Press, 1988.

Freund, David M. *Colored Property: State Policy and White Racial Politics in Suburban America*. Chicago: University of Chicago Press, 2007.

Gelfand, Mark I. *A Nation of Cities: The Federal Government and Urban America*, New York: Oxford University Press, 1975.

Gerhardt, Paul Jr. "Standards of Professional Practice," *Journal of the American Institute of Architects* 9, no. 3 (March 1948), 138.

Gilbert, James. *A Cycle of Outrage: America's Reaction to the Juvenile Delinquent in the 1950s*. New York: Oxford University Press, 1986.

Gill, Jill K. *Embattled Ecumenism: The National Council of Churches, The Vietnam War, and the Trials of the Protestant Left*. DeKalb: Northern Illinois University Press, 2011.

Gitlin, Todd. *The Sixties: Years of Hope, Days of Rage*. New York: Bantam Books, 1987.

Gleason, Bill. *Daley of Chicago*. New York: Simon and Schuster, 1970.

Glessing, Robert J. *The Underground Press in America*. Bloomington: Indiana University Press, 1970.

Goldstein, Brian D. *The Roots of Urban Renaissance: Gentrification and the Struggle Over Harlem*. Cambridge, MA: Harvard University Press, 2017.

Gonzalez, Rodolpho. *Tierra y libertad: two interviews with Corky Gonzales and Cha Cha Jimenez*, pamphlet, Special Collections, Deering Library, Northwestern University.

Graham, Kevin Fox. *Race, Real Estate, and Uneven Development: The Kansas City Experience*. Albany: State University of New York Press, 2002.

Grazian, David. *Blue Chicago: The Search for Authenticity in Urban Blues Clubs*. Chicago: University of Chicago Press, 2003.

Greenberg, Cheryl Lynn. "Liberal NIMBY: American Jews and Civil Rights." *Journal of Urban History* 38, no. 3 (March 22, 2012).

Grossman, James R., Ann Durkin Keating, and Janice L. Reiff, eds. *The Encyclopedia of Chicago*. Chicago: University of Chicago Press, 2004.

Guinier, Lani. "From Racial Liberation to Racial Literacy." *The Journal of American History* 91, no. 1 (June 2004).

Haas, Jeffrey. *The Assassination of Fred Hampton: How the FBI and the Chicago Police Murdered a Black Panther*. Chicago: Lawrence Hill Books, 2010.

Hadden, Jeffrey K. "Clergy Involvement in Civil Rights." *The Annals of the American Academy of Political and Social Science* 387 (January 1970), 118–127.

Halsted, Fred. *Out Now! A Participant's Account of the American Movement Against the Vietnam War*. New York: Monad Press, 1978.

Hauser, Philip M., and Evelyn M. Kitagawa, eds. *Local Community Fact Book for Chicago, 1950*. Chicago: University of Chicago, Chicago Community Inventory, 1953.

Henderson, Stuart. *Making the Scene: Yorkville and Hip Toronto in the 1960s*. Toronto: University of Toronto Press, 2012.

Hertz, Daniel Kay. *The Battle of Lincoln Park: Urban Renewal and Gentrification in Chicago*. Cleveland, OH: Belt Publishing, 2018.

Hirsch, Arnold R. *Making the Second Ghetto: Race and Housing in Chicago, 1940–1960*. Cambridge: Cambridge University Press, 1985.

———. "Massive Resistance in the Urban North: Trumbull Park, Chicago, 1953–1966." *The Journal of American History* 82, no. 2 (September, 1995), 522–550.

Hock, Jennifer. "Bulldozers, Busing, and Boycotts: Urban Renewal and the Integrationist Project." *Journal of Urban History* 39, no. 3 (2013), 433–453.

Hodgdon, Tim. *Manhood in the Age of Aquarius: Masculinity in Two Countercultural Communities, 1965–83*. New York: Columbia University Press, 2008.

Hoffman, Jack, and Daniel Simon. *Run, Run, Run: The Lives of Abbie Hoffman*. New York: G. P. Putnam's Sons, 1994.

Holliman, Irene V. "From Crackertown to Model City? Renewal and Community Building in Atlanta, 1963–1966. *Journal of Urban History* 35, no. 3 (March 2009), 369–386.

Horne, Gerald. *Fire This Time: The Watts Uprising and the 1960s*. Charlottesville: University Press of Virginia, 1995.

Hudnut-Beumler, James. *Looking for God in the Suburbs: The Religion of the American Dream and Its Critics, 1945–1965*. New Brunswick, NJ: Rutgers University Press, 1994.

Hunt, Andrew E. *The Turning: A History of Vietnam Veterans Against the War*. New York: New York University Press, 1999.

Hunter, Albert. *Symbolic Communities: The Persistence of and Change of Chicago's Communities*. Chicago: University of Chicago Press, 1974.

Hutchinson, Ray, ed. *Research in Urban Sociology, A Research Annual: Gentrification and Urban Change*, vol. 2. Greenwich, CT: JAI Press, 1992.

Hyra, Derek F. *The New Urban Renewal: The Economic Transformation of Harlem and Bronzeville*. Chicago: University of Chicago Press, 2008.

Isaacs Jackson, Mandi. *Model City Blues: Urban Space and Organized Resistance in New Haven*. Philadelphia: Temple University Press, 2008.

Isserman, Maurice. *If I Had a Hammer: The Death of the Old Left and the Birth of the New Left*. New York: Basic Books, 1989.

Isserman, Maurice, and Michael Kazin. *America Divided: The Civil War of the 1960s*. Oxford: Oxford University Press, 2015.

Jeffries, Judson. "An Interview with Jose 'Cha Cha' Jimenez: Leader of the Young Lords Organization." *Journal of African American Studies* 22 (2018), 267–273.

———. "From Gang-Bangers to Urban Revolutionaries: The Young Lords of Chicago." *Journal of the Illinois State Historical Society* (Autumn 2003), 288–304.

Jezer, Marty. *Abbie Hoffman: American Rebel*. New Brunswick, NJ: Rutgers University Press, 1993.

Johnson, Michael L. *The New Journalism: The Underground Press, the Artists of Nonfiction, and Changes in the Media*. Lawrence: University of Kansas Press, 1971.

Joseph, Peniel E. *Waiting 'Til the Midnight Hour: A Narrative History of Black Power in America*. New York: Henry Holt and Company, 2006.

Kaiser, Charles. *1968 in America: Music, Politics, Chaos, Counterculture in the Shaping of a Generation*. New York: Wiedenfield and Nicholson, 1997.

Kaplan, Laura. *The Story of Jane: The Legendary Underground Feminist Abortion Service*. Chicago: University of Chicago Press, 1995.

Kempton, Richard. *Provo: Amsterdam's Anarchist Revolt*. New York: Autonomedia, 2007.

Kirkpatrick, Rob. *1969: The Year Everything Changed*. New York: Skyhorse Publishing, 2011.

Kitagawa, Evelyn, ed. *Local Community Factbook: Chicago Metropolitan Area, 1960*. Chicago: Chicago Community Inventory, University of Chicago, 1963.

Klimke, Martin, and Jochim Scharloth, eds. *1968 in Europe: A History of Protest and Activism, 1956–1977*. New York: Palgrave MacMillan, 2008.

Kousser, J. Morgan, and James M. McPherson, eds. *Region, Race, and Reconstruction: Essays in Honor of C. Vann Woodward*. Oxford: Oxford University Press, 1982.

Kurlansky, Mark. *1968: The Year that Rocked the World*. New York: Ballantine Books, 2004.

Kusch, Frank. *Battleground Chicago: The Police and the 1968 Democratic National Convention*. Westport, CT: Praeger Press, 2004.

Laney, James T. "The New Morality and the Religious Communities." *The Annals of the American Academy of Political and Social Science* 387 (January 1970), 14–21.

Lazerow, Jama, and Yohuru Williams, eds. *In Search of the Black Panther Party: New Perspectives on a Revolutionary Movement*. Durham, NC: Duke University Press, 2006.

Leamer, Lawrence. *The Paper Revolutionaries: The Rise of the Underground Press*. New York: Simon and Schuster, 1972.

Lees, Loretta. *The Emancipatory City? Paradoxes and Possibilities*. Thousand Oaks, CA: SAGE, 2004).

——. "A Reappraisal of Gentrification: Towards a 'Geography of Gentrification.'" *Progress in Human Geography*, no. 24 (2000), 389–408.

Lewis, Roger. *Outlaws of America: The Underground Press and Its Context*. Middlesex, England: Penguin, 1972.

Ley, David. "Artists, Aestheticisation, and the Field of Gentrification." *Urban Studies* 40, no. 12 (November 2003), 2527–2544.

——. *The New Middle Class and the Remaking of Central City*. Oxford: Oxford University Press, 1996.

Lieberman, Robbie. *Prairie Power: Voices of 1960s Midwestern Student Protest*. Columbia: University of Missouri Press, 2004.

Liebling, A. J. *Chicago: The Second City*. New York: Alfred A. Knopf, 1952.

Light, Jennifer S. *From Warfare to Welfare: Defense Intellectuals and Urban Problems in Cold War America*. Baltimore: Johns Hopkins University Press, 2003.

——. *The Nature of Cities: Ecological Visions and the American Urban Professions, 1920–1960*. Baltimore: Johns Hopkins University Press, 2009.

Lindberg, Richard C. *To Serve and Collect: Chicago Politics and Police Corruption from the Lager Beer Riot to the Summerdale Scandal*. New York: Praeger, 1991.

Luecke, Richard Henry. "Protestant Clergy: New Forms of Ministry, New Forms of Training." *The Annals of the American Academy of Political and Social Science* 387 (January 1970), 86–95.

Lyons, Paul. *The People of this Generation: The Rise and Fall of the New Left in Philadelphia*. New York: Simon and Schuster, 1999.

Lyttle, Bradford. *The Chicago Anti-Vietnam War Movement*. Chicago: Midwest Pacifist Press, 1988.

Martin, Bradford D. *The Theater Is in the Streets: Politics and Performance in Sixties America*. Amherst and Boston: University of Massachusetts Press, 2004.

Martinez, Miranda J. *Power at the Roots: Gentrification, Community Gardens, and Puerto Ricans of the Lower East Side*. Lanham, MD: Lexington Books, 2010.

Marwick, Arthur. *The Sixties: Cultural Revolution in Britain, France, Italy, and the United States, c. 1958–1974*. Oxford: Oxford University Press, 1998.

Matusow, Allen J. *The Unraveling of America: A History of Liberalism in the 1960s*. New York: Harper and Row, 1984.

May, Elaine Tyler. *Homeward Bound: American Families in the Cold War Era*. New York: Basic Books, 1999.

Mayer, Harold M., and Richard C. Wade. *Chicago: Growth of a Metropolis*. Chicago: University of Chicago Press, 1969.

McEnaney, Laura. "Nightmares on Elm Street: Demobilizing in Chicago, 1945–1953." *The Journal of American History* 92, no. 4 (2006), 1265–1291.

McGirr, Lisa. *Suburban Warriors: The Origins of the New American Right*. Princeton, NJ: Princeton University Press, 2001.

McKee, Guian M. "I've Never Dealt with a Government Agency Before: Philadelphia's Somerset Mills Project, the Local State, and the Missed Opportunities of Urban Renewal." *Journal of Urban History* 35, no. 3 (March 2009).

McMillian, David, and Paul Buhle. *The New Left Revisited*. Philadelphia: Temple University Press, 2003.

Mele, Christopher. *Selling the Lower East Side: Culture, Real Estate, and Resistance in New York City*. Minneapolis: University of Minnesota Press, 2000.

Michel, Greg L. *Struggle for a Better South: The Southern Student Organizing Committee, 1964–1969*. New York: Palgrave Macmillan, 2004.

Miller, James. *"Democracy is in the Streets:" From Port Huron to the Siege of Chicago*. New York: Simon and Schuster, 1987.

Miller, Timothy. *The Hippies and American Values*. Knoxville: University of Tennessee Press, 1991.

Mollenkpf, John H. *The Contested City*. Princeton, NJ: Princeton University Press, 1983.

Monhollon, Rusty. *This Is America? The Sixties in Lawrence, Kansas*. New York: Palgrave, 2002.

Morgan, Edward P. *The 60s Experience: Hard Lessons About Modern America*. Philadelphia: Temple University Press, 1991.

Moretta, John Anthony. *The Hippies: A 1960s History*. Jefferson, NC: McFarland and Company, 2017.

Mumford, Kevin. *Newark: A History of Race, Rights, and Riots in America*. New York: New York University Press, 2007.

Murch, Donna. *Living for the City: Migration, Education and the Rise of the Black Panther Party in Oakland, California*. Chapel Hill: University of North Carolina Press, 2010.

Newman, Oscar. *Defensible Space: Crime Prevention Through Urban Design*. New York: Macmillan, 1972.

O'Connor, Len. *Clout: Mayor Daley and His City.* Chicago: Henry Regnery Company, 1975.

Ogbar, Jeffrey O.G., "Puerto Rico en mi corazon: The Young Lords, Black Power, and Puerto Rican Nationalism in the U.S. 1966–1972." *CENTRO Journal* 18, no. 1 (Spring 2006).

Olsen, Paulina. *Portland in the 1960s: Stories from the Counterculture.* Charleston and London: History Press, 2012.

O'Neil, William L. *Coming Apart: An Informal History of the 1960s.* New York: Quadrangle Books, 1971.

Osman, Suleiman. *The Invention of Brownstone Brooklyn: Gentrification and the Search for Authenticity in Postwar New York.* Oxford: Oxford University Press, 2011.

Pacyga, Dominic A. *Chicago: A Biography.* Chicago: University of Chicago Press, 2009.

Pacyga, Dominic A., and Ellen Skerrett. *Chicago: City of Neighborhoods: Histories and Tours.* Chicago: Loyola University Press, 1986.

Padilla, Felix. *Puerto Rican Chicago.* Notre Dame, IN: University of Notre Dame Press, 1987.

Parsons, David L. *Dangerous Grounds: Antiwar Coffeehouses and Military Dissent in the Vietnam Era.* Chapel Hill: University of North Carolina Press, 2017.

Patterson, Clayton, ed. *Resistance: A Radical Social and Political History of the Lower East Side.* New York: Seven Stories Press, 2007.

Patterson, James. *The Eve of Destruction: How 1965 Transformed America.* New York: Basic Books, 2012.

Pattillo, Mary. *Black on the Block: The Politics of Race and Class in the City.* Chicago: University of Chicago Press, 2007.

Peck, Abe. *Uncovering the Sixties: The Life and Times of the Underground Press.* New York: Pantheon, 1985.

Perez, Gina M. *The Near Northwest Side Story: Migration, Displacement, and Puerto Rican Families.* Berkeley: University of California Press, 2004.

Perkiss, Abigail. *Making Good Neighbors: Civil Rights, Liberalism, and Integration in Postwar Philadelphia.* Ithica, NY: Cornell University Press, 2014.

Perry, Charles. *The Haight-Ashbury: A History.* New York: Wenner Books, 2005.

Peterson, Sarah Jo. *Planning the Home Front: Building Bombers and Communities at Willow Run.* Chicago: University of Chicago Press, 2019.

Pritchett, Wendell. *Brownsville, Brooklyn: Blacks, Jews, and the Changing Face of the Ghetto.* Chicago: University of Chicago Press, 2002.

Ralph, James. *Northern Protest: Martin Luther King, Jr., Chicago, and the Civil Rights Movement.* Cambridge, MA: Harvard University Press, 1993.

Ramos-Zayas, Ana Y. *National Performances: The Politics of Race, Class, and Space in Puerto Rican Chicago*. Chicago: University of Chicago Press, 2003.

Raskin, Jonah. *For the Hell of It: The Life and Times of Abbie Hoffman*. Berkeley: University of California Press, 1996.

Ribeiro, Alyssa. "A Period of Turmoil: Pittsburgh's 1968 Riots and their Aftermath," *Journal of Urban History* 39, no. 2 (March 2013), 141–171.

Rieder, Jonathan. *Canarsie: The Jews and Italians of Brooklyn Against Liberalism*. Cambridge, MA: Harvard University Press, 1985.

Rivera, Marisol V., and Judson Jeffries, "From Radicalism to Representation: Jose 'Cha Cha' Jimenez's Journey into Electoral Politics, *Journal of African American Studies* 23 (2019), 299–319.

Rorabaugh, W. J. *American Hippies*. Cambridge: Cambridge University Press, 2015.

———. *Berkeley at War: The 1960s*. New York: Oxford University Press, 1989.

Rosen, George. *Decision-Making Chicago-Style: The Genesis of a University of Illinois Campus*. Urbana: University of Illinois Press, 1980.

Rossi, Peter H., and Robert A. Dentler. *The Politics of Urban Renewal: The Chicago Findings*. Westport, CT: Greenwood Press, 1961.

Rossinow, Douglas. *The Politics of Authenticity: Liberalism, Christianity, and the New Left in America*. New York: Columbia University Press,1998.

Royko, Mike. *Boss: Richard J. Daley of Chicago*. New York: Dutton, 1971.

Sale, Kirkpatrick. *SDS*. New York: Random House, 1973.

Sarchet, Bettie B. *Block Groups and Community Change: An Evaluation of the Block Program of the Hyde-Park Kenwood Community Conference*. Chicago: University of Chicago, Human Dynamics Laboratory, 1955.

Schulman, Bruce J., and Julian E. Zelizer. *Rightward Bound: Making America Conservative in the 1970s*. Cambridge, MA: Harvard University Press, 2008.

Schultz, Bud, and Ruth Schultz. *The Price of Dissent: Testimonies to Political Repression in America*. Berkeley: University of California Press, 2001.

Secrist, Karen A. "Occupy Lincoln Park: The Militant Drama of the Young Lords Organization." *Journal of African American Studies* 23 (2019), 389–404.

Seligman, Amanda I. *Block by Block: Neighborhoods and Public Policy on Chicago's West Side*. Chicago: University of Chicago Press, 2005.

———. "But Burn—No: The Rest of the Crowd in Three Civil Disorders in 1960s Chicago." *Journal of Urban History* 37, no. 2 (March 2011), 230–255.

Shkuda, Aaron. *The Lofts of SoHo: Gentrification, Art, and Industry in New York, 1950–1980*. Chicago: University of Chicago Press, 2016.

Siegel, Frederick. *The Future Once Happened Here: New York, D.C., L.A., and the Fate of America's Cities*. New York: Free Press, 1997.

Silk, Mark. *Spiritual Politics: Religion and America Since World War II*. New York: Simon and Schuster, 1988.

Singh, Nikhil Pal. *Black Is a Country: Race and the Unfinished Struggle for Democracy*. Cambridge, MA: Harvard University Press, 2004.

Sleeper, Jim. *The Closest of Strangers: Liberalism and the Politics of Race in New York*. New York: W. W. Norton and Company, 1990.

Smith, Neil. *The New Urban Frontier: Gentrification and the Revanchist City*. London and New York: Routledge, 1996.

Smith, Preston H. II. *Racial Democracy and the Black Metropolis: Housing Policy in Postwar Chicago*. Minneapolis: University of Minnesota Press, 2012.

Sonnie Amy, and James Tracy. *Hillbilly Nationalists, Urban Race Rebels, and Black Power: Community Organizing in Radical Times*. New York: Melville House, 2001.

Spinney, Robert G. *City of Big Shoulders: A History of Chicago*. Dekalb: Northern Illinois University Press, 2000.

Sparling, Edward J. et al. *Dissent and Disorder: A Report to the Citizens of Chicago on the April 27 Peace Parade*. Chicago: The April 27 Investigation Commission, 1968.

Stoecker, Randy. *Defending Community: The Struggle for Alternative Redevelopment in Cedar-Riverside*. Philadelphia: Temple University Press, 1994.

Sugrue, Thomas. *Origins of the Urban Crisis: Race and Inequality in Postwar Detroit*. Princeton, NJ: Princeton University Press, 1996.

Suttles, Gerald D. *The Man-Made City: The Land-Use Confidence Game in Chicago*. Cambridge, MA: Harvard University Press, 1993.

Sweet, Jeffrey. *Something Wonderful Right Away: An Oral History of the Second City and the Compass Players*. New York: Proscenium Publishers, 2003.

Taub, Richard B., Garth Taylor, and Jan D. Dunham. *Paths of Neighborhood Change: Race and Crime in Urban America*. Chicago: University of Chicago Press, 1984.

Taylor, Flint. *The Torture Machine: Racism and Violence in Chicago*. Chicago: Haymarket Press, 2019.

Teaford, Jon C. *The Rough Road to Renaissance: Urban Revitalization in America,1940–1985*. Baltimore: Johns Hopkins University Press, 1993.

Thompson, Heather Ann. *Blood in the Water: The Attica Prison Uprising of 1971 and its Legacy*. New York: Pantheon Books, 2016.

Unger, Irwin, and Debi Unger. *The Movement: A History of the American New Left, 1959–1972*. New York: Dodd, Meade and Company, 1974.

Varon, Jeremy. *Bringing the War Home: The Weather Underground, The Red Army Faction, and Revolutionary Violence in the Sixties and Seventies*. Berkeley: University of California Press, 2004.

Viorst, Milton. *Fire in the Streets: America in the 1960s*. New York: Simon and Schuster, 1979.

Von Hoffman, Alexander. "Enter the Housing Industry, Stage Right: A Working Paper on the History of Housing Policy." Joint Center for Housing Studies of Harvard University, February 1, 2008, 8–9. https://www.jchs.harvard.edu/research-areas/working-papers/enter-housing-industry-stage-right-working-paper-history-housing.

Walker, Daniel. *Rights in Conflict: The Violent Confrontation of Demonstrators and National Convention of 1968. A report submitted by Daniel Walker, director of the Chicago Study Team, to the National Commission on the Causes and Prevention of Violence.* New York: Bantam Books, 1968.

Whitzman, Carolyn. *Suburb, Slum, Urban Village: Transformations in Toronto's Parkdale Neighborhood, 1875–2002.* Vancouver: UBC Press, 2010.

Wild, Mark. "Liberal Protestants and Urban Renewal." *Religion and American Culture: A Journal of Interpretation* 25, no. 1 (Winter 2015), 110–146.

——. *Renewal: Liberal Protestants and the American City After World War II.* Chicago: University of Chicago Press, 2019.

Williams, Jakobi. *From the Bullet to the Ballot: The Illinois Chapter of the Black Panther Party and Racial Coalition Politics in Chicago.* Chapel Hill: University of North Carolina Press, 2013.

Williams, Rhonda Y. *Concrete Demands: The Search for Black Power in the 20th Century.* New York: Routledge, 2015.

Wuthnow, Robert. *After Heaven: American Spirituality Since the 1950s.* Berkeley: University of California Press, 1998.

Zaroulis, Nancy, and Gerald Sullivan. *Who Spoke Up?: American Protest Against the War in Vietnam, 1963–1975.* New York: Doubleday and Company, 1984.

Zipp, Samuel, and Michael Carriere, "Introduction: Thinking Through Urban Renewal." *The Journal of Urban History* 39, no. 3 (2012), 359–365.

——. *Manhattan Projects: The Rise and Fall of Urban Renewal in Cold War New York.* Oxford: Oxford University Press, 2010.

——. "The Roots and Routes of Urban Renewal." *Journal of Urban History* 39, no. 3 (2012), 366–391.

Zukin, Sharon. *Loft Living: Culture and Capital in Urban Change.* Baltimore: Johns Hopkins University Press, 1982.

Italicized page numbers indicate figures.

Brian Mullgardt is a professor of history at Millikin University. He has written for *The Journal of Illinois History, Chicago History,* and *The Journal of the Illinois State Historical Society.*